Unwin Critical Library
GENERAL EDITOR: CLAUDE RAWSON

TRISTRAM SHANDY

Tristram Shandy

MAX BYRD

Professor of English
University of California, Davis

London
GEORGE ALLEN & UNWIN
Boston   Sydney

**George Allen & Unwin (Publishers) Ltd,
40 Museum Street, London WC1A 1LU, UK**

George Allen & Unwin (Publishers) Ltd,
Park Lane, Hemel Hempstead, Herts HP2 4TE, UK

Allen & Unwin, Inc.,
Fifty Cross Street, Winchester, Mass. 01890, USA

George Allen & Unwin Australia Pty Ltd,
8 Napier Street, North Sydney, NSW 2060, Australia

First published in 1985

British Library Cataloguing in Publication Data

Byrd, Max
    Tristram Shandy. – (Unwin critical library)
    1. Sterne, Laurence. Tristram Shandy
    I. Title
    823'.6   PR3714.T73
    ISBN 0–04–800033–7

Library of Congress Cataloging in Publication Data

Byrd, Max
    Tristram Shandy.
(Unwin critical library)
Bibliography: p.
Includes index.
1. Sterne, Laurence, 1713–1768. Life and opinions
of Tristram Shandy, gentleman. I. Title. II. Series.
PR3714.L53B97 1984   823'.6   84–9167
ISBN 0–04–800033–7 (alk. paper)

Set in 10 on 11 point Plantin by Computape (Pickering) Ltd
and printed in Great Britain by Billings and Sons (London and Worcester)

CONTENTS

GENERAL EDITOR'S PREFACE

Each volume in this series is devoted to a single major text. It is intended for serious students and teachers of literature, and for knowledgeable non-academic readers. It aims to provide a scholarly introduction and a stimulus to critical thought and discussion.

Individual volumes will naturally differ from one another in arrangement and emphasis, but each will normally begin with information on a work's literary and intellectual background, and other guidance designed to help the reader to an informed understanding. This is followed by an extended critical discussion of the work itself, and each contributor in the series has been encouraged to present in these sections his own reading of the work, whether or not this is controversial, rather than to attempt a mere consensus. Some volumes, including those on *Paradise Lost* and *Ulysses*, vary somewhat from the more usual pattern by entering into substantive critical discussion at the outset, and allowing the necessary background material to emerge at the points where it is felt to arise from the argument in the most useful and relevant way. Each volume also contains a historical survey of the work's critical reputation, including an account of the principal lines of approach and areas of controversy, and a selective (but detailed) bibliography.

The hope is that the volumes in this series will be among those which a university teacher would normally recommend for any serious study of a particular text, and that they will also be among the essential secondary texts to be consulted in some scholarly investigations. But the experienced and informed non-academic reader has also been in our minds, and one of our aims has been to provide him with reliable and stimulating works of reference and guidance, embodying the present state of knowledge and opinion in a conveniently accessible form.

C.J.R.
University of Warwick,
December 1979

ACKNOWLEDGEMENTS

I am very grateful to the following colleagues and friends, who have read portions of the manuscript and discussed Sterne with me most patiently and helpfully: John Bender, W. B. Carnochan, Peter A. Dale, Robert H. Hopkins and Leon Mayhew. I am indebted as well to several of my students for references, phrases and discussion: Amy Baldwin, Martin Regal, Tony Rosso, Mary Uhde and especially Constance Malloy. I am also grateful to the Committee on Research of the University of California, Davis, which has paid for the typing; and to Gary Konas and Anne Cabello, who have processed my words into prose. My greatest debt, of course, is to the General Editor of the series, Claude Rawson, who started me on an entertaining and very challenging project. Professor Rawson and Allen & Unwin have generously permitted portions of Chapters 2 and 3 to appear as 'Swift and Sterne' in *The Age of Johnson*, ed. James Engell (Cambridge, Mass.: Harvard University Press, 1984).

And, finally, Brookes, Kate and David have made it possible for me to work in an updated, California version of 'Crazy Castle'.

ABBREVIATIONS

The following frequently cited titles are given by these abbreviations in the text:

ASJ   Laurence Sterne, *A Sentimental Journey through France and Italy, by Mr Yorick*, ed. Gardner D. Stout, Jnr (Berkeley/Los Angeles, Calif.: University of California Press, 1967)

Cash   Arthur H. Cash, *Laurence Sterne: The Early and Middle Years* (London: Methuen, 1975)

CH   Alan B. Howes (ed.), *Sterne: The Critical Heritage* (London/Boston, Mass.: Routledge & Kegan Paul, 1974)

Croft   John Croft, 'Anecdotes of Sterne', in W. A. S. Hewins (ed.), *The Whitefoord Papers* (Oxford, 1898)

Essay   John Locke, *An Essay Concerning Human Understanding*, ed. Peter H. Nidditch (London: Oxford University Press, 1975). Cited by book, chapter and section

Letters   Lewis Perry Curtis (ed.), *Letters of Laurence Sterne* (Oxford: Clarendon Press, 1935)

Traugott John Traugott (ed.), *Laurence Sterne: A Collection of Critical Essays* (Englewood Cliffs, NJ: Prentice-Hall, 1968)

The following abbreviations for journals are also used:

ELH   *ELH: A Journal of English Literary History*
MP   *Modern Philology*
PMLA   *PMLA: Publications of the Modern Language Association of America*

CHAPTER 1

'A Picture of Myself'

Like other great eighteenth-century novelists, Laurence Sterne came to fiction late in life: he was 46 years old when he sat down in January of 1759 to begin *Tristram Shandy*, an eccentric, moderately unsuccessful clergyman lost to sight in the obscurity of a Yorkshire winter. But unlike Daniel Defoe, who was 59 and notorious when he began *Robinson Crusoe*, or Samuel Richardson, 51 at the publication of *Pamela*, Sterne had virtually no experience as a writer. Defoe, in fact, had filled one long shelf already with volumes of journalism, political tracts and even poetry; and Richardson, a prosperous printer licensed to the House of Commons, had all his life been engaged in some kind of literary production and had even written a book himself of specimen letters on various subjects – polite fictions – for his readers to emulate. In retrospect their steps from journalism and letter-books to the novel seem natural and short. But apart from his sermons, only one of which had ever been published, and a trickle of polemical newspaper articles for the *York Gazetteer*, Sterne had had little more to do with the literary life than any other decently educated provincial minister – one could point to a hundred candidates, younger, with better claims to literary distinction or literary promise. And yet after hastily scribbling in the early days of January 1759 two separate versions of a satirical pamphlet against a local cleric (*A Political Romance*), and starting and abandoning two chapters of an untitled imitation of Rabelais, Sterne exploded into the history of English literature. By the end of May he was offering the first two volumes of *Tristram Shandy* to the eminent London publisher Robert Dodsley, and by March of the next year he was at Dodsley's side in London, overseeing a second edition and signing a contract for two more volumes of *Shandy* at the enormous sum of £630. In another two years he would boast, not without reason, that a letter addressed simply 'Tristram Shandy, Europe' would reach him without delay.[1]

It is familiar enough by now that a book can confer instant celebrity – in the eighteenth century Richardson, Goethe, Rousseau all enjoyed vogues similar to Sterne's. It is plausible as well that a vision and even a style can mature in long, obscure silence, as Proust's did. But it deepens the puzzle of Sterne's genius that these things happened not only without preparation, but also without apparent aptitude. In this chapter, accordingly, I want first to supplement briefly the biographical and bibliographical information usually found in editions of *Tristram Shandy*, then to discuss at somewhat greater length the vexed but central question of Sterne's personality.

(i) BIOGRAPHICAL

His father Roger Sterne was the younger son of a wealthy Yorkshire landowner, descendant of an old and distinguished family whose most notable member, Richard Sterne, had been both Master of Jesus College, Cambridge, and Archbishop of York. Fired perhaps by Marlborough's great victories on the Continent, or possibly angered by a family quarrel, Roger left home in 1710 at the early age of 16 or 17 and enlisted in the 34th Regiment of Foot. Almost a year later he was promoted in the field to ensign, the lowest rank of commissioned officer; and there he remained until a second field promotion to lieutenant four months before his death, although his elder brother Richard could have afforded at any time to purchase him a higher rank. If a quarrel did exist between the two brothers, it can only have been exacerbated by Roger Sterne's rash and ill-advised marriage in 1711 to Agnes Herbert, a woman of low birth, widow of a captain and daughter of an army 'sutler' (camp provisioner). Two years later, the homunculus having been safely escorted by the animal spirits, Laurence was born on 24 November 1713 at Clonmel, Ireland, where his father's regiment had been stationed.

Of his father, Sterne has left us a deft and affectionate sketch in his *Memoirs*:

> My father was a little smart man—active to the last degree, in all exercises—most patient of fatigue and disappointments, of which it pleased God to give him full measure—he was in his temper somewhat rapid, and hasty—but of a kindly, sweet disposition, void of all design; and so innocent in his own intentions, that he suspected no one; so that you might have cheated him ten times in a day, if nine had not been sufficient for your purpose . . . (*Letters*, p. 3)

Of his mother, however, no such affectionate account has survived. Instead, Yorkshire gossip and Sterne's own letters have established a genuine estrangement between mother and son, dating evidently from Sterne's marriage and rising prosperity, when Agnes came forward to demand money, but undoubtedly having its roots in the long separation that began with the boy's removal from Ireland to the protection of his Yorkshire relatives in 1723 or 1724. In the preceding summer two of the Sterne infants had died, a boy and a girl (only three of the children were to survive infancy), and Roger Sterne, fearful perhaps for his eldest son, 'got leave of his colonel to fix me at school' in England (*Letters*, p. 3).

Thereafter Laurence was never to return to Ireland and to the rough, dangerous barrack life his mother and sisters continued to endure – camping and decamping in haste, scrambling after his father's regiment from crowded post to crowded post. Tended by his uncle Richard Sterne and surrounded by his well-connected cousins, he studied Latin and Greek at the Hipperholme Grammar School in a pleasant village near Halifax and the family seat. (At the time of his ordination the school was to present him with a bill for nine years' tuition and supplies.) Meanwhile Roger Sterne, who like Uncle Toby had seen action in earlier sieges, was posted in 1727 to take part in the siege of Gibraltar; there he fought an unlucky duel with a fellow-officer (about a goose, according to the *Memoirs*) that saw him pierced by his opponent's rapier and pinned to the wall. Four years later, constitution still impaired by the injury, Sterne relates, 'he was sent to Jamaica, where he soon fell by the country fever, which took away his senses first, and made a child of him, and then, in a month or two, walking about continually without complaining, till the moment he sat down in an arm chair, and breathed his last' (*Letters*, p. 3). In 1733, supported now by an allowance from a cousin also named Richard, at the relatively advanced age of 20, Sterne entered Jesus College, Cambridge, to which other members of his family had belonged.

From that point on his career was fixed on the church. Whether or not he felt a genuine calling – and his clerical sincerity, like Swift's, has often been questioned – family tradition alone, beginning with the great weight of Archbishop Sterne's example, would have exerted sufficient pressure; and it is entirely possible that his cousin Richard had also insisted on his taking orders as a condition of the allowance. In any case, however, no other realistic possibilities existed. Sterne had been an indifferent student – bored perhaps by the fossilized curriculum at Cambridge, developing already a Shandyesque eye for the ridiculousness of learned lumber – he would have been unlikely to turn in the direction of seeking a place in government or a private house, the only real alternatives for an impoverished university gentleman in the eighteenth century. And a military career like his father's, if he ever considered it, would also have been out of the question: out of the question for a reason that was profoundly to affect the very texture of Sterne's life and of his masterpiece *Tristram Shandy*. His sister Anne – 'this pretty blossom', Sterne wrote in the *Memoirs* – had died at the age of 3 in the Dublin barracks: 'she was, as I well remember, of a fine delicate frame, not made to last long, as were most of my father's babes' (*Letters*, p. 2). 'Lorry Slim', to use his own nickname, had inherited the family delicacy. Six feet tall, with spider legs and a 'thin, dry . . . rarified' figure, at some point during his Cambridge years he suffered the first of a series of terrifying, lifelong consumptive episodes: a vessel burst in his lungs while he slept and filled his bed with blood ('in two hours, thou lost as many quarts of blood', Tristram reports nonchalantly of himself; 'and hadst thou lost as much more, did not the faculty tell thee——it would have amounted to a gallon?').[2] For pulmonary tuberculosis such as that there was no cure. 'That death-looking, long-striding scoundrel of a scare-sinner ... is posting after me,' Tristram would say with a constant backward glance (VII, vii). Thereafter Sterne's whole adult life was to see periods of good health alternating precipitously with disabling fits of weakness, exhaustion, nervous apprehension. Having little choice, and with a foretaste of his own mortality that must have for a time turned every ambition to ashes, Sterne left Cambridge in the spring of 1737 and submitted quietly to the mysterious dispensations of Anglican preferment.

For the next twenty years he served as a cleric at Sutton, near York, at first under the protection of his influential uncle Jacques Sterne, Archdeacon of Cleveland and precentor of York. After a bitter quarrel over politics, however, Jacques withdrew his patronage and Sterne found all further advancement blocked. While resident at Sutton and still on good terms with his uncle, he took the further step of marrying, not rashly and below himself as his father had done, but not well. Elizabeth Lumley was a spinster of 26 when Sterne, after a courtship of nearly two years, married her in York Minster on 30 March 1741. Like Sterne she was consumptive, in delicate health, and like him, too, she had influential relatives in the ecclesiastical hierarchy of York. She brought with her not only a small income derived from her parents' estate, but also a stubborn, intransigent temper that was to sit badly with the increasingly odd, not to say flighty, temper of her husband. By no account is the marriage reported to have been a happy one – '*wife.*—— 'Tis a shrill, penetrating sound of itself,' says Tristram (V, v). 'Sterne and his Wife,' wrote their friend and neighbour John Croft, 'tho' they did not *gee* well together, for she used to say herself, that the largest House in England cou'd not contain them both, on account of their Turmoils and Disputes, they were every day writing and addressing Love Letters to one another . . .' (Croft, p. 234). The chief cause of unhappiness – in the beginning, at least – was not incompatibility of temper, but what Croft bluntly called Sterne's 'infidelity to the Marriage Bed' (Croft, p. 226). A family servant, Richard Greenwood, was much later to recall that 'He used to accompany his master whenever Sterne came to York, & when there he rarely spent a night without a girl or two which Richard used to procure for him. He promised Richard to reward him for keeping these private amours of his secret, particularly from Mrs Sterne.'[3] (York gossip blamed Laurence's quarrel with Jacques on a dispute about a mistress.) It is not the least of the paradoxes of his character that Sterne, undoubted and indefatigable philanderer though he was, could centre his great novel around the theme of sexual impotency.

For the next decade he preached occasional sermons in York Minster, visited his eccentric college friend John Hall-Stevenson at his 'Crazy Castle' in the north of Yorkshire, where a motley group of literary pranksters and Rabelaisian *poseurs* called themselves the 'Demoniacs', and tended with uneven success his farm and parishes. Richard Greenwood remembers him writing sermons: 'In person tall and thin—when [composing] would often pull down his wig over one eye & remove it from side to side'.[4] Other York residents, spurred by Jacques Sterne, remembered his refusal to give money to his mother when she came to York from Chester, where she had been living with Sterne's sister Catherine, a refusal that led apparently to Mrs Sterne's brief imprisonment for a debt in 1751. The scandal, widely circulated in York, was to canker Sterne's reputation in his own time and afterwards to heighten the disgust Victorian critics instinctively felt for a clergyman who wrote indecent novels. ('Ah, I am as bad as that dog Sterne', Byron wrote in his journal, 'who preferred whining over "a dead ass to relieving a living mother".')[5] Recent biographers have tended to exonerate Sterne, however, portraying his mother as unduly grasping and as the victim of Jacques Sterne's machinations against his nephew.

If the quarrels with his mother and uncle did nothing to temper the strains in Sterne's inherently unstable character, the nearer daily skirmishes with Elizabeth Sterne must have intensified them almost beyond measure. Along both of the two great fault-lines that threaten most marriages – sex and money – there were constant rumblings and slippages. 'It was agreed betwixt them,' Croft writes, 'to have a Strong Box with a Nick in the Top and so they were to putt in what each saved out of their private expenses towards raising a Fortune for their Daughter Lidia when unhappily Mrs Sterne fell ill, and she espied Laurie breaking open the Strong Box. She fainted, and unluckily a Quarrel ensued' (Croft, pp. 234–5). And the *Letters* give all too plain evidence of a quite public liaison in 1759 with a visiting actress, Catherine Fourmantel ('What is Honey to the sweetness of thee, who art sweeter than all the flowers it comes from.—I love you to distraction Kitty': *Letters*, p. 83). There is also the story John Croft set down in his 'Anecdotes of Sterne': 'As an instance of his infidelity, his wife once caught him with the maid, when she pulled him out of bed on the Floor and soon after went out of her senses, when she fancied herself the Queen of Bohemia' (Croft, p. 226). In a later collection of Yorkshire stories and jokes he enlarged the episode:

Mrs Shandy, fancied herself the Queen of Bohemia. Tristram, her husband, to amuse and induce her to take the air, proposed coursing, in the way practised in Bohemia; for that purpose he procured

bladders, and filled them with beans, and tied them to the wheels of a
single horse chair. When he drove madam into a stubble field, with the
motion of the carriage and the bladders, rattle bladder, rattle; it
alarmed the hares, and the greyhounds were ready to take them.[6]

Whether or not Croft exaggerates (Bohemia was the name of fields south
of Sutton), it may well have been this sad collapse that Sterne had in mind
when he explained to a friend that 'every sentence' of *Tristram Shandy*
'had been conceived and written under the greatest Heaviness of Heart'.[7]

(ii) BIBLIOGRAPHICAL

In a letter of 23 May 1759, Sterne offered Volume 1 of *The Life and
Opinions of Tristram Shandy* to Robert Dodsley for £50, and promised a
second volume by November if Dodsley liked it. Dodsley, however,
returned the manuscript within a month, explaining that the 'risk' was
too great and the satire too local. Undeterred, Sterne rewrote throughout
the summer ('All locality is taken out of the book—the satire general,' he
told Dodsley), finished a second volume, and returned to Dodsley in
October with a new proposition. He would print a 'lean edition, in two
small volumes, of the size of Rasselas, and on the same paper and type, at
my own expense', and sell them from John Hinxman's bookshop in
York. If the book met with the success he expected, he would then ship
Dodsley a portion of the first printing to be sold by him in London, and
he would bargain with him for future editions and advances.[8]

The book appeared in Hinxman's window during the last days of
December 1759 and almost at once sold two hundred copies. Catherine
Fourmantel promptly carried a letter (undoubtedly written by Sterne) to
the great actor David Garrick in London, puffing the novel and asking
for his endorsement. In March of 1760, leaving sick wife and daughter
behind, Sterne impulsively travelled to London with York friends to
seek news for himself. 'The next morning', wrote Croft

Sterne was missing at breakfast. He went to Dodsley's where on
inquiry for Tristram Shandy's works, his Vanity was highly flattered,
when the Shopman told him, that there was not such a Book to be had
in London either for Love or money ... Soon after Mr Croft and
Cholmley passing by Pall Mall in a coach, who should they see in
Dodsley's Shop but Sterne who accosting them said that he was
mortgaging his brains to Dodsley for £50, the overplus of Six hundred
pounds, that he stood out for above the Bargain of Six hundred
pounds, that he offered him for the Copy of the two volumes of
Tristram Shandy, and for two Volumes of Sermons which he was to
compose in two months time, under the title of Yorick's Sermons, on a

further condition that he was to engage to write a vol. of Tristram
Shandy every year, and so to continue the work during his life . . . The
Gent^n advized him not to haggle, or bargain any longer about the
matter, but to close the agreem^t with Dodsley which he did, after
which he returned to Chapell street and came skipping into the room,
and said that he was the richest man in Europe. (Croft, pp. 227–8)

The bargain was kept. A second, lightly corrected and repunctuated
edition appeared in London soon afterwards, and then seven more
volumes in four instalments, although after Volumes III and IV Sterne
switched from Dodsley to another London publisher, Thomas Becket.
The Sermons of Mr Yorick – a title that offended many, linking a jester
with Holy Scripture – appeared in May 1760, then two more volumes in
1766, and a final two ('the sweepings of [my] study': *Letters*, p. 443, n. 2)
after his death. In the summer of 1766, moreover, wearying of *Tristram
Shandy* and no doubt alert to the critical success of the pathetic vein in its
later volumes, he began to think of a second novel, a tour across Europe
conducted by his *alter ego* Yorick. It would be, he told a friend, a 'work of
four volumes, which when finish'd, I shall continue Tristram with fresh
spirit' (*Letters*, p. 284). It would also, he boasted, fetch him a thousand
pounds. Two volumes of the uncompleted *Sentimental Journey through
France and Italy, by Mr Yorick* were published in early 1768, three weeks
before Sterne died.

Sterne's letters, edited (and in some cases rewritten) by his daughter
Lydia, appeared in 1775. A collected edition of his works in ten volumes
was published in 1780.

The last item in Sterne's bibliography may never have been meant for
publication. Composed during the most stressful period of his final
illness, *Letters from Yorick to Eliza* records Sterne's hysterically sentimental ardour for Elizabeth Draper, the 22-year-old wife of an India
merchant whom Sterne met in London in 1766 and courted notoriously
until she set sail to rejoin her husband in India. Sterne was then 54,
virtually an invalid ('worn down my dear Girl to a Shadow'), and his
epistolary courtship may be only a manifestation of physical desperation
(*Letters*, p. 326). He may have been thinking, too, of Swift's *Journal to
Stella*, published for the first time that year, as a model for his own work:
the most original of eighteenth-century writers was also the most sensi-
tively conscious of predecessors. Mrs Draper herself allowed the letters
to be published in 1773. The Journal to Eliza was edited and published
by Wilbur L. Cross in 1904.

(iii) 'A PICTURE OF MYSELF'

From the beginning, Sterne seems to have had a shrewd, instinctive
sense of how some issue of self-definition and identification is involved in

his writing. To a correspondent who warns against the indecorous bawdry of the first two volumes he replies with uncharacteristic firmness: 'I will use all reasonable caution—Only with this caution along with it, not to spoil My Book;—that is the air and originality of it, which must resemble the Author.' ''Tis ... a picture of myself,' he tells David Garrick when the book appears (*Letters*, pp. 76 and 87). He may well have taken the particular image of self-portraiture from his favourite Montaigne, who claims in his *Essays* to 'paint' himself precisely as he is, in all honesty and candour. But every novelist in fact knows what it is to see himself emerging in his text, as Sterne did in *Tristram Shandy*: the impulse to fiction nearly always contains an autobiographical element, all the more insistent when the fiction is written in the first person, like both of Sterne's novels. Because I cannot see myself whole, as I am, I try to see myself in the characters around me, those I can invent and those I can remember. Hence Tristram's complaint of fateful misfortunes is no doubt a version of Sterne's frustrations in church and marriage and his long struggle with tuberculosis (extended in the epilepsy of his daughter); Mrs Shandy's maddening refusal to be categorical resembles Mrs Sterne's indifferent misunderstanding of her husband; and Uncle Toby and his wars are an innocently nostalgic re-creation of Sterne's boyhood in Ireland with his father.

To many readers, however, Sterne's self-portrait fails in just that honesty and candour by which Montaigne so completely succeeds. W. M. Thackeray, who hated Sterne, and hated him with the virulent, condescending insight of a Victorian occupying high moral ground, writes vividly of what he regarded as Sterne's sentimental hypocrisy.

> I suppose Sterne had this artistic sensibility; he used to blubber perpetually in his study, and finding his tears infectious, and that they brought him a great popularity, he exercised the lucrative gift of weeping: he utilised it, and cried on every occasion. I own that I don't value or respect much the cheap dribble of those fountains. He fatigues me with his perpetual disquiet and his uneasy appeals to my risible or sentimental faculties. He is always looking in my face, watching his effect, uncertain whether I think him an impostor or not; posture-making, coaxing, and imploring me.[9]

This passage, once famous, has been taken as the result of Thackeray's secret identification with Sterne, his own temptation to sentimentality and 'humbug' – no one, after all, stares more intently into the faces of his readers than Thackeray, or tries more obviously to manipulate them. But, despite his complicity (or because of it), Thackeray chooses the essential adjectives: Sterne is 'uneasy', in 'perpetual disquiet'; he is 'uncertain' whether or not we think him an impostor. He signs his letters variously 'Tristram' or 'Yorick' (as if Joyce should sign his letters 'Bloom'). He depends upon disguise for some validation of self only tenuously related to his subject-matter, to his sentiment and jokes. 'I would take the image one step farther', insists a recent biographer, David Thomson, 'and say that Sterne was himself anxious to know whether he was genuine or not.'[10]

We may plausibly give a number of reasons why, beneath the pyrotechnics of his comedy, Sterne makes of his novel an obsessive and irrepressible self-portrait. A history of frustration, for example, humorous in Tristram, disheartening in fact, can produce an anxious counter-pressure of self-assertion. And that pressure may be all the stronger in someone chronically ill as Sterne was, singled out and threatened at every moment; or in someone conscious that life has neglected to keep its childhood promises of endless praise and attention: revealingly, his only anecdote of school concerns the day he wrote his name on the schoolroom ceiling and the master would not have it erased, saying 'I was a boy of genius, and he was sure I should come to preferment' (*Letters*, p. 4). Such uncertainty of self may also spring from the fact, as far as we can guess it, that Sterne was a man of strong, but not of deep emotions. The self-conscious 'blubber' that Thackeray claims Sterne could turn on and off, the apparent absence of long-lasting intimate relationships in his life – these things, too, can be invoked commonsensically to explain some of the frenetic insecurity of identity that readers detect in *Tristram Shandy*. Finally, we may speculate that inevitable feelings of exile – from Ireland, from parents, from siblings – continued into maturity and intensified those twin demons alienation and self-absorption. '*Tristram Shandy* is no less an island drama than *Robinson Crusoe*', as W. B. Carnochan observes.[11]

But the truth is, Sterne turns to self-portrait because his extraordinary personality proves so enigmatic even to himself ('There is not a more perplexing affair in life to me', says Yorick in the *Sentimental Journey*, 'than to set about telling any one who I am': *ASJ*, p. 221). He has, for one thing, that 'galloping' temperament sometimes characteristic of consumptives – we imagine him in constant, contradictory motion, like his prose. He enters a room all teeth and limbs and high-pitched giggles. We know of him as a reasonably conscientious, sometimes quite charitable clergyman; yet we associate him with flirtations and flightiness rather than with authority and dignity. It is often hard indeed to see what he is *serious* about in life, for he seems always ready to sacrifice anything, certainly dignity, to silliness. And yet alongside his frivolity we are conscious of a nervous, fearful, time-haunted self whose comic novels are littered with deaths and tears, a cadaverous jester. All of these elements, moreover, come together in his unsettling attitudes towards sex, a subject never more than a page away in his work, yet never rendered directly or steadily. The element of fantasy present in everyone's sexuality appears to suffuse Sterne's: he imagines strangely bodiless flirtations, concentrated with excruciating sensitivity on extremities, the tips of fingers, pulses. When celebrity and wealth enable him to separate from his wife, he choreographs a series of quite public and mostly harmless affairs, in London, Bath and Paris (though he will tell Eliza, at the appearance of venereal symptoms, that he has had no commerce with the sex 'not even with my wife', these fifteen years: *Letters*, p. 329). Indeed, the superficial hysteria of the *Journal to Eliza* only carries to the limits that bizarre combination of bravado and impotence characteristic of all his fiction. Hence the very public nature of his affair with Eliza convinced his shrewder friends that, for Sterne, nothing more was possible or needed: 'Any other idea of the Matter', writes Richard Griffith, 'would be more than the most abandoned Vice could render probable. To intrigue with a Vampire! To sink into the Arms of *Death Alive!*'[12]

It is fair to say, however, that our sense of flickering identity may also be the logical consequence of Sterne's attitude towards literary form. Twentieth-century academic criticism of *Tristram Shandy* would have astonished Sterne's contemporaries in a number of ways, but perhaps most of all in its tendency to interpret the book as a profound philosophical novel.[13] Yet Sterne's uninhibited subversion of literary conventions – the preface delayed until Volume IV, the fragmented line of narration, the black and blank pages – has naturally raised aesthetic questions that at their limits bear in upon the very nature of fiction, even of art: it is 'the most *typical* novel of world literature', runs Viktor Shklovsky's famous judgement, laying bare with its rebellious antics 'the general laws of novelistic form' (Traugott, pp. 66 and 89). And these aesthetic questions, because they so often come down to Sterne's views of language, have intersected with that central, abiding concern of modern philosophy itself, the unbreakable and unknowable relationship between language and reality. Certainly it is clear that the conversations of Toby and Walter (not to mention those of Walter and Mrs Shandy) raise questions of non-communication and alienation that we now associate with the concerns of philosophy. And it is clear as well that Sterne's arbitrary command of style – the sheer *process* of writing that he displays, as if the novel had a glass window into which we could peer and see its workings – logically provokes questions about the arbitrary nature of language itself, and about its power to thwart and to control our sense of reality. Sceptical readers, of course, responsive to the undoubted skittering quality of Sterne's text, may hesitate to take seriously the philosophic dimensions of a novel that describes itself as a cock and bull story, 'wrote, an' please your worships, against the spleen' (IV, xxii). But more than one critic has protested on Sterne's behalf that comedy and profundity need not be at odds; and, in any case, the best of such academic studies, James Swearingen's *Reflexivity in 'Tristram Shandy'*, has argued that the real philosophical subject of the book is not one or another traditional category like time or language, but a new kind of philosophy altogether. Sterne's novel, Swearingen says, drawing upon the theories of Husserl and Heidegger, is 'an incipient phenomenology the ultimate aim of which is an ontological analysis of the meaning of Tristram's being'.[14] Or, in non-technical language, Sterne's book attempts to interpret the identity of its protagonist (and we can say of its author as well) by rendering in language and symbol his whole field of consciousness, including most particularly those strange creatures in his life who have formed his consciousness and who in turn have made him so strange. Its form therefore represents the realistic motions of a mind struggling to describe itself, and its central philosophical question is the nature of consciousness.

The question arises in part because such a subject-matter is ideally suited to the techniques of fiction, which can hardly sustain systematic argument but is unsurpassed for rendering subjective vision. (If Sterne did not exist, Virginia Woolf would have had to invent him.) But it also arises in part because John Locke and David Hume had prepared the way for it in their discussions of 'personal identity' earlier in the century, discussions that drew a wide audience, including Sterne, into a debate over self-knowledge and continuity which had begun with Descartes' first *cogito*. Sterne's revealing capsule of Locke's *Essay Concerning Human Understanding* suggests, indeed, how far the novelist's mind has gone towards transforming philosophy:

... many, I know, quote the book, who have not read it,——and many have read it who understand it not:——If either of these is your case, as I write to instruct, I will tell you in three words what the book is.——It is a history.——A history! of who? what? where? when? Don't hurry yourself.——It is a history book, Sir, (which may possibly recommend it to the world) of what passes in a man's own mind ... (II, ii)

This 'history', moreover, like the 'life and opinions' of Tristram Shandy, takes place inside, within, secretly, like the successions of sensations that Locke claims make up our personal identities. And, for Locke's famous images of the mind as a *tabula rasa* and a darkened room, Sterne has an equivalent image pattern that runs like a leitmotiv from the beginning to the end of the novel: no writer has ever described the inside of our heads so literally. In *Tristram Shandy* 'the spare places of our brains' are capacious beyond all imagination (III, xx).[15] They can contain a city square of nerves, converging on the cerebellum like streets and alleys (II, xix); Dr Slop's brain can accommodate a flotilla of thoughts 'without sail or ballast ... millions of which, as your worship knows, are every day swimming quietly in the middle of the thin juice of a man's understanding, without being carried backwards or forwards, till some little gusts of passion or interest drive them to one side' (III, ix). Toby's head can be like the inside of a Savoyard's box, or more wonderfully still: 'his head like a smoak-jack;——the funnel unswept, and the ideas whirling round and round about in it, all obfuscated and darkened over with fuliginous matter!' (III, xix). 'Such a head!' Tristram exclaims, identifying at once the real setting of the novel and its dark, unreachable secrecy: '——would to heaven! my enemies only saw the inside of it!' (III, xxxviii). If Sterne has influenced any number of modern writers by his anti-novelistic techniques, he has influenced them still more by the sense he conveys, Cartesian and Lockian in origin, of a second, inner life, an interior consciousness potentially at odds with the face he presents to the world; a less happy, less clear, and more truthful identity.

(iv) 'ROLE DISTANCE'

How can the inside of a head be seen? How can his enemies be drawn forward, to penetrate that interior reality? In a central moment of the *Confessions*, Sterne's great contemporary Jean-Jacques Rousseau begins to condemn his own opacity: 'I should like in some way', he declares, frustrated, 'to make my soul transparent to the reader's eye.' And he goes on to give what is in effect a précis of Tristram's method:

> If I made myself responsible for the result and said to [the reader], 'Such is my character', he might suppose, if not that I am deceiving him, at least that I am deceiving myself. But by relating to him in simple detail all that has happened to me, all that I have done, all that I have felt, I cannot lead him into error ... His task is to assemble these elements and to assess the being who is made up of them.[16]

Like Rousseau, whom he resembles in so many other ways as well, Sterne yearns for transparency, yearns to turn himself inside out, for his friends and enemies to see him in every detail as he really is and therefore to understand him: ''tis a picture of myself'. (Montaigne would 'most willingly have pourtrayed my selfe fully and naked'.)[17] Whether we call it self-portrait or phenomenology, the theme of communication in both writers is really a theme of exhibitionism, not without its literal element of eroticism, but having its source in the fuliginous whirlings of consciousness that make both men depend upon an audience's focus and reaction for their self-definition.

One can almost hear Thackeray, that percipient fellow-traveller, turning away with an impatient snort. The controlling noun of his description, after all, is 'impostor'. He implies, not that Sterne is opaque or perplexed, but that he has deliberately taken a false role and attempted to coax us into seeing him as better than he is. If he knows himself to be an immoral and unfaithful husband, his romantic sentimentality will overlay his vices, obscuring them. If he knows himself an irresponsible clergyman, he moves in the highest circles of society, protected and petted. If he is terrified of a rapacious death that may be understood as punishment (or as meaningless), his 'risible' faculties will laugh away this terror. Sooner or later in speaking of Sterne's self-portrait, however philosophical our temper, we come to Thackeray's challenge that it is all humbug and imposture. Or, to change, 'imposture' into contemporary, neutralized language, we come to the question of Sterne's role-playing.

For many of us, the terms 'role' and 'role-playing' have by now lost all dramatic resonance – a resonance particularly right for Sterne, self-proclaimed friend of David Garrick, and noisy arranger of the stage in *Tristram Shandy* – and have passed into the general din of psychobabble. But the sociologist Erving Goffman, revitalizing the traditional metaphor, has argued that, while we all may be seen as playing roles in our daily lives, there are moments in which, even as we act out a role, we wish to resist it and to suggest some disaffection with it. For illustration he turns to 5-year-old boys on merry-go-rounds. Once a quite solemn, unself-conscious rider, the 5-year-old abruptly changes his behaviour.

Parents are not likely to be allowed to ride along, and the strap for preventing falls is often disdained. One rider may keep time to the music by his feet or a hand against the horse, an early sign of utter control. Another may make a wary stab at standing on the saddle or changing horses without touching the platform. Still another may hold on to the post with one hand and lean back as far as possible while looking up to the sky in a challenge to dizziness. Irreverence begins, and the horse may be held on to by his wooden ear or his tail. The child says by his actions: 'Whatever I am, I'm not just someone who can barely manage to stay on a wooden horse.'[18]

What reader will not recognize Sterne's behaviour as novelist in this account? 'One would think I took a pleasure in running into difficulties of this kind,' Tristram sighs at a point when his plot has collapsed like a clown's chair, 'merely to make fresh experiments of getting out of 'em' (VIII, vi). 'There may be as many chapters as steps,' he threatens, reminding us that it has taken two chapters to get Toby and Walter down one pair of stairs: 'let that be as it will, Sir, I can no more help it than my destiny:——A sudden impulse comes across me——drop the curtain, *Shandy*——I drop it——Strike a line here across the paper, *Tristram*—

—I strike it——and hey for a new chapter!' (IV, x). His whole manner
of proceeding resembles nothing so much as the boy on the merry-go-
round, holding on with one hand and leaning as far back as possible 'in a
challenge to dizziness'. ('The tempo of *Tristram Shandy*', observes Cyril
Connolly, 'reminds one at times of the youthful occupation of seeing
how slowly one can ride a bicycle without falling off.')[19] If he is a
novelist in the tradition of Defoe and Fielding and Richardson, he takes
every possible opportunity to mock that tradition, to lift its curtains and
reveal its absurdities, to distance himself from the role of novelist by
superimposing upon it the role of jester. The boy on the merry-go-
round, however, distances himself from his role as part of his drive to
grow older, to seem more than a child. For adults, there can be
pragmatic reasons – a surgeon may constantly joke as he works in order
to release tension – but an adult may also mock his role as the child does,
in order to show that another, larger, deeper, preferable identity exists:
whatever I am, there is more to me than this frivolous retailer of jokes
and dialogue. 'Explanations, apologies, and joking', Goffman says, 'are
all ways in which the individual makes a plea for disqualifying some of
the expressive features of the situation as sources of definitions of
himself.'[20]

Such a view is consistent with the impression that *Tristram Shandy*
adds up to a portrait of its author; consistent as well with the idea that
Sterne's presentation of consciousness in the book touches profounder
levels than the casual reader may suspect, and indeed makes its
strongest appeal to us now by virtue of the struggle it records to define
and establish a self. Sterne himself expresses impatience with readers
who do not see that his novel is in fact 'a moral work, more read than
understood' ('It is too much to write books and find heads to understand
them,' he complains to a correspondent).[21] In this context role-distancing may have its obvious source in Sterne's other great role, so clearly in
conflict with that of a comic writer: a clergyman, as everybody from the
Bishop of Gloucester down informed him, ought not to write indecent
novels, or perhaps novels at all. I am someone else, the jokes are saying,
someone to be taken seriously, and my book is really a sermon.
Twentieth-century readers may underestimate this conflict between
novelist and cleric – though Victorians would not – but it runs through
all contemporary reactions, contributing to Sterne's scandalous celebrity and intensifying undoubtedly that sense of enigmatic self always
present to his own consciousness.

We can add that the concept of role distance belongs to the larger
movement in sociology sometimes called 'symbolic interaction' or 'perspectivist' theory, which posits at least three other points relevant to
Tristram Shandy:

(1) multiple definitions of the same 'reality' are possible, and depend upon each individual's perspective; hence

(2) objectivity and communication are always problematic, as are the stabilities of meaning; but

(3) from this unsteadiness of objectivity and meaning there arises a concurrent freedom to define the self and to take pleasure in its pure sensibility – that is, to step back and enjoy the spectacle of the self in action.

In one way or another, each of these points will recur over and over again as we take up the questions of Sterne's ambiguity of language and meaning, his insistence that Toby, Walter and the others occupy parallel but different realities, his manipulative delight in Toby's and Yorick's pathetic sensibility. Here, however, it may be enough simply to say that role distance, as Goffman defines it, allows for much more than comic relief by means of detachment: it is the very root of creativity in the self; it permits Tristram to mock his own comic behaviour as a writer, but it also permits Sterne, in theory at least, to stand back and by an act of will compose a more coherent, more satisfactory, even a more genuine self.

It is likewise possible that Sterne's role-distancing, however much it may lead academic readers to suspect philosophy or sociology, derives simply from a trick of Fielding's that Sterne has begun by imitating. 'I would again invoke the Muse, (which the good-natured Reader may think a little too hard upon her, as she hath so lately been violently sweated),' the narrator of *Tom Jones* characteristically remarks after the famous battle in 'Homerican' style. 'I ask Pardon for this short Appearance, by Way of Chorus on the Stage . . . As I could not prevail on any of my Actors to speak, I myself was obliged to declare.'[22] Fielding's voice is always verging like this on a mockery of himself as well as of his material, always slipping a certain distance to expose a personality more expansive and more authoritative than those of his invented characters; and when he drops the urbane tone for a moment altogether, as he does in praising the very real virtues of Ralph Allen, for example, we find ourselves in the presence of a genuinely serious personality, at once moral and secure. If Sterne took up this trick of voice as one of many imitable novelistic techniques, he transformed it instantly into the compulsive hysterical chatter that makes *Tristram Shandy*, among other things, so brilliant a parody of Fielding's kind of novel. When his parodic voice slips, however, as it sometimes does, and discovers another narrator, the moment is infinitely more vulnerable, more intimate than anything in Fielding:

No——I think, I said, I would write two volumes every year, provided the vile cough which then tormented me, and which to this hour I dread worse than the devil, would but give me leave . . . I swore it should be kept a going at that rate these forty years if it pleased but the fountain of life to bless me so long with health and good spirits. (VII, i)

And so, with this moral for the present, may it please your worships and your reverences, I take my leave of you till this time twelve-month, when (unless this vile cough kills me in the mean time) I'll have another pluck at your beards, and lay open a story to the world you little dream of. (IV, xxxii)

Whoever he is, the writer's concerns plunge farther and deeper than the boundaries of Shandy Hall. 'My good friend,' Tristram declares to the commissary in Lyons

... sure as I am I——and you are you——
——And who are you? said he——Don't puzzle me; said I. (VII, xxxiii)

(v) CHILD'S PLAY

In his wild subversion of decorum, finally, Sterne may be only expressing a form of that exuberance for which the eighteenth century is famous: his manic energy may belong to the same order of vitality as Moll Flanders's determination to survive or Tom Jones's robust masculinity. In the singular freedom of his self-portrait, we may see, not Sterne's tuberculosis or his phenomenology or his neurosis, but simply Sterne as he is: his book exactly reflecting, as he claimed from the first, the unfettered spirit of its author. 'We are free', writes Henri Bergson in *Time and Free Will*, 'when our actions emanate from our total personality, when they express it, when they resemble it in the indefinable way a work of art sometimes does the artist.'[23]

What kind of self is thus synonymous with such pure freedom? Let me suggest one last image. The composite character who emerges laughing from the pages of Sterne's novel – the Sterne so inappropriately named – is in one way the most childlike and childish of writers. Not even Rabelais, with all his uproar – certainly not Swift or Cervantes, to name his nearest models – maintains so completely the guise of mischievous childishness that Sterne achieves. ('If I thought you was able to form the least judgment or probable conjecture to yourself, of what was to come in the next page,——I would tear it out of my book': I, xxv). The child laughs, Freud tells us, out of pure pleasure, and when we laugh with him we experience for a moment 'an awakening of the infantile'. But we always laugh in any case, Freud also says, because of an unconscious comparison going forward in our minds; and when we laugh at the immoderate, uninhibited actions of infantile humour it is because we are comparing those actions with the way we ourselves, now sober and adult, would perform them. 'The complete comparison which leads to the comic would run: "That is how he does it – I do it in another way – he does it as I used to do it as a child." '[24] The 5-year-old has dismounted the merry-go-round and taken up a pencil, capering wildly and scribbling a wavy line across his pages. Parody or inspiration, Sterne writes a novel just as a child would write it.

None of this is intended to rob Sterne of the dignity to which all comic writers aspire. What Freud calls 'infantile humour' has inevitably its serious meaning, all the more serious because of the deeply primitive energy it draws upon. It is important for the reader of *Tristram Shandy* to remember, as it was impossible for Sterne to forget, that its author was all his life a man on the edge, as Tristram puts it, of time's abyss, a man in the grip of death, whose vile asthma was rattling in his throat. However much it may be true that Sterne was trying to render himself transparent, or trying to distance himself from his novel in order to reconcile one role with another, it is also true that he was writing to disarm as well as distance. For humour, Freud declares, represents

> the triumph of narcissism, the victorious assertion of the ego's invul-nerability. The ego refuses to be distressed by the provocations of reality, or to let itself be compelled to suffer . . . It means: 'Look! here is the world, which seems so dangerous! It is nothing but a game for children – just worth making a jest about!'[25]

And into Freud's classic humanism we can also absorb the notion in role-distance theory of another self struggling towards assertion. If a man laughs at himself 'in order to ward off possible suffering', Freud asks, can we not say that he 'is treating himself like a child and is at the same time playing the part of a superior adult towards that child'?[26] 'When DEATH himself knocked at my door', Tristram recounts in an address to his 'spirits', 'ye bad him come again; and in so gay a tone of careless indifference, did ye do it, that he doubted of his commission——' (VII, i). This is the humour, infantile, impervious and heroic, that exposes a self and yet preserves it.

We would do Sterne an injustice, however, to conclude with an image of naïve simplicity, inadvertently stumbling upon literary achievement. Like that visionary comedian of the next generation, William Blake, Sterne possesses the extraordinary ability to combine the child's self-delighting innocence with the most baffling artistic sophistication. And, like Blake, Sterne required more than a century before his achievement began to be understood and influential. Novelists will perhaps always be first in his debt, for the sheer technical possibilities his virtuosity opened up. But general readers of all kinds will value him for other reasons. If his

world contains a tragic centre, revealed best in Volume VII, it none the
less encloses that dark core, like a great star, in a radiant humour that
requires neither critical nor philosophical theory to understand, only a
shared (and farcical) humanity.

NOTES: CHAPTER 1

1   For the dates of composition given here I rely on Cash, chs. 13–14. Margaret R. B.
    Shaw argues for an earlier date in *Laurence Sterne: The Making of a Humorist,
    1713–1762* (London: Richards Press, 1957), pp. 161–70. On the letter, see Croft, p.
    231.

2   Laurence Sterne, *The Life and Opinions of Tristram Shandy, Gentleman*, ed. Melvyn
    New and Joan New (Gainesville, Fla: University Presses of Florida, 1978), Vol. VIII,
    ch. vi. Cited parenthetically by volume and chapter in the text.

3   James Kuist, 'New light on Sterne: an old man's recollections of the young vicar',
    PMLA, vol. 80 (1965), p. 549.

4   ibid., p. 550.

5   George Noel Gordon, Lord Byron, *Letters and Journals*, ed. Leslie A. Marchand
    (Cambridge, Mass.: Harvard University Press, 1973–82), Vol. 3, p. 229.

6   John Croft, *Scrapeana*, 2nd edn (York, 1792), p. 22.

7   *European Magazine*, March 1792, p. 170; quoted in Cash, p. 287.

8   See *Letters*, pp. 74–5, 80–1. Important discussions of the whole subject are Lewis
    Perry Curtis, 'The first printer of *Tristram Shandy*', *PLMA*, vol. 47 (1932), pp.
    777–89, and Kenneth Monkman, 'The bibliography of the early editions of *Tristram
    Shandy*', *The Library*, 5th ser., vol. 25 (1970), pp. 11–39.

9   William Makepeace Thackeray, 'Sterne and Goldsmith', in *The English Humorists of
    the Eighteenth Century*, in *Works* (New York, 1898), Vol. 11, pp. 320–1.

10 David Thomson, *Wild Excursions: The Life and Fiction of Laurence Sterne* (London:
    Weidenfeld & Nicolson, 1972), p. 5.

11 W. B. Carnochan, *Confinement and Flight: An Essay on English Literature of the
    Eighteenth Century* (Berkeley/Los Angeles, Calif.: University of California Press,
    1977), p. 55.

12 Richard Griffith, *A Series of Genuine Letters between Henry and Frances* (London,
    1786), Vol. 5, pp. 199–200; quoted in Thomson, op. cit, p. 259.

13 See, for example, Arthur H. Cash, 'The sermon in *Tristram Shandy*', *ELH*, vol. 31
    (1964), p. 416: 'Sterne is the most philosophic of novelists.' Also, Martin Price, *To the
    Palace of Wisdom: Studies in Order and Energy from Dryden to Blake* (Garden City, NY:
    Doubleday, 1964), p. 327; and Robert Alter, '*Tristram Shandy* and the game of love',
    American Scholar, vol. 37 (1968), p. 317.

14 James E. Swearingen, *Reflexivity in 'Tristram Shandy': An Essay in Phenomenological
    Criticism* (New Haven, Conn.: Yale University Press, 1977), p. 44.

15 David Thomson discusses the same image pattern (op. cit., pp. 12–20).

16 Jean-Jacques Rousseau, *Confessions*, trans. J. M. Cohen (Harmondsworth: Penguin,
    1954), p. 169. For further discussion of this point in Rousseau, see J. Starobinski,
    Jean-Jacques Rousseau, la transparence et l'obstacle (Paris: Gallimard, 1957), pp.
    216–39.

17 Michel de Montaigne, 'The Author to the Reader', *Essays*, trans. John Florio, The
    Tudor Translations, ed. W. E. Henley (London: David Nutt, 1892; reprinted New
    York: AMS, 1967), Vol. 1, p. 12.

18 Erving Goffman, *Encounters: Two Studies in the Sociology of Interaction* (Indianapolis,
    Ind.: Bobbs-Merrill, 1961), p. 107.

19 Cyril Connolly, *The Condemned Playground: Essays: 1927–44* (New York: Macmillan, 1946), p. 24.
20 Goffman, op. cit., p. 105. A good introduction to perspectivist sociology is Peter L. Berger and Thomas Luckmann, *The Social Construction of Reality: A Treatise in the Sociology of Knowledge* (Garden City, NY: Doubleday, 1966).
21 Sterne, 'Advertisement' to 'Sermon XII', *The Sermons of Mr Yorick*, in Sterne's *Works* (Oxford: Basil Blackwell, 1927), Vol. 7, p. 66; *Letters*, p. 411.
22 Henry Fielding, *The History of Tom Jones, A Foundling*, ed. Martin C. Battestin and Fredson T. Bowers (London: Oxford University Press, 1975), bk IV, ch. viii; bk III, ch. vii.
23 Henri Bergson, *Time and Free Will*, trans. R. L. Pogson (London: George Allen, 1910), p. 172.
24 Sigmund Freud, *Jokes and Their Relation to the Unconscious*, trans. James Strachey *et al.*, *The Standard Edition of the Complete Psychological Works of Sigmund Freud* (London: Hogarth Press, 1960), Vol. 8, pp. 224-5.
25 Sigmund Freud, 'Humour', in *The Future of an Illusion and Other Works*, trans. James Strachey *et al.*, *Standard Edition* (London: Hogarth Press, 1961), Vol. 21, pp. 162 and 166.
26 ibid., p. 164.

CHAPTER 2

The Line of Wit:
Literary Backgrounds

It is possible to speak of the advantages of influence as well as the anxiety. In his recent theoretical speculations, elaborating what might be called the poetics of neurosis, Harold Bloom has sketched a picture of literary history as a series of baroque, subliminal psychic rivalries between modern poets and their predecessors. 'Belated' modern poets, he contends, are at once inhibited and inspired by the accomplishments of earlier writers; they fall back from the challenge of an overpowering tradition, they can free themselves to write only by taking arms against a sea of fathers. They take arms and by 'misreading' end them. To find his own voice, that is, the filial poet must distort or reinterpret the 'precursor' who tyrannizes his imagination, much as Blake recasts *Paradise Lost* to make Satan the hero and Milton the poet of the Devil's party. What Bloom calls 'anxiety' W. J. Bate more accurately and dramatically terms 'the burden of the past', and traces it to the specific historical situation of the mid and later eighteenth century in England, when 'originality' and 'novelty' for the first time become conscious critical ideals and young writers feel an urgent pressure to differ from earlier writers, by sheer force of singularity if nothing else.[1]

Sterne's extravagant assault upon literary convention has sometimes caused him to be placed among these anxious experimental writers – among pre-romantic names like Ossian, Chatterton and Blake – but Sterne's originality, for all its subversion of convention, has more to do with eccentricity than with experiment. He belongs to an earlier generation of writers, his point of view and – so far as we can judge them – his intentions are profoundly conservative, hard to distinguish from those of Johnson, Pope or Swift. In spite of the celebrated 'oddness', Sterne seems less like someone striking out a new path than like someone cartwheeling back and forth across familiar terrain, merely capering to absurd extremes. Indeed, in his self-absorption, in his effort to use the novel to establish or clarify his own identity, Sterne scarcely looks up to see what is being written around him – his letters and books are striking for their lack of reference to contemporary literature; and he seems unaware even of the existence of his immediate predecessors Fielding and Richardson. His glance instead turns automatically to the past, to the writers of what D. W. Jefferson has suggestively called the 'tradition of learned wit'; and his use of them – his cock-eyed imitation of their best voices and gags – conveys nothing at all of anxiety, everything of irreverent glee.[2]

What kind of book did he think he was writing?

(i) SOURCES AND PLAGIARISM

When Sterne offered the first volume of *Tristram Shandy* to Robert Dodsley in May of 1759, his account was vague in the extreme: 'The Plan, as you will percieve, is a most extensive one,—taking in, not only, the Weak part of the Sciences, in wch the true point of Ridicule lies—but every Thing else, which I find Laugh-at-able in my way—' (*Letters*, p. 74). And when he submitted a revised version and a second volume in September of that same year – having written at breakneck pace through the summer – he explained his changes only in a postscript, an apparent response to Dodsley's criticisms: 'P.S. All locality is taken out of the book—the satire general; notes are added where wanted, and the whole made more saleable—about a hundred and fifty pages added.' From this and other evidence, it is fair to guess that the first version of *Tristram Shandy* probably followed closely the satirical character of the little pamphlet Sterne had written in the early days of January 1759, and entitled *A Political Romance*. That pamphlet has little else but locality in it. Dr Francis Topham, the primary target of its satire (interestingly renamed 'Trim'), had for six months been labouring noisily to induce the new dean of York, John Fountayne, to grant him a certain clerical stipend, and moreover to guarantee the same stipend to his son Edward after his death. (Edward was then 7 years old.) Sterne, long experienced in ecclesiastical scrimmages, took the opportunity to court Fountayne's favour himself by writing a farcical account of Topham's heavy-handed (and unsuccessful) appeals, called at first 'The History of a Good Warm Watch-Coat', a mildly licentious imitation of Swift's inherited-coat allegory in the *Tale of a Tub*. Before Sterne could have this 'History' printed, however, Topham had caused a public uproar with a series of pamphlets of his own, and Sterne was inspired to add both a 'Postscript' and a 'Key' to the allegory, the latter a conversation among various gentlemen around a fire who offer interpretations from politics, history or their professions of the 'History' (a tailor thus finds that Topham's boots stand for Italy, his breeches Sicily). If the first part of the completed book shows the undeniable influence of Swift, the enlargements are sometimes taken to show Sterne's more novelistic gift of drawing humorous characters in the amiable manner of the *Spectator*; but beyond these debts it is also clear that the 'Key' affords our first glimpse of Sterne's characteristic juxtaposition of conflicting, not to say cancelling, views of reality – a technique that was to reach its perfection in the opaque, voluble, criss-crossing solitudes of Toby and Walter. Sterne was persuaded by Fountayne and others to suppress his book, and *A Political Romance* was never actually published – it remains one of the rarest works in English literature – though several hundred copies were run off in late January 1759. If he objected to this suppression, Sterne never said so; but, according to one witness at least, 'it was to this Disappointment that the World is indebted for Tristram Shandy' (Cash, p. 277).

When he moved almost without a pause from *A Political Romance* to *Tristram Shandy* – he was offering a completed manuscript of some bulk to Dodsley by May – Sterne's idea of what he was doing could not yet have clarified into Uncle Toby, Walter or the triple disaster of nose, name and sash. His friend John Croft, writing fifteen years after Sterne's death, recalled a satiric Grand Tour:

> Sterne said that his first Plan, was to travell his Hero Tristram Shandy all over Europe and after making his remarks on the different Courts, proceed with making strictures and reflections on the different Governments of Europe and finish the work with an eulogium on the superior constitution of England and at length to return Tristram well informed and a compleat English Gentleman. (Croft, p. 228)

An unidentified gentleman visiting York in mid-1759 met Sterne somehow, read part of the new manuscript, and talked through a night with him about it. 'The design . . . is to take in all Ranks and Professions,' he explained in a subsequently published letter, revealing the names of specific satiric victims and the persistence of the allegorical mode:

> A system of Education is to be exhibited, and thoroughly discussed. For forming his future Hero . . . a private Tutor . . . no less a Person than the great and learned Dr. W[arburton, Bishop of Gloucester]: Polemical Divines are to come in for a slap. An Allegory has been run up on the Writers on the Book of Job. The Doctor [Warburton] is the Devil who smote him from Head to Foot, and G[re]y P[ete]rs and Ch[appel]ow [commentators on Job] his miserable Comforters. (Cash, p. 279)

And, almost as if to counter the impression of glib self-confidence in Sterne's letters to Dodsley, the unidentified gentleman notes that Sterne was 'haunted with Doubts and Fears of its not taking'. (Croft says that when Sterne read part of the book aloud after dinner his audience 'fell asleep at which Sterne was so nettled that he threw the Manuscript into the fire', from which Croft claims he rescued it: p. 229.)

The scale and satirical elasticity of these schemes (as well as their changeableness) will bring to mind predecessors like Lucian, Martinus Scriblerus, Rabelais, Swift and, perhaps above all, Robert Burton, and these are in fact writers whom Sterne enjoyed and some of whose names actually turn up in *Tristram Shandy*. An exact genealogy would expand the list into a formidable literary ancestry – others named at one time or another include Petronius, Apuleius, Varro, Bruscambille, Scarron, Bouchet, Beroalde, Bacon, Dunton, Montaigne, Erasmus, and Bishop Hall – and Northrop Frye has boldly traced Sterne back to the lost works of the Greek cynic Menippus. Such a miscellany, breathlessly cited as 'sources' in some critical and biographical studies, has two unfortunate effects: first, it makes Sterne look much more learned than he actually was – he had read widely but not systematically – and, second, it obscures what in a general way he could have inherited from such precursors. Northrop Frye catches the essential formal quality that they had in common: '*Tristram Shandy* may be ... a novel, but the digressing narrative, the catalogues, the stylizing of character along "humor" lines, the marvellous journey of the great nose, the symposium discussions, and the constant ridicule of philosophers and pedantic critics are all features that belong to the anatomy' – his useful term for the kind of loose-jointed narrative that extends past *Tristram Shandy* and on through *Nightmare Abbey, Sartor Resartus* and *Moby Dick*.[3] This is the careless, conversational form whose 'originality' Sterne ironically found himself constantly defending and which he insisted 'must resemble the Author'.

Any beginning writer will clutch at whatever security he can find in rummaging through earlier writers – as advice, 'write like an author you admire' comes second only to 'write about what you know' – but Bloom's idea of anxiety is a misleadingly subjective way to describe the relationship. What writers generally steal are small things, not big. What a novice wants is technique, not vision. The real relationship of writer to source is less like a crouching son, teeth bared, to an imposing father, and more like a passing burglar to an open window. In the case of Sterne, although many of his contemporaries were puzzled by his extravagant formlessness, others recognized at once that his starting-point was an imitation, if not of a Menippean anatomy, at least of a whole family of sixteenth- and seventeenth-century jesters. 'It was not the business of Sterne to undeceive those, who considered his Tristram as a work of unfathomable knowledge,' wrote John Ferriar in a little book called *Illustrations of Sterne* (1812), intended precisely to do that business.

His imagination, untamed by labour, and unsated by a long acquaintance with literary folly, dwelt with enthusiasm on the grotesque pictures of manners and opinions, displayed in his favourite authors. It may even be suspected, that by this influence he was drawn aside from his natural bias to the pathetic; for in the serious parts of his

works, he seems to have depended on his own force, and to have
found in his own mind whatever he wished to produce; but in the
ludicrous he is generally a copyist, and sometimes follows his original
so closely, that he forgets the changes of manners, which give an
appearance of extravagance to what was once correct ridicule.[4]

From these 'favourite authors' Ferriar draws a long catalogue of
Sterne's borrowings that still makes startling reading – a whole chapter
of examples from Burton alone! – and, although his initial intention is
friendly, not to accuse Sterne of plagiarism, the effect of so many
parallels, paraphrases and sheer liftings is none the less to suggest a
writer often lazy and opportunistic, the 'copyist' of other wits that
Ferriar thinks him. ''Tis an inevitable chance——,' sighs Walter
Shandy; 'the first statute in *Magnâ Chartâ*——it is an everlasting act of
parliament, my dear brother,——*All must die*' (V, iii). Beside which
Ferriar quietly places the passage from Burton: *"T is an inevitable
chance, the first statute in Magna Charta, an everlasting act of Parliament,
all must die*' (p. 74).
    Modern scholarship had added more borrowings to the debt, and not
only from Ferriar's sixteenth- and seventeenth-century wits, but also
from such unlikely sources as Dr John Burton's textbooks on obstetrics, Rapin's *History of England*, and Ephraim Chambers's *Cyclopaedia:
or, An Universal Dictionary of Arts and Sciences*. This last title, in fact,
turns out to be the nearly verbatim storehouse of Uncle Toby's erudi-
tion about warfare and sieges. In Sterne's defence, however, some of
the borrowings have turned out to be witty enough in themselves, and
none wittier than the plagiarized passages at the beginning of Volume
V.II denouncing the practice of plagiarism, themselves largely plagiarized in turn by Sterne's source Robert Burton. But few studies of
Sterne's petty larceny have gone beyond the sharp-eyed citation of
parallels and phrases to recognize how even his simplest 'copying'
reshapes material into new and significant patterns. In the denunciation
of plagiarism, for example, Ferriar has discovered Sterne's declamation
'word for word' in Burton:

Shall we for ever make new books, as apothecaries make new mixtures, by pouring only out of one vessel into another?
    Are we for ever to be twisting, and untwisting the same rope? for
ever in the same track——for ever at the same pace? (V, i)

'As apothecaries, [says Burton,] *we make new mixtures every day, pour
out of one vessel into another; and as those old Romans robbed all the
cities of the world, to set out their bad-sited Rome, we skim off the cream
of other men's wits, pick the choice flowers of their tilled gardens, to set out*

our own sterile plots.' Again, '*We weave the same web still, twist the same rope again and again*' (p. 67).

But Sterne imposes a rhetorical unity that Burton utterly lacks – the parallel syntax of Sterne's questions – and, far more important, a thematic unity: the theme of the passage of time, never far from Tristram's consciousness, emerges here in the drumbeat of repeated phrases. 'Shall we *for ever* make new books ... *for ever* to be twisting ... *for ever* in the same track——*for ever* at the same pace?' And he goes on to repeat the syntactical form with a variation on the idea of time passing: 'Shall we be destined to the days of eternity ... ?' Ferriar adds incredulously that the very next paragraph is also a plagiarism from Burton.

> Who made MAN, with powers which dart him from earth to heaven in a moment——that great, that most excellent, and most noble creature of the world——the *miracle* of nature, as Zoroaster in his book περι φύσεωσ called him ... the *marvel* of *marvels*, as Aristotle——to go sneaking on at this pitiful——pimping——pettifoggying rate?

> *Man*, says Burton, *the most excellent and noble creature of the world, the principal and mighty work of God, wonder of nature as Zoroastes calls him; audacis naturae miraculum; the marvel of marvels, as Plato ...* ' (pp. 67–8)

But these are parallels that veer sharply apart. Sterne, who had begun the page with a comparison of the speed of a 'madcap' carriage and a heavy London wagon, has in his last clause adapted Burton to this comparison (already adumbrated in 'the same pace') and rewritten his entire source to incorporate both the ideas of speed and of time: 'powers which dart him from earth to heaven in a moment'. Such reshaping amounts to something more than plagiarism, something less than anxiety; and it must be said that Sterne almost always similarly imposes the form of his own obsessions upon his sources. '*But where am I? into what subject have I rushed? What have I to do?*' Ferriar quotes Burton (p. 86), without seeing the urgency of Sterne's revision: 'but where am I? and into what a delicious riot of things am I rushing? I——I who must be cut short in the midst of my days' (VII, xiv). In any case, such pilferings are no more than five-finger exercises for a writer so sensitive to style as Sterne. Only three predecessors stand out as influential as well as imitable: Rabelais, Cervantes and Swift.

(ii) RABELAIS

'The author of *Tristram Shandy*, with all his merit,' observes an anonymous reviewer in 1762, 'is not so much of an original as he is commonly imagined. Rabelais dealt in the same kind of haberdashery' (*CH*, p. 139). Not altogether a compliment – Johnson defines 'haberdasher' as a 'pedlar' – but an inescapable comparison. Sterne's contemporaries made it over and over again: 'Oh rare Tristram Shandy!' apostrophized one critic (touching instinctively the question of Tristram's identity), 'Thou very sensible—humorous—pathetick—humane—unaccountable!—what shall we call thee?—Rabelais, Cervantes, What?' (*CH*, p. 52) 'The English Rabelais,' Bishop Warburton declared pompously to everyone who would listen; 'England's second Rabelais,' Voltaire corrected, giving precedence to Swift (*CH*, pp. 56 and 390). Sterne, of course, did nothing to discourage the connection. In his letters he acknowledges Rabelais' example; and in *Tristram Shandy* itself he quotes from him frequently, even transcribes in Volume V an entire chapter from Yorick's copy of *Gargantua and Pantagruel*, and proudly invokes 'Pantagruelism' with the same medical imagery that delighted Rabelais:

> True *Shandeism*, think what you will against it, opens the heart and lungs, and like all those affections which partake of its nature, it forces the blood and other vital fluids of the body to run freely thro' its channels, and makes the wheel of life run long and cheerfully round. (IV, xxxii)

If an occasional reviewer drew the parallel in greater detail than Sterne must have relished ('the same sort of apostrophes to the reader, breaking in upon the narrative, not unfrequently with an air of petulant impertinence ... the same whimsical digressions; and the same parade of learning'), it must have served none the less to reassure him of his place in a celebrated line of wit. Had not Pope dedicated *The Dunciad* to Swift with a similar identification?

> Whether thou chuse Cervantes' serious air,
> Or laugh and shake in Rab'lais' easy chair.[5]

Sterne may well have come across Rabelais' works during his undergraduate years at Cambridge, as Cash speculates (p. 51). He certainly encountered or re-encountered him at 'Crazy Castle', the home of his college friend John Hall-Stevenson (Tristram's 'Eugenius'), where Sterne often took refuge from the frustrations of marriage and church. For into the huge Norman fortress at the northern border of Yorkshire Hall-Stevenson frequently gathered a group of men self-named the 'Demoniacs' (after the 'Franciscans' of Sir Francis Dashwood's notorious 'Hell-Fire Club'), who gave each other Rabelaisian nicknames and engaged in Rabelaisian contests and conviviality. And the large and eclectic library at 'Crazy Castle' was particularly well stocked with the works of those exotic later Rabelaisians like Scarron, Bouchet and Bruscambille that Sterne might not otherwise have known – that same Bruscambille whose prologue on long noses Walter Shandy bought in London for three half-crowns. (Afterwards, when Hall-Stevenson published some bawdy imitations of *Tristram Shandy*, Sterne disavowed the friendship to a shocked Bishop Warburton, but continued their friendly correspondence uninterrupted.) In any case, whether or not the Demoniacs first placed Rabelais in Sterne's hands – or, as Arthur Cash surmises, simply encouraged his taste for eccentrics and misfits – it is clear that *Tristram Shandy* was begun with a copy of Rabelais almost literally beside him (Cash, p. 190).

The copy, as it happened, was by Sterne himself. First published and given its title by his daughter in 1775, Sterne's 'Fragment in the Manner of Rabelais' was written at an undetermined point in 1759 or 1760. Wilbur Cross argued for the later year, suggesting that Sterne meant to incorporate it into *Tristram Shandy*; Melvyn New more persuasively dates it in January 1759, between *A Political Romance* and the first version of *Tristram Shandy*.[6] The interest of the 'Fragment' is in any case slight – the whole text is amateurish, sluggish, unalive, and one can easily imagine Sterne beginning and abandoning it in a morning. The plot amounts to no more than the Rabelaisian device of a gathering of wits – Panurge, Triboulet, Gymnast – to hear 'Longinus Rabelaicus' discuss his 'Kerukopaedia', the elaborately impractical system of sermon-writing that will ultimately issue in Walter's 'Tristra-paedia', while 'Homenas' sits in the next room plagiarizing the sermon he is to preach on Sunday. Here we are very far from the genuine world of Rabelais, that unique combination of morality and silliness, carnality and learning. Instead, what comes through most clearly in the 'Fragment' is no more than the surprising extent to which Sterne is already sensitive to Rabelais' tricks of style, not merely the humorous names, but the very phrases and verbal constructions that he has appropriated in detail from the translation by Thomas Urquhart and Peter Motteux (it is clear that Sterne read and quoted from this translation, as edited by John Ozell: London, 1750). Larger debts, however, would require a hero around whom Rabelaisian themes could cluster.

Tristram, of course, is such a hero, and the broad outlines of his early life invite comparisons with a central motif in Rabelais. For one of Sterne's early plans, we recall, was to satirize a 'system of Education'. And although the plan materializes only briefly, in Walter's doomed 'Tristra-paedia', it is entirely possible to see its impulse as deriving from Rabelais' great Third Book, the satiric story of Panurge's quest to learn whether he should marry or burn.[7] Tristram does not himself resemble Panurge – though Walter with his besotted ingenuity comes close – and the broad comedy of Panurge's fear of cuckoldry and madcap interroga-

tion of sybils and philosophers has no exact parallel in Sterne. But both
stories may be understood to treat in their own ways the general theme of
the 'education of a fool', in which every well-meaning attempt to bring
learning to bear upon a question results only in confusion. Yet where
Rabelais, as it is sometimes said, advanced the Erasmian concept of Folly
by splitting it into dynamically opposed characters – wise Pantagruel and
foolish Panurge – no such split can be discerned in *Tristram Shandy*.
More precisely, no figure of serene, genuine wisdom like Pantagruel
exists to counter-balance the foolishness of Walter or Tristram. Or only
Yorick exists, insignificant after Volume I and in any case never serenely
wise. In both books the education concludes in disarray, Panurge no
wiser than before, the 'Tristra-paedia' rendered useless as Tristram
grows faster than Walter can write. But, though Panurge turns away
mulishly from every oracle of truth that he encounters, the *Tiers Livre*
itself ends with the sane, authoritative voice of father Gargantua (the very
opposite of Walter) and the profound celebration of Pantagruelion, while
Tristram Shandy ends (if it does end) with a bull and a pun.

It is not the parallelism of abstract themes, however, that made Sterne
the English Rabelais. For most contemporary readers he resembled
Rabelais in his grossness and fantasy and especially in his self-contained
sallies of learned wit: the physiological humour, for example, that leads
Panurge to describe borrowing and lending in terms of cosmic blood and
gall, and Tristram to speak familiarly of animal spirits and homunculi.
Or the paradoxical satire against lawyers that concludes Panurge's
education and that, at the Visitation dinner of Volume IV, demonstrates
how a mother is not legally related to her children. Or the bold (and
abusive) addresses to the reader that interrupts even digressions: 'You
Pettifoggers, Garbellers, and Masters of Chicanery, speak not to me, I
beseech you,' Rabelais mocks.[8] 'And pray who was *Tickletoby*'s mare?'
asks one of Sterne's readers (the allusion is to Rabelais' fourth book).
''Tis just as discreditable and unscholar-like question, Sir,' replies
Tristram,

> as to have asked what year (*ab urb. con.*) the second Punic war broke
> out.——Who was *Tickletoby*'s mare!——Read, read, read, read, my
> unlearned reader! read ... (III, xxxvi)

LANGUAGE

For a twentieth-century audience, however, Sterne's debt to Rabelais
will seem less important in such particulars – painstakingly assembled in
scholarly notes for unlearned readers – than in the extraordinarily
imperial and peremptory attitude towards language that they share. In
one respect this attitude hardly differs from other borrowings. Sterne is

fond of ternary rhythm in his sentences, as is Rabelais; he likes the Rabelaisian effect (filtered through Urquhart) of pairs and rhymes – 'a sot, a pot, a fool, a stool', says Rabelais; 'pell mell, helter skelter, ding dong', writes Tristram (III, iv).[9] Rabelais' names range from 'sister Fatbum' and 'young Stiffly-stand-to't' to 'Epistemon' and 'Raminagrobis', while Sterne trots behind with 'Kysarcius', 'Kunastrokius' and 'Gastripheres'. But the imperial attitude emerges less in these puns and sounds, and more in such devices as the Rabelaisian list, which Sterne imitates from time to time, though never with Rabelais' appetite:

> Accounts to reconcile:
> Anecdotes to pick up:
> Inscriptions to make out:
> Stories to weave in:
> Traditions to sift:
> Personages to call upon:
> Panegyricks to paste up at this door:
> Pasquinades at that . . . (I, xiv)

At other points he imitates (more successfully) Rabelais' delight in simple noise, giving a whole chapter over to the imitation of a fiddle, and duplicates happily his chain-reaction sentence structure: 'shall I be call'd as many blockheads, numsculs, doddypoles, dunderheads, ninny-hammers, goosecaps, joltheads, nicompoops, and sh--t-a-beds——and other unsavory appelations, as ever the cake-bakers of *Lernè*, cast in the teeth of King Gargantua's shepherds . . .' (IX, xxv). In every case he is lobbing words into place, juggling them with one hand as if they were mere things, round, solid, palpable, with which a writer plays, the handiest toys in the authorial nursery, the surest, and most inexhaustible, source of amusement in the world, linked in a continuum of pleasure with sex and drink.

In another mood, this irreverence towards language crosses over into scepticism. There is, for example, the excessive, burlesque precision that Sterne could have got only from Rabelais: Gargantua mourns his wife with mathematical grief – 'my sweeting, my honey, my little c . . . (yet it had in circumference full six acres, three rods, five poles, foure yards, two foot, one inche and a half of good woodland measure' (bk II, ch. iii). And in a choreographed duel with Loupgarou 'Pantagruel was very nimble, and had alwayes a quick foot, and a quick eye, and therefore, with his left foot did he step back one pace, yet not so nimbly but that the blow, falling upon the bark, broke it in foure thousand, fore score and six pieces' (bk II, ch. xxix). This device Sterne can replicate in a metaphor of painting: Trim

stood,——for I repeat it, to take the picture of him in at one view, with
his body sway'd, and somewhat bent forwards,——his right-leg firm
under him, sustaining seven-eighths of his whole weight,——the foot
of his left-leg, the defect of which was no disadvantage to his attitude,
advanced a little,——not laterally, nor forwards, but in a line betwixt
them . . . (II, xvii)

And in his slow-motion account of Dr Slop's fall from his horse Sterne
uses words as a kind of strained net to hold in a bulging disorder, but
fully aware that the net consists more of holes than of cord:

> . . . in crossing himself he let go his whip,——and in attempting to
> save his whip betwixt his knee and his saddle's skirt, as it slipp'd, he
> lost his stirrup,——in losing which, he lost his seat;——and in the
> multitude of all these losses . . . the unfortunate Doctor lost his
> presence of mind. So that, without waiting for *Obadaiah's* onset, he
> left his pony to its destiny, tumbling off it diagonally, something in the
> stile and manner of a pack of wool . . . (II, ix)

Burlesque of this kind, for all its good-humour, amounts in the end to a
satiric criticism of language; its dependence upon numbers and geometry
reminds us how far short even the most carefully chosen words will fall of
invoking and enclosing simple physical reality. For this reason both
Rabelais and Sterne are unusually interested to explore those com-
plementary languages of sign and gesture (and in Sterne's case painting
and music as well):

> Then Panurge knocked one hand against another, and blowed in his
> palm, and put again the forefinger of his right hand into the overture or
> mouth of the left, pulling it often in and out. Then held he out his chin,
> most intentively looking upon Thaumast. The people there, who
> understood nothing in the other signs, knew very well that therein he
> demanded, without speaking a word to Thaumast——What do you
> mean by that? (II, xix)

Panurge's virtuosity is not limited to hand-signs, of course – he literalizes
figures of speech by wearing an actual flea in his ear and by trying to sit
between two stools – but in such antics the final effect is always the same:
to make words disappear, to substitute actions. We may defer until a
later chapter the further implications of such literalization for Sterne's
style, especially for his use of metaphor; here it is enough to say that in
these Rabelaisian codes of gesture the mock signs can theoretically be
retranslated into words ('What do you mean by that?'): Rabelais raises
only to laugh aside all questions of alienation and communication. But

this assurance vanishes in *Tristram Shandy*, even as Panurge's gigantic system of signs is there reduced to single gestures like Trim's eloquent dropping of his hat to the floor, whose meaning is at bottom untranslatable: 'Nothing could have expressed the sentiment of mortality, of which it was the type and fore-runner, like it,——his hand seemed to vanish from under it,——it fell dead,——the corporal's eye fix'd upon it, as upon a corps,——and *Susannah* burst into a flood of tears' (V, vii). In the end, Rabelais' criticism of language is withheld: his prodigious style belongs to the giants who speak it, an expansive, unbounded multiplicity, fully commensurate with the Renaissance world it overlays and measures, nothing less than total wish-fulfilment. In the end, Rabelais' peremptory attitude towards language is in the service of his pleasure. For all its greatness, however, Sterne's style lacks this last, Gargantuan richness, and his fantasies are fantasies of inhibition.

BAWDRY

What is true of Sterne's attitude towards language is true of his bawdry as well. It seems unlikely that any reader could confuse Rabelais' and Sterne's indecencies, yet curiously those are precisely the grounds on which Sterne himself saw their resemblance. 'Still I promise to be Cautious,' he tells a correspondent, responding to the charge that his humour in *Tristram Shandy* is too 'free', especially coming from a clergyman. 'But I deny I have gone as farr as Swift—He keeps a due distance from Rabelais—& I keep a due distance from him—Swift has said a hundred things I durst Not Say—Unless I was Dean of St Patricks' (*Letters*, p. 76). It is a revealing afterthought, mercenary and ambitious, but few people opening the first volume of *Tristram Shandy* in 1760 could have felt that there was anything at all that Sterne dare not say – he who began his novel at the very moment of his hero's conception, who explained hobbyhorses with a reference to Dr Kunastrokius' delight 'in combing of asses tails, and plucking the dead hairs out with his teeth' (I, vii), who proposed 'after the ceremony of marriage, and before that of consummation, the baptizing all the HOMUNCULI at once, slap-dash, by *injection*' (I, xx). And yet, despite these unceasing salvos of indecency, Sterne has accurately pointed to the secret of his bawdy humour, and its essential difference from Rabelais': there are 'a hundred things I durst Not Say'.

It is impossible, of course, to be freer than Rabelais. He begins *Gargantua*, as Sterne begins *Tristram Shandy*, with the marriage-bed; but, where Sterne screens the actual sexuality with physiological jargon and a cryptic joke of non-communication, Rabelais (through Urquhart) renders it with unforgettable directness:

These two did oftentimes do the two-backed beast together, joyfully rubbing and frotting their Bacon 'gainst one another, in insofarre, that at last she became great with childe of a faire sonne, and went with him unto the eleventh moneth; for so long, yea longer, may a woman carry her great belly, especially when it is some masterpiece of nature, and a person predestinated to the performance, in his due time, of great exploits. (I, iii)

If a deliberate contrast with Rabelais may have been at the back of Sterne's mind all along – parents who rarely make the beast with two backs, a son, destined for impotence and failure, whose *'misfortunes began nine months before ever he came into the world'* (I, iii) – that would have been in part because the Rabelaisian directness is simply beyond him.

Here within is [said Panurge], (in shewing her his long Codpiece) Master John Thursday, who will play you such an Antick, that you shall feel the sweetnesse thereof even to the very marrow of your bones: He is a gallant, and doth so well know how to finde out all the corners, creeks, and ingrained inmates in your carnal trap, that after him there needs no broom, he'l sweep so well before, and leave nothing to his followers to work upon. (II, xxi)

Against this style we may set an incident early in Volume II when Toby credits to modesty Mrs Shandy's reluctance to see Dr Slop. 'My sister, I dare say, added he, does not care to let a man come so near her ✱✱✱✱.' Tristram coyly declines to explain: 'I will not say whether my uncle *Toby* had compleated the sentence or not;——'tis for his advantage to suppose he had,——as, I think, he could have added no ONE WORD which would have improved it' (II, vi). And, as if to keep the discussion on the driest, most scholarly level, he proceeds to wonder pedantically if we have just witnessed the rhetorical figure Aposiopesis, the breaking off or suppression of a thought. Far from suppressing a thought, of course he has ensured its appearance in every mind – what reader has ever failed to count the asterisks? Or what reader has ever failed to interpret the visual metaphor in the following chapter, when an angry Walter has accused Toby of not knowing the right end of a woman? 'Right end,——quoth my uncle *Toby*, muttering the two words low to himself, and fixing his two eyes insensibly as he muttered them, upon a small crevice, form'd by a bad joint in the chimney-piece.——Right end of a woman!'

   Suspending for a moment the questions of language and interpretation that these incidents also pose, we can agree that they are typical of Sterne's bawdry throughout the novel – teasing or sniggering, depending upon one's mood and the success of the wit – in any case the very opposite of Rabelais' practice, which admits puns but eschews *double entendres*. Like the two nuns in Volume VII who split an obscenity into syllables and alternate speaking them, Sterne 'durst not say' directly what he means: the joke lies entirely in manipulating us to say it for him. And the discomfort of the joke for many of us, as Coleridge shrewdly says, lies in

> A sort of *knowingness*, the wit of which depends, first on the modesty it gives pain to; or secondly, the innocence and innocent ignorance over which it triumphs; or thirdly, on a certain oscillation in the individual's own mind between the remaining good and the encroaching evil of his nature ... so that the mind has in its own white and black angel the same or similar amusements as might be supposed to take place between an old debauchee and a prude ... We have only to suppose society *innocent* – and [this sort of wit] is equal to a stone that falls in snow; it makes no sound because it excites no resistance. (*CH*, p. 354)

Despite their differences, therefore, Freud's well-known analysis of 'smutty humour' holds true for both Rabelais and Sterne. 'One of the primitive components of our libido', he declares in *Jokes and Their Relation to the Unconscious*, 'is the desire to see the sexual exposed.' And obscene humour he defines as 'the intentional bringing into prominence of sexual facts or relations through speech'. Hence the smutty joke

> is like an exposure of the sexually different person to whom it is directed. By the utterance of the obscene words it compels the person who is assailed to imagine the part of the body or the procedure in question and shows her that the assailant is himself imagining it. It cannot be doubted that the desire to see what is sexual exposed is the original motive of smut.[10]

Rabelais obviously names the thing itself, abundantly, delightedly, and joins us in uproarious pleasure at the pictures we share. Sterne, however, pretends not to name it and furthermore, as Coleridge intimates, engages in mock-hostile reprimand of the invariably female reader who tumbles to the hidden meaning: 'Nor is there anything unnatural or extravagant in the supposition, that my dear *Jenny* may be my friend.——Friend!——My friend.——Surely, Madam, a friendship between the two sexes may subsist, and be supported without——Fy! Mr *Shandy*:——Without any thing, Madam, but that tender and delicious sentiment, which ever mixes in friendship ...' (I, xviii). If he keeps a 'due distance from Rabelais', the effect is only to bring the picture into sharper focus. 'Soon after *Tristram* had appeared', Sir Walter Scott recounts,

Sterne asked a Yorkshire lady of fortune and condition whether she
had read his book. 'I have not, Mr Sterne,' was the answer; 'and, to be
plain with you, I am informed it is not proper for female perusal.'—
'My dear good lady,' replied the author, 'do not be gulled by such
stories; the book is like your young heir there,' (pointing to a child of
three years old, who was rolling on the carpet in his white tunics,) 'he
shows at times a good deal that is usually concealed, but it is all in
perfect innocence!' (*CH*, pp. 371–2)

(iii) CERVANTES

Of Sterne's affection for Cervantes his letters and novels leave no doubt –
'by the ashes of my dear *Rabelais*, and dearer *Cervantes*,' Tristram swears
(III, xix). More than any other book *Don Quixote* springs to his memory
continually in everything he writes, in allusions, similes and anecdotes
(Sterne had little or no Spanish and read Cervantes in the translation by
Peter Motteux, revised by John Ozell: London, 1719). But affection is
not necessarily influence, and of Cervantes' actual effect upon *Tristram
Shandy* it is more difficult to speak precisely. Defending the description
of Dr Slop's fall, for example (quoted a few pages earlier), Sterne saw
nothing Rabelaisian at all in the passage: 'I will reconsider . . . my too
Minute Account of it,' he tells a correspondent, '—but in general I am
perswaded that the happiness of the Cervantic humour arises from this
very thing—of describing silly and trifling Events, with the Circumstantial Pomp of great Ones' (*Letters*, p. 77). He may indeed have taken this
notion of mock-heroic from *Don Quixote*, but he might equally well have
taken it from Pope or Swift or Fielding (whose *Joseph Andrews* bore on its
title page 'Written in Imitation of the Manner of Cervantes'), and it
would in any case be difficult to point to anything in Cervantes quite like
the geometric precision of Slop's slow-motion tumble. Elsewhere Sterne
speaks of the Cervantic humour in other terms, as 'sweet' or 'serious' or
'gentle', 'spiritual and refined', and these words perhaps better suggest
Sterne's aspirations (and difficulties) as he was finding his way into the
early chapters of his novel.

His first reference is to Don Quixote's horse Rosinante, 'full-brother'
to Parson Yorick's broken-winded nag; two pages later the momentum
of allusion leads him to extend the comparison to Yorick himself, who
has perversely refused to explain his charitable motive for riding such a
'sorry jade' and thereby chosen 'to bear the contempt of his enemies, and
the laughter of his friends'.

I have the highest idea of the spiritual and refined sentiments of this
reverend gentleman, [Tristram declares,] from this single stroke in his
character, which I think comes up to any of the honest refinements of

the peerless knight of *La Mancha*, whom, by the bye, with all his follies, I love more, and would actually have gone further to have paid a visit to, than the greatest hero of antiquity. (I, x)

Appropriately for a book so much concerned with establishing identity – a preoccupation not absent from the early pages of *Don Quixote* – this invocation of Cervantes falls at the beginning of Sterne's most obvious self-portrait, for the reverend gentleman (unnamed at this point), as lanky and 'spare a figure as his beast', lives the kind of double life that Sterne himself lived in his parsonage at York: outwardly eccentric and a misfit, inwardly 'spiritual and refined'. And into this misunderstood but lovable character Sterne pours those contradictions that so absorbed him in his own personality, the self that captures 'the attention of both young and old' wherever he goes, but that will not or cannot explain its nature, the inveterate jester who mocks 'himself going off fast in a consumption', and who studies the poor nag as he rides, 'like a death's head before him'. When a chapter later Sterne invents a name and a Shakespearian ancestry for Yorick, the self-portrait moves a long step away from Cervantes, though the melancholy-sweet Cervantic humour reappears in Yorick's last words, a death-bed allusion in 'the *cervantick* tone' to Sancho Panza's 'bruised and mis-shapen'd head' (I, xii).

A second Shandian character may also be traced to Cervantes, though less directly. I have in mind not Uncle Toby's modesty or implausibility as a soldier, but his sentimental gentleness. For like Don Quixote, though he enters the novel as an object of ridicule – Toby owns as many books on siegecraft as the Don on chivalry – he quickly becomes an altogether admirable figure of kind sensibility, who literally acts out (like Panurge) the figurative saying 'he would not hurt a fly'. Stuart Tave has demonstrated how Fielding ('the English Cervantes') and Sterne together transform the received idea of Don Quixote in the eighteenth century, making him over from a crack-brained lunatic into the complex, lovable, amiable humorist he is only towards the end of Cervantes' novel.[11] This Don's madness represents idealism, if not insight; his mournful countenance is like Hamlet's and has its source in exquisite sensitivity rather than in buffets and pratfalls. To this new strain Sterne had added in Toby and Trim a version of the Don's and Sancho's master–servant relationship, though its innate tension (which Diderot was fully to explore in *Jacques le fataliste*) is almost done away with, transferred in fact along with the bond of affection to the stormier partnership of Walter and Toby.

NARRATOR

In his important article 'The self-conscious narrator in comic fiction before *Tristram Shandy*', however, Wayne Booth has argued that Cervantes' influence upon Sterne appears chiefly, not in such sentimental lineage, but in the technical device of an intrusive author, who engages in dialogue with both his audience and his characters and emerges as a character in his own right. The 'editor' of *Don Quixote* is a 'fully self-conscious narrator', Booth says, whom we see 'at his desk as intimately as we ever see Tristram'.[12] He recognizes, of course, that Tristram takes over his story in a way Cid Hamet never does – and he finds convincing precedent for that expansion of role in comic novels of the 1750s with similarly intrusive narrators – but he insists that 'it is primarily to this aspect that Sterne refers when he talks of his master Cervantes'. Yet other readers may think that Sterne's whole effect of self-portraiture in Tristram differs too strikingly to be called Cervantic – Cid Hamet is in fact an aspect of *Don Quixote* to which Sterne refers only once – and may recall that similar intrusions punctuate the works of Rabelais and Swift. Sterne's technical debt to Cervantes actually seems to lie in the general nature of the self-reflexive novel he created: a novel whose hero first attempts to impose his fiction on reality and then in part II becomes aware of himself as simultaneously real and fictional, a character in other people's books who must nevertheless persist in the 'reality' of his own. For such ambivalences and tensions Sterne has obvious relish; but what he learns from Cervantes in this regard has far more to do with focus of plot than with the personality of Tristram.

He learns first of all, for example, that comedy can be automatically generated by collisions (between 'trifling events' and 'circumstantial pomp', as he informs his correspondent); and in particular he learns the comic possibilities inherent in the collision of two kinds of reality, a collision between the outward, exterior world we and Sancho commonly agree on and the interior world of Don Quixote's mind, where inns are castles and doxies maidens. Rabelais' world, of course, was relentlessly external – its only interior setting is Pantagruel's mouth! – and even its words are palpable things, cascading out of a cornucopia and on to the page: a world of immense interest to someone experimenting with style, largely irrelevant to someone faced with problems of narrative. But Cervantes, in the simplicity of his genius, offers Sterne a version of narrative in which every physical element of his novel – from the windmills of La Mancha to the fist of an unpaid landlord – ricochets harmlessly off a single consciousness, a rival reality that cannot be bruised or bloodied. In this version, moreover, we almost never enter any mind but Don Quixote's; the novel focuses virtually its whole attention upon the wilfulness of that single consciousness, and all its narrative energy is bent upon assaulting it and recovering it for the ordinary world. Perhaps because he has so little taste for the ordinary world in that way, Sterne alters the model of *Don Quixote* only here: instead of choosing a single consciousness, he plunges inside every head he sees – Tristram's, Phutatorius', the foolish fat scullion's – reporting gleefully on the strange forms of life he finds floating or rotting or whirling there. And where Cervantes' rendering of interior consciousness is tentative – we see the metamorphosis of the inn, but not the process itself – Sterne luxuriates at length in the consciousness of his characters, unfolding them as one might fan a deck of cards. Where Cervantes' characters physically embody their differences, Sterne's are opposed not by their physical appearance or by their social rank, but entirely by their process of thought, by Toby's obsessive association of everything with siegecraft and Walter's obsessive assimilation of everything to theory. The physical world is not therefore absent from *Tristram Shandy* – far from it: a whole battery of real-world forces is always colliding (precisely) with its people, circumcising, crushing, diseasing. But Sterne's extension of an interior consciousness to all his characters lessens that world's prominence; at the same time it re-emphasizes, if it does not actually alter, the great theme of interpretation that runs through all of *Don Quixote*.

INTERPRETATION

In a limited way, it is true, Sterne could have encountered the theme of interpretation in the *Tiers Livre* or in the *Tale of a Tub*; but there the idea is restricted to a single question – whether to marry, how to read the father's will – and a 'correct' interpretation is constantly available. Cervantes, however, raises the idea in an inexhaustible series of paradoxes, as we have seen, and applies it not only to the action he narrates, but even to the act of narration. When the Don, for example, declares to a bemused Sancho that the barber's basin before them is in reality Mambrino's magic helmet, enchanted into another form, the question of interpretation centres (as it most often does) upon a physical thing, challenging our vision in both a literal and a figurative sense. When the Don attacks and destroys a group of puppets, whom he takes to be real, the question becomes how to interpret a fiction or, more enigmatically, how our fictions become 'false' when we believe them to be true. And when, in the great Dulcinea episode, enchantment is suddenly understood as art the Don himself transfers the theme of interpretation to the related example of drama, which he declares a 'mirror' held up to nature, like his own book. To this kind of question Sterne is ever attuned. His mysterious sense of style, of ambiguity in style, is always pressing him to jokes of misunderstanding like Cervantes'. A physical symbol like a nose becomes a sign to be interpreted, a word like 'Zounds!' or a gesture like the dropping of a hat an expression to be retranslated into ordinary language. Competing consciousnesses offer competing interpretations – Toby understands the Widow Wadman's question about the location of his wound in one way, she understands his answer in another. But no correct interpretation buffers their collision: each consciousness rebounds and rolls free again, loose cannons on the deck of Tristram's narration. Meanwhile Tristram himself, with his black and blank pages, his typographical gimmicks, and his self-conscious chatter, calls our attention repeatedly to the arbitrary nature of his book and our own misinterpretations as we read it, so that the reader himself is drawn into the dialectic of interpretation, and the ultimate collision occurs between our own consciousness and Tristram's. Who shall impose his fiction most successfully?

> ——How could you, Madam, be so inattentive in reading the last chapter? I told you in it, *That my mother was not a papist.*——Papist! You told me no such thing, Sir. Madam, I beg leave to repeat it over again, That I told you as plain, at least, as words, by direct inference, could tell you such a thing. (I, xx)

For good reasons do the critics of Sterne and Cervantes sound so much alike, dwelling on the fundamental principles of art that each novelist lays bare, insisting that each novel represents an exfoliation of structure, a critical analysis in fiction of the nature of illusion. The first European novel and the most 'typical' novel have in common not so much their self-conscious narrators as their preoccupation with the way two or more minds can confront a word, a thing, an action, and arrive at contradictory understandings of it.[13] They have in common also the perception – Swift was to make it a moral rather than an artistic principle – that misinterpretation is madness.

(iv) SWIFT

The fundamental difference between Sterne and Swift may be felt in their characteristic images for the brain – that spacious, enclosed ocean in the Sternian scheme where ideas swim and spout like playful whales, or whirl about like smoke in a funnel. Swift, however, does not simply arrive at this inner space in the turning of a simile, as Sterne does. His entry is accomplished by the officious Reason, 'with Tools for cutting, and opening, and mangling, and piercing'; and when the brain is finally laid open we see chiefly its disappointing 'Defects . . . in Number and Bulk' (*Tale*, pp.. 173–4).[14] Or if we consider ideas as like the mist that rises from a dunghill, contends the narrator of *A Tale of a Tub*,

> it will follow, that as the Face of Nature never produces Rain, but when it is overcast and disturbed, so Human Understanding, seated in the Brain, must be troubled and overspread by Vapours, ascending

from the lower Faculties, to water the Invention, and render it fruitful. (*Tale*, p. 163).

Elsewhere, in the course of explaining the usefulness of quilted caps, he repeats

> the Opinion of Choice *Virtuosi*, that the Brain is only a Crowd of little Animals, but with Teeth and Claws extremely sharp, and therefore, cling together in the Contexture we behold like the Picture of *Hobbes*'s *Leviathan*, or like Bees in perpendicular swarm upon a Tree, or like a Carrion corrupted into Vermin, still preserving the Shape and Figure of the Mother Animal. (*Tale*, p. 277)

Every comparison of Swift and Sterne turns into a contrast like this, in which an initial similarity of purpose collapses, as here Sterne's brief surrealistic images, his rapid-fire fantasy, shrivel before Swift's relentless development of simile into monstrous analogy. Sterne himself makes comparisons with Swift into contrasts: unlike Swift he has no such title as Dean of St Patrick's, he remarks to a friend; unlike Swift he has not yet been persecuted by his enemies into great fame. But this is not to say that Swift exerts no influence on him. To the contrary, it is clear that in a general way Sterne identifies with Swift, seeing himself as a second Anglo-Irish clergyman frustrated by the politics of the church, too clever for his own good, writing himself out of favour and into scandal as Swift did in *A Tale of a Tub*. He describes proudly to Eliza how old Lord Bathurst, the former patron of Pope and Swift, told him in London that 'despairing ever to find their equals, it is some years since I have closed my accounts, and shut up my books, with thoughts of never opening them again: but you have kindled a desire in me of opening them once more before I die; which I now do; so go home and dine with me' (*Letters*, p. 305). The *Journal to Eliza* itself, we recall, appears to have been inspired by Swift's *Journal to Stella*, which was published for the first time in 1766.

As a writer, Sterne responded chiefly to *A Tale of a Tub* – *Gulliver's Travels* seems hardly to have interested him – and what he responded to is very clear: of all the books we have so far mentioned, the formal elements of *Tristram Shandy* most nearly resemble those of the *Tale* – the digressions piled precariously upon digressions, the mock-scholastic parodies of literary decorum (Swift's endless Apology, Dedication, Preface and Introduction), the volleys against critics, the proposals for other books, the division of emphasis between actual narration and the encroaching personality of the narrator. 'What has this book done more than the Legation of Moses,' Tristram demands, 'or the Tale of a Tub, that it may not swim down the gutter of Time along with them?' (IX, viii) Even certain preoccupying images of the *Tale* – brains, horses, noses – appear transplanted to *Tristram Shandy*. At the most general level these resemblances disappear, of course – Swift is writing a satire, Sterne a novel – but similar forms have a way of generating similar themes. Sterne's bawdry, his interest in language as a subject of interpretation and corruption, and his view of madness undoubtedly have many sources, including most significantly his own enigmatic and vexing personality; but his predispositions to those themes are surely mobilized by Swift's example, even if from a common starting-point they tend to go racing in utterly different directions.

BAWDRY

If Sterne occupies a position halfway between Rabelais and the Victorians, Swift stands closer by far to Rabelais: there is nothing of the nudging elbow in his humour, nothing of Sterne's characteristic wink and snigger. On the other hand, there is little of Rabelais' gaiety, either. Swift's indecent humour, when it concerns sexuality, strikes most readers as coarse rather than direct, without pleasure. And when it grows scatological most readers pull back from the grim anger it discharges, an anger that sometimes seems directed at the sheer inescapable fact of the human body's functions.[15] In his account of the Aeolist priests, for example, Swift's Hack first explains that large funnels stuck up their posteriors bring on the literal inspiration of strong winds and eloquent eructations. More impressive still, he adds, are the

> *Female* Officers, whose Organs were understood to be better disposed for the Admission of those Oracular Gusts, as entring and passing up thro' a Receptacle of greater Capacity, and causing also a Pruriency by the Way, such as with due Management, hath been refined from a Carnal, into a Spiritual Extasie. (*Tale*, p. 157)

This sardonic refinement ('refined' is one of the most common adjectives in the *Tale*) has long been recognized as Swift's version of sublimation, the displacement of psychic affects from an appropriate to a disguised object, though Swift states it in Aristotelian rather than psychological terms: '*the Corruption of the Senses is the Generation of the Spirit*' (*Tale*, p. 269). Nor does he limit its application to female pruriency. As the Hack narrator of the *Tale* undertakes to survey the uses of madness in a commonwealth, he begins with the case of a 'certain great Prince' (Henry IV of France), who suddenly raises a mighty army and fleet and threatens universal conquest.

It was afterwards discovered, that the Movement of this whole Machine had been directed by an absent *Female*, whose Eyes had raised a Protuberancy, and before Emission, she was removed into an Enemy's Country ... The very same Principle that influences a *Bully* to break the Windows of a Whore, who has jilted him, naturally stirs up a Great Prince to raise mighty Armies, and dream nothing but Sieges, Battles, and Victories. (*Tale*, pp. 163–5)

Whatever the remoter origins of Uncle Toby – the memory of Sterne's father, or the eccentric Captain Robert Hinde proposed by some scholars – it is impossible to avoid seeing Swift's version of sublimation at work in him, spurring the hobbyhorse of siegecraft into genial lunacy, his 'Fancy ... *astride* on his Reason' as firmly as any Bedlam inmate's (*Tale*, p. 171).[16] Sterne makes the connection between repressed sexuality and warfare almost as plain, in fact, as Swift: when Trim utters the words 'A rood and a half of ground to do what they would with', Toby begins to blush immoderately, and a moment later Tristram draws the necessary comparison, adding only a teasing note on the importance of privacy to miniature warfare.

Never did lover post down to a belov'd mistress with more heat and expectation, than my uncle *Toby* did, to enjoy this self-same thing in private ... The idea of not being seen, did not a little contribute to the idea of pleasure preconceived in my uncle *Toby*'s mind. (II, v)

For Sterne this displacement of erotic energy apparently represents no more than a joke on human nature, a Shandian variation on a topos that, one way or another, stretches back to the *Iliad*. For Swift, however, the joke is made through clenched teeth. Its serious point is that our politics derives from our illogical psychology, that our collective corruption has its source in the ease with which our lower faculties control our higher. More seriously still, such sublimation reveals a moral error as well, the preference of illusion to truth, for we know these things about ourselves, or ought to, and yet choose to remain mired in appetite, wilfully blind to realities. Swift makes the consequences of this self-deceit as violent and repellent as he can, he pitches it all in the place of excrement, and with the climactic image of Bedlam hospital and its iron bars he makes clear that when we choose this way we choose to be enslaved, not to be free. But Sterne, freest of writers, simply turns away from the satiric possibilities implicit in the preference of illusion over truth. His voice returns no echo of Swift's fierceness. Toby's mock warfare leaves flies unharmed and widows unravished. Apart from that rood and a half of sublimation, in fact, Sterne's bawdry far more than Swift's depends upon ambiguity and ambivalence, matters for lingustic rather than moral interpretation.

LANGUAGE

Swift's personality is a mysterious mixture of absoluteness and irony. In his hands the Augustan concept of correctness becomes a moral as well as an aesthetic standard, which he applies with obsessive force to every possible kind of expression. By contrast, Sterne's view of language is an elusive and complex matter, the subject of prolonged scholarly study, and it is probably true that Locke more than anyone else sets out the basic terms and problems for him. But at the practical, larcenous level from which novelists usually regard other fiction Sterne unquestionably discovered in Swift's allegory of the brothers Martin, Peter and Jack the problem of interpretation in its most suggestive form.

Their father's will had expressly commanded the three brothers never to alter the appearance of their inherited coats; but motivated by lust, their desire to court three grand ladies, they concoct a series of sophistic rereadings of the will that begins with shoulder-knots and oral tradition, proceeds to gold lace and Aristotle's *de Interpretatione* ('which has the Faculty of teaching its Readers to find out a Meaning in every Thing but it self': *Tale*, p. 85), and concludes with satin linings and sheer forgery. And, though Swift's satiric target here is primarily the Catholic Church, he makes the same general point throughout his career: words have at once a single meaning and endless meanings. Like Locke, that is, he holds to the view that words should mean definite things, precisely and obviously (Swift proposes an English Academy, modelled after the French, to fix in place meanings and forms). But unlike Locke, who finds the problem in the inherent ambiguity of language itself, Swift blames instead its corrupt users, the politicians, priests and rabble who pervert what can and should be clear. '*I charge and command my three sons*', booms the will,

> *to wear no sort of Silver Fringe upon or about their said Coats* ...
> However, after some Pause the Brother so often mentioned for his
> Erudition, who was well Skill'd in Criticisms, had found in a certain
> Author, which he said should be nameless, that the same Word which
> in the Will is called *Fringe*, does also signifie a *Broom-stick* ... (*Tale*,
> p. 88)

Sterne, no one has ever doubted, delights in the ambiguity that so discourages Swift. In his world, no word stands still for a single meaning: they dart continually like sea-birds into our subconscious, returning every moment with fresh and outrageous evidence of our disposition to pervert. And where Swift directs his comedy at the brothers' willingness to make words mean whatever they want – in the service of power, vanity and illusion as well as of lust – Sterne limits the alternative meanings to a single kind: whatever we say, we are thinking of sex.

————Here are two senses, cried *Eugenius*, as we walk'd along, pointing with the fore finger of his right hand to the word *Crevice*, in the fifty-second page of the second volume of this book of books,————here are two senses,————quoth he.————And here are two roads, replied I, turning short upon him,————a dirty and a clean one,————which shall we take?————The clean,————by all means, replied *Eugenius*. *Eugenius*, said I, stepping before him, and laying my hand upon his breast,————to define————is to distrust. (III, xxxi)

Crevices, whiskers, noses: fanned by the south winds of the libido, every word turns gently over to reveal another meaning. So infectious, in fact, is Tristram's habit of sexualizing his language that after a time no word at all seems innocent. Scholars read with dictionaries of slang open beside them ('toby' can mean 'posterior', 'hobbyhorses' can be 'whores'), and a sentence justifying digressions can bring explication to a blushing halt: 'when a man is telling his story in the strange way I do mine, he is obliged continually to be going backwards and forwards to keep all tight together in the reader's fancy' (VI, xxxiii).[17] I depend, Tristram says, quite truthfully, 'upon the cleanliness of my reader's imaginations' (III, xxxi).

Swift indulges in no such trust. If Sterne offers us a choice of meanings, either possible, neither wrong, for his part Swift insists that interpretation aims at nothing less than truth. Peter, having locked away the will and seized power over his brothers, thrusts a piece of bread before them and calls it mutton. They protest; they

> never saw a Piece of Mutton ... so nearly resembling a Slice from a Twelve-peny Loaf. Look ye, Gentlemen, cries Peter in a Rage, to convince you, what a couple of blind, positive, ignorant, wilful Puppies you are, I will use but this plain Argument; By G—, it is true, good, natural Mutton as any in Leaden-Hall Market; and G— confound you both eternally, if you offer to believe otherwise. Such a thundring Proof as this, left no farther Room for Objection: The two Unbelievers began to gather and pocket up their Mistake as hastily as they could. (*Tale*, p. 118)

This, as Gulliver was later to learn, is to say the thing that is not. It is Quixotic madness gone sour, fiction turned to lies. Worse still, it is a moral failing for which language is not responsible. Here, of course, Swift assigns responsibility for misrepresenting truth to his characters, the mad Peter and his cowardly brothers, and by extension to the religious factions they represent. But, as so often happens in his work, the page never contains his anger. Elsewhere and generally throughout the *Tale*, responsibility for misinterpretation widens to include not only the Hack and his puppets, but also each of us, the 'Gentle Reader', and our flawed human nature, torn perpetually between the state of being a knave or a well-deceived fool. 'I am wonderfully well acquainted with the present Relish of Courteous Readers', says the Hack in an ostensible compliment to us, 'and have often observed with singular Pleasure, that a *Fly* driven from a *Honey-pot*, will immediately, with very good Appetite alight, and finish his Meal on an *Excrement*' (*Tale*, p. 207). Sterne may have taken from Swift the technique of reaching out to include the reader in the 'conversation' of the book, but he never duplicated the intimacy Swift so ferociously achieves: his clowning references to 'Madam', 'Sir', 'Your Reverence' create only a curiously impersonal familiarity. Nor did he duplicate the technique of irony that places so crushing a burden of interpretation on him. For Swift's irony finally extends the question of interpretation beyond the action or the texts within his text: it challenges the reader directly to understand the writer himself, and it works to ensure that he cannot. The relationship between the reader and author is the ultimate question of truthful interpretation that Swift raises, and raises only to deny. Beneath Tristram's mad dashes, the chatter and puppyish cajoling, we detect a self in the making, a personality that we (and Sterne) can eventually 'read'. A far stronger self lies beneath Swift's metamorphoses – a face glimpsed and lost at every moment – but it is the last illusion to think that we can know him.

NARRATOR

The only Swiftian character whom we do in fact know is insane. Those formal resemblances between *Tristram Shandy* and the *Tale* with which we began – the digressions, parodies and subversions – have their common, summarizing source in the personalities of the narrators: if Sterne learned anywhere how to divide the focus of his text between the story-line and the speaker, he learned it from the jabbering example of the Hack. But where Swift's narrator serves him as a mask, a satiric target by no means to be identified with the actual Swift, Tristram exists as a plausible enough version of Sterne, a recognizable and deliberate 'portrait'. And, where the Hack's madness begins in eccentricity and concludes in a nightmarish Bedlam, Tristram's 'madness' exists only in the 'Shandy' name – Yorkshire dialect for crack-brained, addled – and in an early imitative passage, and thereafter dwindles into eccentricity. It is the image of the hobbyhorse that provokes Tristram's admission:

> for happening, at certain intervals and changes of the Moon, to be both fiddler and painter, according as the fly stings:——Be it known to you, that I keep a couple of pads myself, upon which, in their turns, (nor do I care who knows it) I frequently ride out and take the air;——tho' sometimes, to my shame be it spoken, I take somewhat longer journies

than what a wise man would think altogether right.——But the truth is,——I am not a wise man ... (I, viii)

To be long on the road, to be addled, not to be wise – these confessions hardly bear comparison with the Hack's declaration that he has long been a student in Bedlam; nor do Tristram's hobbyhorsical 'pads' show anything like a Swiftian spirit: 'I my self, the Author of these momentous Truths, am a Person, whose imaginations are hard-mouth'd, and exceedingly disposed to run away with his *Reason*, which I have observed from long Experience, to be a very light Rider, and easily shook off' (*Tale*, p. 180). For the Hack's kind of madness, which Swift insists he shares with every other Modern, is about the embracing of false values. His madness, like his deranged idea of good writing, indicates a cultural crisis of enormous proportions to Swift's mind, a destructive folly that is wilful, poisonous and sinful. In his preference for '*Delusion*' and all 'Artificial *Mediums*, false Lights, refracted Angles, Varnish, and Tinsel' (*Tale*, p. 172), the Hack reflects the very madness he describes in the three brothers, their demented blindness without insight. But Tristram's comic 'madness' upsets conventional values without bringing them into crisis; it concerns a cultural breakdown far less than it concerns the profound and abiding subjectivity that determines our relationships with other people. And Sterne never turns on Tristram or anyone with Swift's excremental ammunition, Shandy Hall never becomes more than an imperfect bunker against reality's fitful sallies. Toby's miniature illusions of war or Walter's disembodied theories belong to a later, less anxious vision than that shared by Swift, Pope and the other Augustans: on the stage where Tristram so cheerfully capers, Great Anarch has not yet let her curtain fall. Or as C. J. Rawson puts it in a genuinely Shandian speculation about literary influence: 'what the *Tale of a Tub* is really parodying is Sterne, in advance'.[18]

NOTES: CHAPTER 2

1   Harold Bloom, *The Anxiety of Influence: A Theory of Poetry* (New York: Oxford University Press, 1973); W. Jackson Bate, *The Burden of the Past and the English Poet* (Cambridge, Mass.: Harvard University Press, 1970).

2   D. W. Jefferson, '*Tristram Shandy* and the tradition of learned wit', *Essays in Criticism*, vol. 1 (1951), pp. 225–48; in Traugott, pp. 148–67.

3   Northrop Frye, *Anatomy of Criticism: Four Essays* (Princeton, NJ: Princeton University Press, 1957), p. 312.

4   John Ferriar, *Illustrations of Sterne*, 2nd edn (London, 1812; reprinted New York London: Garland, 1974), pp. 6–7.

5   Alexander Pope, *The Dunciad, in Four Books*, ed. James Sutherland, The Twickenham Edition (London: Methuen, 1943; revised 1963), p. 270, bk I, ll. 21–2.

6   Melvyn New, 'Sterne's Rabelaisian fragment: a text from the holograph manuscript', *PMLA*, vol. 88 (1972), pp. 1083–92.

7   Jefferson draws this comparison in interesting detail; see Traugott, pp. 162–3. See also
    the eloquent discussion of the *Tiers Livre* in Walter Kaiser, *Praisers of Folly: Erasmus,
    Rabelais, Shakespeare* (Cambridge, Mass.: Harvard University Press, 1963), pp.
    103–92.

8   François Rabelais, *Gargantua and Pantagruel*, trans. Thomas Urquhart and Peter le
    Motteux, The Tudor Translations, ed. W. E. Henley (London: David Nutt, 1900;
    reprinted New York: AMS, 1967), bk III, 'The Author's Prologue'. Cited parentheti-
    cally by book and chapter in the text.

9   ibid., bk III, ch. xvi. For a detailed but unsystematic comparison, see Huntington
    Brown, *Rabelais in English Literature* (Cambridge, Mass.: Harvard University Press,
    1933), pp. 188–206.

10 Sigmund Freud, *Jokes and Their Relation to the Unconscious*, trans. James Strachey *et
    al.*, in *The Standard Edition of the Complete Psychological Works of Sigmund Freud*
    (London: Hogarth Press, 1960), Vol. 8, p. 98.

11 Stuart M. Tave, *The Amiable Humorist: A Study in the Comic Theory and Criticism of the
    Eighteenth and Early Nineteenth Centuries* (Chicago, Ill.: University of Chicago Press,
    1960), pp. 140–63.

12 Wayne Booth, 'The self-conscious narrator in comic fiction before *Tristram Shandy*',
    PMLA, vol. 67 (1952), p. 166.

13 For a very different reading of Cervantes' influence on Sterne, see Walter L. Reed, *An
    Exemplary History of the Novel: The Quixotic versus the Picaresque* (Chicago, Ill.:
    University of Chicago Press, 1981), pp. 137–61.

14 Jonathan Swift, *A Tale of a Tub*, ed. A. C. Guthkelch and D. Nichol Smith, 2nd edn
    (London: Oxford University Press, 1958). Cited parenthetically by page number in
    the text.

15 See, for instance, A. E. Dyson, *The Crazy Fabric: Essays in Irony* (London: Mac-
    millan, 1965), pp. 1–13.

16 For Captain Hinde, see C. J. Rawson, 'Two notes on Sterne', *Notes and Queries*, NS,
    vol. 4 (1957), pp. 255–6.

17 See Frank Brady, '*Tristram Shandy*: sexuality, morality, and sensibility', *Eighteenth-
    Century Studies*, vol. 4 (1970), pp. 41–4.

18 C. J. Rawson *et al.*, 'Sternian realities', in Arthur H. Cash and John M. Stedmond
    (eds), *The Winged Skull: Papers from the Laurence Sterne Bicentenary Conference at the
    University of York* (London: Methuen, 1971), p. 92.

CHAPTER 3

An Age of Sensibility

In academic literary history, periods follow each other with the well-defined, plausible order of chapters in a book. Born in the Augustan Age, Sterne comes into his own as a writer in the succeeding period, the Age of Johnson, publishing the first volumes of *Tristram Shandy* less than a year after *Rasselas* had appeared, instructing his printer in fact to duplicate the very size and typeface of *Rasselas*, as if to present a passport to respectability. But we have already noted that to many readers Sterne's discordant originality makes him seem out of place in his own time, a writer strayed from his proper chapter. For one thing – difficult to grasp now, when the novel dominates all other forms of imaginative literature – in 1760 the novel is still an experimental genre, unsettled and exploring various shapes, as the quite different formal constructions of Defoe, Richardson and Fielding demonstrate; to be a novelist is almost by definition to be outside convention. For another thing, the Age of Johnson is a great age of intellectual prose, but not of self-consciousness and bawdry. On the two or three occasions that we know Johnson and Sterne to have met in London, nothing seems to have passed except thunder on the one side and uncomprehending chatter on the other; and it is Johnson who is the source of the most quoted (and unlucky) critical assessment of Sterne's novel: 'nothing odd will do long. "Tristram Shandy" did not last.'[1]

Interleaved in the Age of Johnson, however, exists another literary period that has long resisted an academic label. For many years the non-Johnsonian literature of the later eighteenth century has been known to scholars as 'pre-romantic', a usefully imprecise term that brings together such diverse ideas as 'the sublime and the beautiful', 'sincerity' and 'Gothic', and such diverse writers as Burns, Cowper, Smart, Blake, Ossian and Radcliffe; but a label that has, in Northrop Frye's words, 'the peculiar demerit of committing us to anachronism before we start, and imposing a false teleology on everything we study ... The "pre-romantics" did not know that the Romantic movement was going to succeed them.'[2] 'Pre-romantics' is an evaluative term, of course: none of the writers of this grouping energizes its ideas with anything like the genius of the great Romantics (Blake is always an inaccessible exception) and, in so far as we talk of work that still exerts a pull on our imaginations, we will rightly see the pre-romantics as signposts to something better. But Frye's own suggestion, the 'age of sensibility', has been widely adopted as a preferable way of calling attention to what is new and distinctive in the period, its characteristic emphasis upon irrationality and delicacy of feeling. Widely adopted, too, is his distinction between the Augustans and Johnsonians as authors of a literary 'product', finished, polished, regular, and the new age that presents instead a work in the very act or 'process' of becoming, as Christopher Smart chants a poem into existence, for example, and Boswell and Richardson give the illusion of 'writing to the moment'. Not surprisingly, Frye thinks Sterne an unusually pure example of a process writer and places him at the centre of change: 'when we turn to *Tristram Shandy* we not only read the book but watch the author at work writing it: at any moment the house of Walter Shandy may vanish and be replaced by the author's study'.

I have already declared my bias for seeing Sterne at the extreme of the Augustan generation, a moralist in the tradition of Pope and Swift and Locke. Yet in many ways Frye's placement of Sterne is obviously correct and helps to link the formal qualities of his fiction with its sentimental and self-conscious content, and in turn to link both these things with a wider literary movement. From the great 'sensorium' of sensibility, we can certainly find our way by three major paths to the doors of Shandy Hall.

(i) THE LEGACY OF RICHARDSON: FROM *PAMELA* TO *THE MAN OF FEELING*

British literature of 'the age of reason' had always stressed the importance of the passions, and its criticism stressed as well the psychological effect of those literary passions upon the reader. Long before Burke's famous *Philosophical Enquiry into the Origin of Our Ideas of the Sublime and Beautiful* (1757), Addison had celebrated the 'sublimity' of Milton in his series of *Spectator* papers on *Paradise Lost*, and John Dennis (known as 'tremendous Dennis' because of his favourite adjective) had devoted his *Grounds of Criticism in Poetry* to an analysis of the enthusiastic emotions that great poetry excites. But it is none the less true that in the period of the 1740s and 1750s, the two decades before *Tristram Shandy*, English writers had begun to present emotion in a way different in degree and finally in kind from the earlier satiric and critical emphasis on irrationality. A cult of feeling, indeed, begins to appear in the very un-Augustan poetry of melancholy and transcendence of such mid-century writers as Collins and Gray: a theatrical, numinous poetry that transforms poet into bard and poetic impulse into otherwordly trance.[3] And it has a prose analogue in the intense, sensational psychological dramas of Samuel Richardson, whose *Pamela* and *Clarissa*, although pedestrian in language and shapeless in design, turn the focus of the novel inwards and portray subjective life with a power never before seen in English fiction. In them, feeling overmasters craft. Thus Diderot, in a passage typical of the response Richardson generated, praises him as an artist of feeling: 'C'est lui qui porte le flambeau au fond de la caverne; c'est lui qui apprend à discerner les motifs subtils et déshonnêtes qui se cachent et se dérobent sous d'autres motifs ... Dans son ouvrage, comme dans le monde, les hommes sont partagés en deux classes: ceux qui jouissent et ceux qui souffrent.'[4]

The new values of sensibility are emerging here, of course, particularly in the division of human nature according to predominant feelings and in the suggestion that the imaginative work of the artist has less to do with elegance and order than with rendering emotional states directly. (Geniuses like Shakespeare, it begins to be said, compose by association of ideas rather than by rules.)[5] This belief in the truthfulness and the central importance of our emotions, moreover, is powerfully bolstered by those mid-century developments in English philosophy so often cited by critics of Sterne: the tendency, beginning with Locke, to address problems in epistemology instead of problems in objective knowledge, and to generate theories that concentrate on the subjective and unpredictable character of human nature. Richardson's success and the vogue of the new poets, therefore, represent not a simple shift in literary taste, but a new emphasis in talking about human nature. Indeed, the great subject of eighteenth-century thought in general can perhaps be called the question of human nature: whether it is good or evil, malleable or intractable, rational or depraved. For major works of the century in all languages tend to ask forms of these questions over and over. What constitutes a man? What constitutes the essentially human? Are we gigantic creatures like Gulliver's Brobdingnagians, or insignificant like Lilliputians? Are we Yahoos or Houyhnhnms? In fictive terms, the new sensibility answers that human nature is essentially emotional and irrational, driven by secret forces stronger than laws, institutions or conventions.[6]

In its classical form, obviously, such a view of human nature will be profoundly conservative, verging on the tragic. Johnson's moral thought, for example, rests upon the dark conviction that passions like envy and pride, unchecked by social institutions, will always storm and scale the barriers of reason. Even a more tempered voice in this tradition can undercut its praise of our emotional complexity with a revealing image: 'The passions are so contagious,' writes David Hume in the *Treatise on Human Nature*, 'that they pass with the greatest facility from one person to another, and produce correspondent movements in all human breasts. Where friendship appears in very signal instances, my heart catches the same passions, and is warm'd by those warm sentiments, that display themselves before me.'[7] The age of sensibility, however, no longer understands emotionalism as a source of satire or 'contagious' pain, but as an ennobling power: our feelings constitute our essential human strength, they bring us closest to divinity. 'Dear sensibility!' exclaims Yorick near the end of *A Sentimental Journey*,

> source inexhausted of all that's precious in our joys, or costly in our sorrows! thou chainest thy martyr down upon his bed of straw—and 'tis thou who lifts him up to HEAVEN—eternal fountain of our feelings!—'tis here I trace thee—and this is thy divinity which stirs within me—not, that in some sad and sickening moments, *'my soul shrinks back upon herself, and startles at destruction'*—mere pomp of words!—but that I feel some generous joys and cares beyond myself—all comes from thee, great—great SENSORIUM of the world! (*ASJ*, pp. 277–8)

The sensibility Sterne celebrates, as his image of martyrdom suggests, includes not merely the capacity for intense emotion, but more characteristically a tremulous readiness of compassion for the suffering of others: 'cares beyond myself'. Cowper defines the attitude with exemplary benevolence in *The Task*:

> I would not enter on my list of friends
> (Tho' grac'd with polish'd manners and fine sense,
> Yet wanting sensibility) the man,
> Who needlessly sets foot upon a worm.[8]

And compassion is not without its compensation. 'Praised be God for my sensibility!' Sterne writes in a very late letter. 'Though it has often made me wretched, yet I would not exchange it for all the pleasures the grossest sensualist ever felt' (*Letters*, p. 396). There is a clear hierarchy of emotions here: what Sterne and his contemporaries value most in sensibility is the heightened *delicacy* of feeling it permits, rather than the 'grossest' sensuality it transcends. Figures in distress, instances of friendship or love all excite the heart, but true sensibility goes beyond simple warmth of feeling to represent a purposeful focusing of soul, a purified intensity that amounts to an apprehension of life itself. Henry Mackenzie's lachrymose hero in *The Man of Feeling* (1771) vibrates with exquisite compassion for the misery of others and finds, like Yorick, that he has thereby achieved a stammering transcendence: 'There are some feelings which are perhaps too tender to be suffered by the world,' he sighs. '... I cannot think but in those regions which I contemplate, if there is any thing of mortality left about us, that these feelings will subsist;—they are called, perhaps they are—weaknesses here;—but there may be some better modifications of them in heaven, which may deserve the name of virtues.'[9]

Frequently Sterne seems to assert that all the ingredients of sensibility – reason, compassion, sexuality – are in a state of flux and beyond our control: all one can do is to savour the sensations as they occur. But at its extreme limits such delicacy requires a new name – one that Sterne almost singlehandedly established in its special usage. 'Sentimentalism', as he created it for the eighteenth century, describes a state of compassionate emotion in excess of its apparent cause: Yorick's outburst on behalf of the caged starling in the *Journey*, for example, or his communion with the very soul of the *grisette* whose pulse he takes (and gloves he buys).[10] But it is by no means confined to *A Sentimental Journey*. Every reader has noticed an evolution in the later volumes of *Tristram Shandy*, as Toby begins to predominate, towards the same pathos. (Contemporary reviewers applauded the new emphasis.) The death of Le Fever surely marks the point of change, when Toby's natural compassion for a fellow-soldier in distress (Sterne's soldier father died of a fever) leads to scenes of comic mawkishness. And the apostrophes to the mad Maria of Volume VII, the declarations of eternal friendship between Toby and Trim that punctuate Volumes VIII and IX intensify our impression of emotion released from some hidden source of energy. 'He was an honest, light-hearted lad,' Trim declares of his brother Tom,

an' please your honour, as ever blood warm'd——
——Then he resembled thee, Trim, said my uncle Toby rapidly.
The corporal blush'd down to his fingers ends——a tear of sentimental bashfulness——another of gratitude to my uncle Toby——and a tear of sorrow for his brother's misfortunes, started into his eye and ran sweetly down his cheek together; my uncle Toby's kindled as one lamp does at another and taking hold of the breast of Trim's coat (which had been that of Le Fevre's) as if to ease his lame leg, but in reality to gratify a finer feeling——he stood silent for a minute and a half . . . (IX, v)

Although the vogue of sentimentality was to be genuinely European, and was to issue in such masterpieces as Goethe's *Sorrows of Young Werther*, there were from the beginning robuster minds that turned away suspiciously. ('This world is a comedy to those that think,' observed Horace Walpole at the full tide of urbanity, 'a tragedy to those that feel.')[11] To some, the excesses of overwrought delicacy suggested self-deceit and hypocrisy – Clarissa's punctiliousness on the subject of marriage impresses even her friend Anna Howe as 'over-delicate', and Lovelace pays reluctant tribute to the same womanly refinement: 'Never, I believe, was there so true, so delicate a modesty in the human mind as in

that of this lady.'[12] But Johnson catches at the undercurrent of wilful
delusion in this modesty when he says, 'you may observe there is always
something which she prefers to truth' (just as Fielding had earlier
satirized the greedy hypocrisy of *Shamela*).[13] The source of the
emotional energy, moreover, was thinly hidden. Distresses of poverty or
old age or the warmth of friendship might occasionally provoke the
complacent ecstasy of the sentimentalist, but more often than not he
turns his tearful gaze upon a beautiful young woman in *déshabillé*. Desire
is refined into sympathy. ('Sentimental affection', rumbles the Reverend
Vicesimus Knox, '. . . is but lust in disguise': *CH*, p. 253.) Yorick's
apostrophe to Sensibility follows a series of chapters describing the
alluring mad girl Maria, whom he entreats to lie in his 'bosom, and be
unto me as a daughter' (in his letters and journals Sterne often compares
his passion for Eliza to the love of a father for his daughter). The Man of
Feeling himself peers through a moist blur upon a succession of prosti-
tutes or madwomen tragically frustrated in love: in a crowded Bedlam
cell, one beauty, having told her story, 'press'd his hand to her bosom,
then holding her head in the attitude of listening' sobbed farewell to her
lost Billy. The sentimentalist 'burst into tears, and left them'.[14] Even
Clarissa's genuinely tragic dignity gains its force from her suppression,
exquisite and masterful, of her erotic nature. Lovelace had intended 'to
prove her either angel or woman': it is her heroic delicacy that lifts her up
to heaven.[15]

If Fielding or Johnson (and half of England) could laugh at sentimental titillation – an Academy of Sensibility was sarcastically proposed
– Sterne possessed the more remarkable ability to yield to his own
sentimentalism and at the same time to stand back, detached, and mock
it. Such detachment may very well be Sterne's version, as Martin Price
suggests, of a 'central paradox' in eighteenth-century thought: the idea,
given classic expression in Diderot's *Paradoxe sur le comédien*, that an
actor 'must be free of emotion in order to call up emotion in others'.[16] Yet
if, like Thackeray, we credit Sterne with a certain hypocritical calculation of effect it is hard not to credit him as well with an overlay of genuine
emotion. This ambivalence between sentimentalism and mockery or
detachment forms the principal aesthetic experience (and problem) of *A
Sentimental Journey*, but it is present as well in *Tristram Shandy*, developing out of Tristram's stylistic self-consciousness at first, yet moving
steadily towards a kind of lyricism that arches over comic tensions. Here,
for example, Tristram apostrophizes Toby in the accents of David's
lament for Absalom:

> stop! my dear uncle *Toby*,——stop! go not one foot further into this
> thorny and bewilder'd track,——intricate are the steps! intricate are
> the mases of this labyrinth! . . . O my uncle! my uncle *Toby*. (II, iii)

After which he begins a new chapter and airily tells why:

> I would not give a groat for that man's knowledge in pencraft, who
> does not understand this,———That the best plain narrative in the
> world, tack'd very close to the last spirited apostrophe to my uncle
> *Toby*———would have felt both cold and vapid upon the reader's palate.

When Le Fever dies, Tristram intrudes himself in the same manner, but
so abruptly that few readers know whether to hear the famous sentence as
a joke or as a tremor of sensibility: 'Nature instantly ebb'd again,———the
film returned to its place,———the pulse fluttered———stopp'd———went
on———throb'd———stopp'd again———moved———stopp'd———shall I go
on?———No' (VI, x). If we call it 'role-distancing', we have still not quite
accounted for the haunting quality of a moment like that in the last
volume, when Tristram lifts tearful eyes from his page and speaks to his
lover in the ordinary condition of creatures:

> Time wastes too fast: every letter I trace tells me with what rapidity
> Life follows my pen; the days and hours of it, more precious, my dear
> Jenny! than the rubies about thy neck, are flying over our heads like
> light clouds of a windy day, never to return more———everything
> presses on———whilst thou art twisting that lock,———see! it grows
> grey; and every time I kiss thy hand to bid adieu, and every absence
> which follows it, are preludes to that eternal separation which we are
> shortly to make.———
> ———Heaven have mercy upon us both! (IX, viii)

He undercuts it with a single-sentence chapter ('Now, for what the world
thinks of that ejaculation———I would not give a groat'), but not before
the compassion of true sensibility, purified of all overt sensuality, has
raised his imagery, his very hand, heavenwards. It may be true of all
sensibility – Richardson knew it better than anyone else – that when
eroticism is suppressed ideas of death rise to the surface like the
counter-balance of a scale. In Sterne's sensibility, however, something
further happens. As the theme of time exerts its familiar pressure upon
him to bring the thought of 'eternal separation' upwards, he steps openly
into the scene himself, waving his characters aside, and turns to face his
ever-present audience of one.

(ii) SELF-CONSCIOUSNESS AND SUBJECTIVITY

'To feel', writes Georges Poulet of eighteenth-century sensibility,

> is to feel oneself. To feel everywhere, is to feel oneself everywhere. At
> the extremity of the antennae that the man of feeling stretches out,

everywhere, there are not only things, there is the self that perceives the things. Thus, sensation is the universal means through which a human being extends himself in space, and, in so diffusing himself, everywhere gains consciousness of himself.[17]

Sentimentalism is not always erotic, but it is always self-conscious. The focus of all the great sentimental scenes draws the man of feeling forward, magnified, between the reader and the initial object of emotion, just as Tristram interferes at Le Fever's death. Here, for example, is Sterne in the *Journal to Eliza*, three days after Elizabeth Draper has sailed to India to rejoin her husband:

> 5 in the afternoon—I have just been eating my Chicking, sitting over my repast upon it, with <no> Tears—a bitter Sause—Eliza! but I could eat it with no other—when Molly spread the Table Cloath, my heart fainted with in me—one solitary plate—one knife—one fork—one Glass!—O Eliza! twas painfully distressing,—<I look'd> I gave a thousand pensive penetrating Looks at the Arm chair thou so often graced on these quiet, sentimental Repasts—& Sighed & laid down my knife & fork,—& took out my handkerchiff, clap'd it across my face, & wept like a child . . . (*Letters*, pp. 323–4)

In this consumptive rhapsody every reader will notice how Eliza herself has vanished and how Sterne's fantasy centres upon himself, solitary; like one of those pre-romantic poets striding into a graveyard or seeking out a storm, a cliff, a prospect, he assembles the little totems, the things, the knife, the fork, the glass that will stimulate him into an ecstasy at once tumescent and tearful. We may put this down in part to the same strain of exhibitionism that runs through his bawdry – what if Eugenius should see Yorick feeling a woman's pulse, 'and in an open shop!': '—So much the better: for when my views are direct, Eugenius, I care not if all the world saw me feel it' (*ASJ*, p. 165). But a concluding sentence underscores the extent to which his feelings are first of all literary material, unalive until recorded: 'I shall read the same affecting Acc[t] of many a sad Dinner w[ch] Eliza has had no power to taste of, from the same feelings & recollections.' The last sentence of an alternative version, perhaps copied out by Sterne's daughter after his death and altered to refer to his wife, makes the point more sharply still, in yet another of Sterne's expert sketches of himself at his desk, pen in hand: 'I do so this very moment, my L. for as I take up my pen my poor pulse quickens, my pale face glows, and tears are trickling down upon the paper, as I trace the word L——' (*Letters*, p. 11; but see Cash, pp. 81–2). Like Boswell, Sterne self-consciously 'quickens' when he writes, his emotions assemble obediently beneath his upraised baton. And, when he cannot

write, both emotions and self threaten to vanish. 'Ap. 22^{d} . . . 4 o'clock
They are making my bed—how shall I be able to continue my Journal . . .
in it?' (*Letters*, p. 326)

Scribo, ergo sum. To be self-conscious therefore means to produce an
image of the self, to contemplate an identity: 'I think of *me*.' One
consequence of such self-consciousness, however, is the projection of the
imagined self outwards until, overtly or not, it fills up the whole screen of
consciousness. The man of feeling extends himself everywhere in space.
Poets of the age of sensibility, for example, frequently take up an
oracular tone and monitor themselves in the very act of composing. And
the shadowy personifications that flit across their poems like the ghosts of
gods – 'rosy Pleasure', 'frantic Fear' – represent for all practical purposes
aspects of their own psyches, invoked deliberately as if for contemplation. They stand for objectified aspects of the Self, that is, just as
Arete and Aphrodite do, and they tend to usurp the foreground of the
poem, transforming the natural setting into a psychic landscape. Sterne
(whose own prose is notably given to this trick of personification) has
nothing of the oracular or incantatory about him, of course; but, as we
have already noted, it is evident that in *Tristram Shandy* he has created a
psychic landscape; or, to vary the figure, he has filled his stage with
partial versions of himself. His whole project of self-discovery, indeed –
his attempt to account for himself and his oddity – makes the novel into a
kind of chase after himself. But it must be added that his ability to mock
his sensibility extends to the self-images he produces. In contrast Defoe's
characters, projections no less than Sterne's, merely yield to their
author's obsessions and moralize upon their erring selves. Richardson's
Clarissa possesses her self and feelings in an apparent continuity strikingly different from the staccato of Tristram's consciousness. She may
analyse her motives and actions but, in James Swearingen's words, 'she
never detaches herself from the stream of experience or suspends her
engagement with events to reflect on her own awareness. Hence the
theme of what or who exactly she is never arises.'[18] Her power of feeling,
like that of the poets, is largely unconscious – she cannot interpret her
dreams any more than they can analyse their personifications – she draws
her greatest strength, a strength often called mythic, from reservoirs of
self she does not imagine she possesses. But Tristram has no such depths.
He is no dreaming creature. It is precisely his self-awareness that swamps
his story, interrupts chapter and sentence, and ultimately – paradoxically
– limits the self he can imagine. The true subject of the book is the nature
of his consciousness, not of his unconscious.

There is a second consequence to this self-consciousness as well. When
the self functions as a centring-point, in the literature of sensibility, the
objective world tends to dissolve into subjectivity. Outward things serve
to stimulate inward vision, as in the poetry of Wordsworth or the reveries

of Rousseau, or disappear altogether, as they do in the virtually pure subjectivity of Blake, for whom the natural world exists only as imagined. Writers in the grip of such subjectivity are no doubt pursuing the problem raised in philosophical terms for the whole century by Locke: the relationship between the outward, sensory world and the inward brain – that bowl of liquid and space so often described by Tristram – activated by the senses. In psychological terms, they may be said to be pursuing the nature of the pure self, as distinguished from the self changing in time and from those layers of self indissolubly linked to outward objects, including the body: the literature of sensibility is exhibiting a self, probing for an authentic self. Hence the characteristic appearance in the later eighteenth century of works like Diderot's *Paradoxe sur le comédien* and *Le Neveu de Rameau*, which distinguish self from all its subordinate social and physical parts, as a biologist might distinguish the membrane of a cell from its nucleus.

In this regard, Sterne at first appears to belong to an older tradition and to be aligned with a moralist like Swift, who holds that no 'essential' self in this life will ever be free of the physical world. Matter directly affects mind; subjectivity is delusion. When we fail to recognize the determining effect of outward things, we are like the madmen of *A Tale of a Tub*, blind, in Swift's stupendous adjective, to the 'mechanical operation of the spirit'.[19] Tristram chooses a less cruel image than 'mechanical', but he understands the inextricable relationship of inward and outward in the same way: 'A Man's body and his mind, with the utmost reverence to both I speak it, are exactly like a jerkin, and a jerkin's lining;——rumple the one——you rumple the other' (III, iv). Just as those fortifications of Toby's, which so much resemble the walls of the skull around the brain, are always being breeched, so 'REASON is, half of it, SENSE' (VII, xiii). But the difference between Swift's and Sterne's view is instructive. For, as we have already seen in the context of Cervantes' influence, Sterne follows his theme of interpretation out of the world of language and into the world of things. Objects change according to the consciousness that perceives them, Mambrino's helmet switches to a barber's basin and back again, like a figure in a *trompe l'œil* drawing. On the level of words, such change is perpetual in *Tristram Shandy* (what is meant by 'auxiliary'? Corporal Trim wonders while Walter discusses verbs: V, xlii). And the linguistic uncertainty reaches out to unsettle the objective world itself. What is meant by nose or whiskers? Does Walter's word 'ass' refer to body or soul (VIII, xxxii)? Nothing stands apart; nothing exists except in relationship to someone's inward self. Every object is slowly absorbed into a rising tide of consciousness.

A remarkable variation on this theme of subjectivity occurs in an untitled 'Fragment' discovered by Paul Stapfer in 1870 and attributed to Sterne. It begins with a narrator's account of his meditations as he walks in an orchard by starlight and ponders the question of whether on other planets other creatures likewise look up and imagine themselves alone in the centre of the universe. He then stops beside a plum-tree and recalls that the microscope has made possible the discovery of another universe of beings, infinitesimally small, who may look up from a drop of water and think themselves, too, at the centre of all things. Human beings, he theorizes,

> are situate on a kind of isthmus, wch separates two Infinitys. The mind can in Idea multiply and increase any finite space or quantity infinitely, and also infinitely divide and subdivide it: nor can it find any where on either side any necessity of setting bounds to the works of creation, or fixing ye stage where ye scale of being must end.[20]

From such a vision of subjectivity, where the mind alters physical scale as it likes, the narrator goes on to wonder if with a differently made brain we might not as easily alter our ideas of time; if a civilization might play out its history in an instant, on a grain of sand or a leaf. The second part of the 'Fragment' then describes a dream in which the narrator is transformed into a new self, born into a new world whose luminous, starlit sky puzzles him. Inexplicably exempt from the ordinary cycle of life and death, he travels and studies the sky from every point, for many generations, finally declaring that their world is a globe and that the great light long shimmering on the black horizon will eventually rise and overpower the stars. A sudden shaking and dislocation of the constellations then follows, and he wakes to see, of course, that day is breaking after a windstorm and that he had dreamed a life carried out as a microscopic creature on the surface of a plum.

'I could be bounded in a nutshell, and count myself a king of infinite space' – we may defer a discussion of Sterne's delight in the miniature until a later chapter. Here we can simply say that to imagine other worlds, other bodies, other dimensions is typical of later eighteenth-century thought in many ways; it takes its beginning in Fontenelle's conception of the plurality of worlds, and it belongs to the general context of the century's preoccupation with the question of human nature. To imagine a character like Tristram, however, who cannot understand the world he lives in and whose travels and opinions provoke laughter, seems more closely related to Sterne's own preoccupations. And it seems likewise typical of Sterne to give the question of multiple perspectives its social analogue in the persistent mockery and misunder-standing that the narrator encounters. Multiple perspectives of this kind, in fact, form one of the comic principles of *Tristram Shandy*, where the Cervantic themes of perspective and interpretation begin in the very first chapter. And, although misunderstanding on the Shandyesque scale is

without question humorous, a vaudeville version of the idea of subjectivity, it has a serious implication as well: there is a tragic potential in the
resultant personal isolation each character displays, the feeling we take
away that Walter and the others are unreachable in their eccentricity.
Poets of sensibility, addressing only abstractions or landscapes, may be
solitary by choice; in Shandy Hall, solitude is neither a choice nor a good.
Everyone speaks unceasingly to everyone else, but no one speaks so as to
be understood. Each character gazes on a different part of the sky. Each
one gallops his hobbyhorse in a different direction – Toby whistling
'Lillabulero', Walter scattering theories in his dust, Mrs Shandy dodging
every outcrop of idea. Nearly the whole action of the novel is conversation, yet it is conversation perpetually at cross-purposes, conversation
interrupted, broken off, left unfinished.

Sterne 'was concerned almost exclusively with the problem of communication among men', writes John Traugott, summarizing (if not over-
stating) a critical consensus.[21] But the problem cannot be solved or the
tragedy averted by language. When words fail, as literally they do – 'My
uncle *Toby* looked brisk at the sound of the word *siege*, but could make
neither head nor tail of it' (IV, xxv) – communication becomes the
business of sensibility: 'A satirist loathing his species', observes J. B.
Priestley, 'could have taken such tragi-comical little creatures, each in
the separate mechanical box of his mind, and made out of them a scene or
narrative that would have jangled the nerves of a dozen generations.
Sterne, however, . . . preserves the balance by emphasising the kinship of
his people. If the Shandies cannot share one another's thoughts, they can
share one another's feelings.'[22] Subjectivity yields only to sentiment. No
Shandy appears to possess the sympathetic imagination that later
eighteenth-century critics so often invoke – the ability like Shakespeare's
to enter into another's personality – but nearly all of them rise eagerly to
shake hands, beg pardon, shed tears of ready compassion:

> As soon as my father had done insulting his HOBBY-HORSE,——he
> turned his head, without the least emotion, from Dr. *Slop*, to whom he
> was addressing his discourse, and look'd up into my father's face, with
> a countenance spread over with so much good nature,——so placid;—
> —so fraternal;——so inexpressibly tender towards him;——it pene-
> trated my father to his heart: He rose up hastily from his chair, and
> seizing hold of both of my uncle *Toby*'s hands as he spoke:——Brother
> *Toby*, said he,——I beg thy pardon;——forgive, I pray thee, this rash
> humour which my mother gave me. (II, xii)

Traugott calls this sentimentalism 'Sterne's greatest glory' because it
re-establishes community where reason, in the form of language, threatens to destroy it (Traugott, p. 15). In any case, it is important to note that

this precarious community differs in a fundamental way from community as celebrated by the great Augustans like Pope and Swift. For their idea is based upon order and hierarchy rather than upon kinship and feeling. Their vision, apparent in politics and architecture as well as in literature, is corporate, concerned with a whole, a classical city set as a standard against a disintegrating present reality. But Shandy Hall sits in a hollow of subjectivity. Neither a real nor an ideal city makes an appearance, only a remote London, sucked instantly into a maw of theories. In Sterne's world, each individual consciousness establishes itself at the centre of a universe of feeling and ignores any such thing as objective reality, until the subject of *Tristram Shandy* finally seems to be the nature of fiction itself.

What remains to be considered, of course, is the possibility that consciousness and fiction are the same thing.

(iii) THE METAMORPHOSIS OF SATIRE: THE IDEA
OF MADNESS

'Walter is wise, he is witty, he is humane', writes Traugott; '—and he is mad.' 'Is Uncle Toby mad too?' John Preston asks, comparing him to Swift's demented Jack. All of the inhabitants of Shandy Hall, observes V. S. Pritchett, 'live shut up in the madhouse of their own imaginations, oysters itching voluptuously upon the pearl within'. 'The real point about Walter and Toby', says Michael DePorte, 'is not so much that Sterne thinks them mad, or even that most contemporary readers would have thought them mad; the point is rather that given the psychiatric criteria of the day they *are* mad.'[23]

This is not true, of course. Swift's Hack in the *Tale*, that self-confessed former inmate of Bedlam, is a genuine madman by the criteria of the day. The madness of Sterne's characters is only a critical metaphor imposed on his books by later readers (Sterne's contemporaries seem never to have used the term in reference to him). Yet the metaphor of madness appears in so many modern discussions because it does disclose certain important issues in *Tristram Shandy*. It helps, for one thing, to underscore that link which many readers feel between Sterne and the Augustan satirists generally, for whom madness is a key image, a recurring synonym for Folly. In writers like Pope and Swift, the classical idea of madness as supernatural inspiration is largely absent (as it would be in Toby or Walter), surrendered to Bedlamite armies of dunces and fools. In the early nineteenth century, by contrast – to skip past Sterne's lifetime for a moment – the classical idea of madness will reappear, almost casually in such instances as Wordsworth's allusion to poets who begin in joy and end in madness ('Resolution and Independence'), and profoundly in such instances as Coleridge's spectral images of inspiration. Some Romantic poets, like Byron and Shelley, will also represent madness as a sign of alienation from a prosaic world that is indifferent to higher truth, insensitive to the madman's sensitivity. And in both Romantic criticism and poetry the faculty of imagination – which Augustans named the primary agent of madness – will be described as the source of this higher apprehension.[24] Obviously the age of sensibility – to return now to Sterne's lifetime – lies closer to Romantic than to Augustan values. Without ever elaborating the systematic aesthetics that raise imagination to the level of creative principle, the literature of process lays stress upon the non-logical powers of the mind, revealing consciousness at work in all its erratic, uplifting motions; poets stand apart from other men; obscurity becomes incantatory, a hypnotic release of inner powers repressed or disvalued by rationality. The characteristic figure of the age, Frye claims, is the *poète maudit*, crushed by his own sensibility, not yet able to make of his sentimental feelings a basis of strength ('The list of poets over whom the shadows of mental breakdown fell is far too long to be coincidence').[25] But such speculations in literary history tend to yield more abstraction than information. For most readers, Tristram in all his good-natured, moonstruck energy hardly seems related to the mad Ossian or the prophetic Blake. Toby puttering about his fortifications belongs to a world different from that of Christopher Smart chanting a liturgy to his cat Jeoffry. What kind of madness do so many modern critics actually find in Sterne's novel?

In fact, *Tristram Shandy* offers two strikingly different kinds of madness. The first, to which all my critical quotations refer, is simply eccentricity – hobbyhorses like Toby's siegecraft and Walter's theories – described as 'madness'. And, if these critical metaphors are put aside, such repetitive, automatic eccentricity represents no more than an eighteenth-century version of an abiding comic principle: as Henri Bergson says, laughter arises from 'a certain *mechanical inelasticity*, just where one would expect to find the wideawake adaptability and the living pliableness of a human being'.[26] But Tristram himself cites another comic principle that links such eccentricity with a genuine and widely known theory of madness: Locke's chapter 'Of the *Association* of Ideas in the *Essay Concerning Human Understanding*, which Tristram says offers an explanation of why 'my poor mother could never hear the ... clock wound up,——but the thoughts of some other things unavoidably popp'd into her head' (I, iv). One of the real services of recent scholarship has been to correct the older notion that Sterne wrote (and his characters talk and act) according to something called vaguely 'the association of ideas'. A school of 'associationist' psychology did certainly exist in mid-eighteenth-century England, led by the philosopher David Hartley, and maintained that our minds function by the recall and evocation of associated ideas. (Hartley postulated physical 'vibrations' or 'vibratiuncles' in the brain.) But Locke's chapter on that subject, though it introduced the phrase to English philosophy, was not inserted before the fourth edition of the *Essay*, and it plays no part in his general account of human understanding. Instead, it concerns only a particular, limited example of association. 'Some of our *Ideas*,' he says, 'have a natural Correspondence and Connexion one with another' (*Essay*, II, xxxiii, 5); others are joined in our minds simply by 'Chance or Custom', as Walter Shandy had made it a habit on the first Sunday night of each month to wind the clock and likewise take care of 'some other little family concernments' (I, iv). Of these random and habitual associations, 'wrong Connexions', Locke speaks with unusual anger: they are at the 'root' of *all* madness. 'I shall be pardon'd for calling it by so harsh a name as *Madness*,' he adds,

> when it is considered that opposition to Reason deserves that Name, and is really Madness; and there is scarce a Man so free from it, but that if he should always on all occasions argue or do as in some cases he constantly does, would not be thought fitter for *Bedlam* than Civil Conversation. (*Essay*, II, xxxiii, 4)

His subsequent illustration of these unnatural associations begins moderately enough, with examples of musicians who habitually follow certain tunes and of a man who still cannot bear honey after a childhood 'overdose' of it; but he gradually increases the force of his analysis, granting the principle of association greater and greater influence over our actions, until he ends by describing a veritable Bedlam of hobbyhorsical eccentrics – one man associates a past injury and a person and is driven to uncontrollable hatred; another cannot bear to enter a room that resembles the one in which his friend died; a young gentleman can only dance when a certain old trunk has a certain position in the room.

> A Friend of mine knew one perfectly cured of Madness by a very harsh and offensive Operation. The Gentleman who was thus recovered, with great sense of Gratitude and Acknowledgement owned the Cure all his Life after, as the greatest Obligation he could have received; but, whatever Gratitude and Reason suggested to him, he could never bear the sight of the Operator: That Image brought back with it the *Idea* of that Agony which he suffer'd from his Hands, which was too mighty and intolerable for him to endure. (*Essay*, II, xxxiii, 14)

In Locke's hands 'this sort of unreasonableness', which he calls perhaps our 'greatest' source of error, constitutes a criticism of human nature (*Essay*, II, xxxiii, 18). In Sterne's hands it constitutes a criticism of reason. Or, rather, of the view that places reason sovereign over human nature. For no principle of logic, no 'natural' connection, is strong enough to penetrate Walter's mesh of theory or Toby's defences, or to make Tristram follow an orderly pattern of narration; and even that notorious eighteenth-century symbol of divine and human reason, the clock, takes its place in a wildly unnatural association of ideas. If we object that Sterne is merely describing obsession or the Renaissance psychology of 'humour', the explicit reference to Locke's *Essay* still complicates what would otherwise be familiar techniques of comedy, and encourages us to speak seriously, even philosophically, of Shandian eccentricity, as we cannot, for example, of Sir Epicure Mammon's greed or Lord Emsworth's dottiness about pigs. The emphasis Sterne brings to bear on language and interpretation, moreover, connects it to the Cervantic tradition, in which madness becomes, not a matter of reason or unreason, but a matter of point of view. (It can be no accident that the Shakespearian play to which *Tristram Shandy* most often alludes is *Hamlet*, where themes of illusion, interpretation and madness – not to mention repressed sexuality – are paramount.) Neither Cervantes nor Sterne, of course, goes so far as to say that reason has no part in our make-up; but in the mirror of Toby's monomania, in Walter's approximately plausible theories and the Don's ready explanations of enchantment they obviously parody its operations and its claims; and at extreme moments their parody raises the possibility that reason bears no necessary relationship to reality at all. 'Herein seems to lie the difference between Idiots and mad Men,' Locke says: 'that mad Men put wrong *Ideas* together, and so make wrong Propositions, but argue and reason right from them; But Idiots make very few or no Propositions, and reason scarce at all' (*Essay*, II, xi, 13). The difference, that is, lies finally between Locke's thoroughly Augustan position that madness is 'wrong' – the moral connotation of his language resembles Swift's, who holds his Bedlamites accountable for choosing to be 'well-deceived' – and Sterne's more equivocal view that every consciousness contains a fiction, every subjectivity a truth.

Sterne's second kind of madness, however, is fundamentally unengaged with these philosophical ideas. The account of Maria (IX, xxiv), the pathetic madwoman whom Tristram meets near Moulins, belongs to a subgenre invented and perfected in the age of sensibility: the portrait of madness designed to evoke, not satire, not awe, but quivering, tearful pity. For this is the same Maria who triggers Yorick's apostrophe to 'sensibility' in *A Sentimental Journey* and whose sisters we have already met in Mackenzie's Bedlam cells and elsewhere, a stock figure of pathos, adumbrated perhaps in *Clarissa*, grotesquely distorted in the madwomen of Gothic fiction to come. Sterne's sketch of her follows, significantly, an invocation to the 'Gentle Spirit of sweetest humour' who guided Cervantes in his prison. And Tristram declares that his mood as they met was one of perfect sensibility, in which 'every thing I saw, or had to do with, touch'd upon some secret spring either of sentiment or rapture'. At such a moment Maria's music on her pipe takes on an irresistibly appealing character, faintly connected to the supernatural by the fact that, although no one has taught her to play, she has somehow learned the service to the Virgin Mary. Her madness combines this hint of literal inspiration with the eroticism never far from such feminine vulnerability ('she was beautiful; and if ever I felt the full force of an honest heart-ache, it was the moment I saw her'). Yet the manic energy, at once menacing and obscene, that we discovered in Swift's Bedlam has given way here to passivity and melancholy. And the idea of madness as wilful, blameable folly has likewise disappeared, along with the idea of madness as a way to higher truth. Maria's madness, indeed, like all such 'sensible' insanities, reveals no content of idea whatsoever; it faintly suggests repressed sexuality (she has been thwarted in love), but it otherwise exists only in a spreading puddle of emotion. The self-consciousness of the sentimental observer will find its characteristic expression in Yorick, who makes Maria's plight a means of admiring his own power of sympathy. But Tristram, equally self-conscious, maintains a comic, disarming distance, calling his initial heartache by that most Augustan of perjoratives, 'my enthusiasm', and breaking her spell with a crude, insensible joke:

> MARIA look'd wistfully for some time at me, and then at her goat——and then at me——and then at her goat again, and so on, alternately——
> ——Well, Maria, said I softly——What resemblance do you find?

When we compare either of Sterne's versions of madness to an account like Swift's in the *Tale* or Pope's chattering dunces in *The Dunciad*, we are likely to be struck by the absence of satire in them. Toby, Walter, Tristram are all objects of mockery at the beginning, to be sure, but we have already noticed how, as the novel proceeds, that mockery is replaced by a warm and sentimental affection. And in both visits to Maria sympathy, not satire, predominates. Nowhere, in fact, does Sterne show more clearly the values of the age of sensibility than in his explicitly mad characters – the gentle unfettering of irrationality, the delicacy of feeling, the fascination with subjectivity. And, if we wish to confirm this general impression that satire is here metamorphosing into sensibility, we can point to a parallel movement in social and medical history, classically documented by Dorothy George: the progressive humanitarian changes in the treatment of the poor and the insane that characterize middle and later eighteenth-century England.[27]

When we compare Sterne's presentation of madness to Johnson's

best-known account, however, we are likely to be surprised by the extent
of their common assumptions and their hidden continuity with the
earlier Augustans. In *Rasselas*, Johnson portrays a learned astronomer, a
recluse, who confides to the sage Imlac his conviction that he 'possesses
the regulation of the weather, and the distribution of the seasons'; and, in
a gesture reminiscent of Johnson's belief that he had inherited a 'vile
melancholy' from his father, the astronomer offers to appoint Imlac his
successor. As Rasselas' sister and maid laugh at this madness, Imlac
replies heavily (in the voice of Johnson himself):

> 'Ladies,' said Imlac, 'to mock the heaviest of human affliction[s] is
> neither charitable nor wise. Few can attain this man's knowledge, and
> few practise his virtues; but all may suffer his calamity. Of the
> uncertainties of our present state, the most dreadful and alarming is
> the uncertain continuance of reason.'[28]

Nothing could be less like the delicately prurient, dimly sublime
Bedlam of the man of feeling. Nothing, for that matter, could be less like
the aloof savagery of Swift's scorn for madness. Johnson's sympathy for
the astronomer's madness grows out of his profound identification with
him, and then out of his general belief that madness can strike any of us,
that indeed none of us is ever truly sane. For 'disorders of the intellect',
Imlac goes on to say,

> happen much more often than superficial observers will easily believe.
> Perhaps, if we speak with rigorous exactness, no human mind is in its
> right state.

In the amiable (and curable) figure of the astronomer, moreover,
Johnson has rendered entirely harmless Swift's vision of the world as
madhouse. Swift, after all, drawing upon the ancient tradition of
madness as a link to supernatural power, had presented the mad world as
dangerous and revolutionary, populated by genuinely destructive fools
and knaves. His madmen in the *Tale* are murderous princes and generals
like Henry IV, subversive philosophers like Hobbes, religious enthusiasts like the Dissenters: they threaten the stability of church and state
literally, as any English reader with a memory of the Civil Wars would
understand. Yet, while there may be some suggestion of astrology in the
astronomer's delusion of control over the sky, Johnson makes clear that
this power is mere hallucination, the fever of subjectivity, and not a
supernatural connection. And Sterne, of course, takes the 'world as
madhouse' to its ultimate point of harmlessness in Shandy Hall, where
no human mind is in 'its right state' and where madness, unconnected to

power, simply joins the general air of impotence that hangs over every character in the novel.

None the less, while he displays an un-Augustan sympathy for his madman – a sympathy that intercepts and humanizes his satire – Johnson analyses human nature precisely as do Swift and Pope and Locke: 'There is no man whose imagination does not sometimes predominate over his reason', Imlac insists, 'who can regulate his attention wholly by his will, and whose ideas will come and go at his command. No man will be found in whose mind airy notions do not sometimes tyrannise, and force him to hope or fear beyond the limits of sober probability.' (Compare Swift's remark: 'If the wisest man would at any time utter his thoughts, in the crude indigested manner, as they come into his head, he would be looked upon as raving mad.')[29] This is Sterne's view as well, translated from rationalistic, moralizing language into the figure of the hobbyhorse:

> Nay, if you come to that, Sir, have not the wisest of men in all ages, not excepting *Solomon* himself,——have they not had their HOBBY-HORSES;——their running horses,——their coins and their cockle-shells, their drums and their trumpets, their fiddles, their pallets,——their maggots and their butterflies?——and so long as a man rides his HOBBY-HORSE peaceably and quietly along the King's highway, and neither compels you or me to get up behind him,——pray, Sir, what have either you or I to do with it? (I, vii)

In a mad world, that is to say, we are all hobbyhorsical, governed by fancies more or less harmless, instead of by reason. And Tristram's first example of a madman, Dr Kunastrokius, recalls, as it must have been intended to do, the hard-mouthed imagination of Swift's *Tale*, that mad equine force 'exceedingly disposed to run away with [our] *Reason*' (*Tale*, p. 180). In the sober context of his sermons, he makes the same point more conventionally, through language that we can hardly distinguish from Johnson's:

> will the coolest and most circumspect say, when pleasure has taken full possession of his heart, that no thought nor purpose shall arise there, which he would have concealed?—In those loose and unguarded moments the imagination is not always at command—in spite of reason and reflection, it will forceably carry him sometimes whither he would not ...[30]

'All power of fancy over reason', Imlac declares, 'is a degree of insanity.'

In so far as Toby and Tristram are typical examples of how our minds work, then, we are still far from the prevailing value of sensibility, the belief that irrationality releases some inward power and guides us towards a higher consciousness. We are even farther from something like Wordsworth's vision on Snowdon of 'The perfect image of a mighty mind,/Of one that feeds upon infinity', a mind that resembles the highest possibility of the poet's mind.[31] The strongest argument against including Sterne in the age of sensibility may be, in fact, the absence of this high sublimity, towards which satire in the eighteenth century has been slowly evolving. For Sterne's vision of mind reaches no higher than hobbyhorses or those bizarre metaphors for the brain that he sprinkles throughout *Tristram Shandy*. His presentations of madness lead no one towards an elevated consciousness or a profounder reality. Or, to put it more positively, we might say that Sterne, like Johnson, displays the classic Augustan faith that human nature is primarily social, that reality (not hell) is other people. If his idea of community is sentimental and non-hierarchical, he none the less shares the impulse that makes Imlac advise the mad astronomer to forsake his solitude and to correct his madness by conversation and society. Thus, there is misunderstanding in every social exchange in *Tristram Shandy*, but not alienation. There is subjectivity, but not solitude. A sense of human limitations, defined in the familiar Johnsonian terms of time and death, crowds his characters together and renders them foolish and mad only in the ordinary human sense. From this point of view Sterne is drawing on a third tradition of madness, common to preachers: like Johnson, he is writing a comic version of Ecclesiastes. And, if he writes in a style that seems to place him in conflict with the values of the age of Johnson, that may only be because we have not yet fully considered the puzzle of his style.

NOTES: CHAPTER 3

1   James Boswell, *The Life of Samuel Johnson, with a Journal of a Tour to the Hebrides*, ed. G. B. Hill, revised by L. F. Powell (Oxford: Clarendon Press, 1934–50), Vol. 2, p. 449.

2   Northrop Frye, 'Towards defining an age of sensibility', in his *Fables of Identity* (New York: Harcourt, 1963), pp. 130–7.

3   The best short account of the new poetry of sentiment is Martin Price, 'The sublime poem: pictures and powers', *Yale Review*, vol. 58 (1969), pp. 194–213. A more systematic survey can be found in chapter 3 of John Butt and Geoffrey Carnall, *The Mid-Eighteenth Century*, Vol. 8 of the Oxford History of English Literature (Oxford: Oxford University Press, 1979).

4   Denis Diderot, 'Eloge de Richardson', in *Oeuvres esthétiques*, ed. Paul Vernière (Paris: Garnier, 1968), pp. 32–3: 'It is he who carries the torch to the depths of the cavern; he who learns to discern the subtle and dishonest motives that hide and steal away under the guise of other motives . . . In his work, as in the world, men are divided into two classes: those who enjoy and those who suffer.'

5   The whole topic receives full-scale treatment in James Engell, *The Creative Imagination: Enlightenment to Romanticism* (Cambridge, Mass.: Harvard University Press, 1981), chs 4 and 11.

6   For more on this question, see Tony Tanner, 'Reason and the grotesque: Pope's *The Dunciad*', *Critical Quarterly*, vol. 7 (1965), pp. 145–60, and Max Byrd, '"Tintern Abbey" and metamorphosis: two notes', *MP*, vol. 81 (1983), pp. 24–37.

7   David Hume, *A Treatise of Human Nature*, ed. L. A. Selby-Bigge (Oxford, 1888), p. 605.

8   William Cowper, *The Task*, bk VI, ll. 560–3, in *The Poetical Works of William Cowper*, ed. H. S. Milford (London: Oxford University Press, 1926), p. 231.

9   Henry Mackenzie, *The Man of Feeling*, ed. Brian Vickers (London: Oxford University Press, 1967), pp. 128–9.

10   By 'sentiment' in the Dictionary, Johnson understands the older meaning of 'Thought; notion; opinion; the sense considered distinctly from the language or things; a striking sentence in a composition'. When he, therefore, advises a friend to read Richardson for the 'sentiment' (Boswell, *Life*, Vol. 2, p. 175), he is pointing to the moral truth embodied in the novelist's portrayal of emotions. This idea of the *truth* of our feelings is subsumed in Sterne's 'sentimentalism', which retains it but stresses much more the act of feeling. Johnson's word 'pathetick' comes close to the sentimentalist's idea of feeling for the sake of feeling; but then he denied that Sterne possessed this quality: a young lady 'insisted that some of Sterne's writings were very pathetick. Johnson bluntly denied it. "I am sure (said she) they have affected *me*."—"Why (said Johnson, smiling, and rolling himself about,) that is, because, dearest, you're a dunce"' (ibid., Vol. 4, p. 109).

11   Horace Walpole, *Correspondence*, ed. W. S. Lewis *et al.* (New Haven, Conn.: Yale University Press, 1937–83), Vol. 32, p. 315. To the Countess of Upper Ossory, 16 August 1776.

12   Samuel Richardson, *Clarissa* (London: Dent, 1932), Vol. 2, p. 475.

13   *Johnsonian Miscellanies* ed. G. B. Hill (Oxford, 1897; reprinted New York: Barnes & Noble, 1966), Vol. 1, p. 297.

14   *The Man of Feeling*, p. 35.

15   *Clarissa*, Vol. 2, p. 208.

16   Martin Price, *To the Palace of Wisdom: Studies in Order and Energy from Dryden to Blake* (Garden City, NY: Doubleday, 1964), p. 328.

17   Georges Poulet, *The Metamorphoses of the Circle*, trans. Carley Dawson and Elliot Coleman (Baltimore, Md: Johns Hopkins University Press, 1966), p. 72.

18   James E. Swearingen, *Reflexivity in 'Tristram Shandy': An Essay in Phenomenological Criticism* (New Haven, Conn.: Yale University Press, 1977), p. 53.

19   'A Discourse Concerning the Mechanical Operation of the Spirit' is printed as a 'Fragment' at the end of the *Tale of a Tub*.

20   Paul Stapfer, *Laurence Sterne: sa personne et ses ouvrages* (Paris, 1870), p. xx.

21   John Traugott, *Tristram Shandy's World: Sterne's Philosophical Rhetoric* (Berkeley/Los Angeles, Calif.: University of California Press, 1954), p. 72.

22   J. B. Priestley, *The English Comic Characters* (London: Bodley Head, 1925), p. 156.

23   Traugott, *Tristram Shandy's World*, p. 59; John Preston, *The Created Self: The Reader's Role in Eighteenth-Century Fiction* (London: Heinemann, 1970), p. 171; V. S. Pritchett, *Books in General*, p. 175; Michael V. DePorte, *Nightmares and Hobbyhorses: Swift, Sterne, and Augustan Ideas of Madness* (San Marino, Calif.: Huntington Library, 1974), p. 116.

24   This is the subject of DePorte's book, cited above, and also of Max Byrd, *Visits to Bedlam: Ideas of Madness in the Eighteenth Century* (Columbia, SC: University of South Carolina Press, 1974).

25   Frye, op. cit., p.136.

26   Henri Bergson, *Laughter: An Essay on the Meaning of the Comic*, trans. Cloudesley Brereton and Fred Rothwell (London: Macmillan, 1913), p. 10.

27   M. Dorothy George, *London Life in the Eighteenth Century* (London: Kegan Paul, 1925), pp. 1–20.

28 Samuel Johnson, *Rasselas*, ed. G. B. Hill (Oxford, 1887), ch. xliii.
29 Jonathan Swift, 'Some Thoughts on Free-Thinking', in *Prose Works*, ed. Herbert Davis (Oxford: Basil Blackwell, 1939–68), Vol. 4, p. 49.
30 'Sermon II', *The Sermons of Mr Yorick*, in *Works* (Oxford: Basil Blackwell, 1927), Vol. 6, p. 19.
31 William Wordsworth, *The Prelude* (1805), bk XIII, ll. 69–70, in *The Prelude 1799, 1805, 1850*, ed. Jonathan Wordsworth *et al.* (New York: Norton, 1979), p. 460.

CHAPTER 4

Style

The Reverend Baptist Noel Turner recalled in 1818 a visit Johnson had made to Cambridge in 1765. When the question of Sterne arose, Turner said, Johnson drew himself up and told his audience an anecdote:

> In a company where I lately was, Tristram Shandy introduced himself; and Tristram Shandy had scarcely sat down, when he informed us that he had been writing a Dedication to Lord Spencer; and sponte suâ, he pulled it out of his pocket; and sponte suâ, for nobody desired him, he began to read it; and before he had read half a dozen lines, sponte meâ, sir, I told him it was not English, sir. (*CH*, p. 138)

Virtually no one has ever agreed. Long after the typographical jokes, the *double entendres* and eighteenth-century allusions may have grown stale, readers of all kinds have continued to admire Sterne's English. Professional writers in particular comment on his surprising art. 'The intensity that Sterne lacked in emotion he retrieved in style,' observes Cyril Connolly, for example: 'such is Sterne's mastery, his ease and grace, that one is always upheld by a verbal expectancy; slow though the action moves, he will always keep his balance and soon there will follow a perfect flow of words that may end with a phrase that rings like a pebble on a frozen pond'.[1] Virginia Woolf, indebted in a general way herself to Sterne's originality, passes over the famous 'sensibility' and humour to describe in extraordinary terms the unexpected, even poetic flavour of his prose.

> The jerky, disconnected sentences are as rapid and it would seem as little under control as the phrases that fall from the lips of a brilliant talker. The very punctuation is that of speech, not writing, and brings the sound and associations of the speaking voice in with it. The order of the ideas, their suddenness and irrelevancy, is more true to life than to literature. There is a privacy in this intercourse which allows things to slip out unreproved that would have been in doubtful taste had they been spoken in public. Under the influence of this extraordinary style the book becomes semi-transparent. The usual ceremonies and conventions which keep the reader and writer at arm's length disappear. We are as close to life as we can be.[2]

Like so many others, Virginia Woolf's tribute points towards the matter
of Sterne's subjective realism, his capacity, as she puts it, to transfer 'our
interest from the outer to the inner'. 'No writing', she adds, 'seems to
flow more exactly into the very folds and creases of the individual mind,
to express its changing moods, to answer its lightest whim and impulse,
and yet the result is perfectly precise and composed.' But she points as
well towards the very technical elements like punctuation that make his
prose so strangely realistic, and with these we can begin.

(i)   THE ELEMENTS OF STYLE

'Mr S—— might have saved himself the trouble of signing his name to
each volume of this performance . . .', declared the *Critical Review* in
1762, 'as it would be impossible for any reader, even of the least
discernment, not to see in the perusal of half a page, that these volumes
can be the production of no other than the original author of *Tristram
Shandy*' (*CH*, pp. 138–9). What any reader would notice first in half a
page, of course, is Sterne's punctuation. Not the notorious squiggles,
however, or the marbled pages and serpentine diagrams of the plot.
Dramatic though these devices are, they appear infrequently in the novel
and may be only parodying the typographical high jinks of such neo-
Rabelaisian volumes as John Dunton's *Voyage round the World* (1691).
Sterne's real signature is obviously his dashes – those nervous and
irrepressible scratches that mark his page, in David Thomson's words,
'like skid marks and places where he has had to brake or accelerate'.[3] It
can be shown that Sterne uses dashes in the conventional eighteenth-
century manner to set off quotations in dialogue and also sometimes to
introduce a long summary or appositive: readers 'who are no readers at
all,——who find themselves ill at ease, unless they are let into the whole
secret from first to last, of everything which concerns you' (I, iv). And
clearly he sometimes uses them in a conventional way to indicate a
theatrical pause: 'Why, Madam,——he was all that time afflicted with a
Sciatica' (I, iv). But for the most part his dashes, like those in Keats's
letters, simply enact the drama of his consciousness arriving at articu-
lation, the volatile motion of a mind whose ideas are crowding in upon
each other, tumbling out in a rush.

> In all nice and ticklish discussions,——(of which, heaven knows,
> there are but too many in my book)——where I find I cannot take a
> step without the danger of having either their worships or their
> reverences upon my back——I write one half *full*,——and t'other
> *fasting*;——or write it all full,——and correct it fasting;——or write it
> fasting,——and correct it full, for they all come to the same thing. (VI,
> xvii)

At first glance, nothing in these dashes suggests repression or compress-
ion of thought – as Emily Dickinson's, for example, do – a mind
calculating, squeezing, deflecting its ideas; nor do they suggest anything
like struggle or diffidence of speech. In an important essay on Sterne's
style, Ian Watt notes that dashes serve him chiefly as a means of arriving
at a multiplicity of viewpoints, as a way of subverting orderly syntax to
reveal the free associations, 'the sudden interruptions and oscillations of
thought and feeling, which characterise Tristram both as a person and as
a narrator'.[4] Yet it is also true that Sterne's dashes do not work in the
service of Tristram alone. They appear in the same disruptive way in
everything we know he wrote: letters, sermons, journal, other fiction.
And it is also true that, partly because he varies their actual typographical
length, Sterne's dashes achieve the paradoxical effect of both speeding
up and slowing down his tempo:

——————————————— Shut the door. ——————————————(I, iv)

At other times they interpose themselves to hold the voice back when it
wants to run: 'My father thrust back his chair,——rose up,——put on
his hat,——took four long strides to the door,——jerked it
open,——thrust his head half way out,——shut the door again . . .' (III,
xli). At some level, we can speculate, the restraining, checking power of
Sterne's dashes also creates, in Watt's suggestive phrase, a drama of
'inhibited impulse'. We are not accustomed to associating Tristram with
inhibition, of course (and Watt says no more on the subject – he may refer
only to theatrical pauses); but, as Thomson reminds us, skid marks
appear when we suddenly brake as well as when we accelerate. If Sterne's
dashes usually zig-zag because they represent the spontaneous discontinuities of thought, at times they may zig-zag as well because they are
approaching forbidden territory. Or, if that is too solemn and psychological a way of putting it, they ricochet because Sterne's whole style, like
his humour, is built upon the principle of never saying quite directly
what he means: 'Take hold of my whiskers, said the lady *Baussiere*—
—The page took hold of her palfrey' (V, i).
   Most readers, however, understand the discontinuities of Sterne's
punctuation as Virginia Woolf did: they are signs of speech, the dashes
are the impulsive gestures of a man in animated conversation. And
Sterne himself first suggests that image, in one of the most quoted
passages of the novel:

Writing, when properly managed (as you may be sure I think mine is)
is but a different name for conversation: As no one, who knows what
he is about in good company, would venture to talk all;——so no
author, who understands the just boundaries of decorum and good

breeding, would presume to think all: The truest respect which you can pay to the reader's understanding, is to halve this matter amicably, and leave him something to imagine, in his turn, as well as yourself. (II, xi)

Writing as conversation: certainly no one could confuse Sterne's syntax with the balanced periodic sentences of Johnson's Imlac or even with the Augustan formality of novelists like Fielding ('Endeavour, madam, to comfort yourself and Miss Nancy as well as you can. I will go instantly in quest of Mr Nightingale').[5] To that extent, his syntactical antics seem daringly close to real speech. But it has often been noted that actual conversation, even of the most educated speakers, tends to collapse into inelegant sentence fragments and broken phrases, with a very different effect from Sterne's brilliancy of rhetoric (Louis Milic cruelly quotes the transcript of an academic seminar to make this point).[6] Sterne asserts in any case not that his prose reproduces speech but, rather, that it enables the reader to enter into his conversational circle and to participate in what he images. Observing 'decorum and good breeding', he issues no Swiftian challenges of interpretation to his gentle reader, no polite address that ends with insult and betrayal. Ordinarily he does no more than either tease us into supplying indecent meanings or else cajole us, as he declares, into picturing mentally what he is saying: 'Let the reader imagine, then, that Dr *Slop* has told his tale;——...Let him suppose, that *Obadiah* has told his tale also ... Let him imagine that my father has stepp'd up stairs to see my mother ...' (II, xi).

In one sense, this is a kind of conversation intended really to benefit the speaker, to allow him to assert and define himself by means of his controlled relationships with other people, and it works naturally to forward the project of self-explanation that we have posited at the heart of Sterne's novel:

> Not that I can be so vain or unreasonable, Madam, as to desire you should therefore think, that my dear, dear *Jenny* is my kept mistress:——no,——that would be flattering my character in the other extream, and giving it an air of freedom, which, perhaps, it has no kind of right to ... It is not impossible, but that my dear, dear *Jenny*! tender as the appellation is, may be my child. (I, xviii)

On the other hand, the technique of instructing the reader to imagine something is familiar to many preachers of sermons – it has an analogue in the 'Bidding Prayer' of the Anglican liturgy – and Sterne himself employs it over and over in the pulpit, as he describes novelistically the characters he talks about, gives them speeches, and turns repeatedly to the congregation: 'Would not one have imagined,' he asks in a typical sermon on Joseph; 'one would be apt, you will say, to imagine here'; 'it is natural to imagine'.[7]

From the largest point of view, finally, Sterne's metaphor of conversation may be understood as one of several contemporary responses to a general change in literary culture, from an élite or coterie readership such as Chaucer, Donne or even Pope enjoyed to an unseen, impersonal audience. 'The gradual detachment, through print, of the writer from a present and familiar audience is one of the most far-reaching influences of modern times in our Western civilization,' Bertrand Bronson observes; 'and its special problems emerge with crucial insistence for the first time in the eighteenth century'.[8] Hence, as Bronson says, Richardson in his novels attempts to regain a sense of audience participation by means of his epistolary technique, just as Fielding tries to insert himself as Master of Ceremonies in *Tom Jones*: the Augustan value of community exerts its pressure even upon the solitary reader and writer, incorporating their private exchanges into the public forum of conversation. But no one goes so far as Sterne, who not only invokes and addresses his community of readers, but also furnishes their dialogue, their sex, their very chairs around the circle: 'Gentleman, I kiss your hands,——I protest no company could give me half the pleasure,——by my soul I am glad to see you,——I beg only you will make no strangers of yourselves, but sit down without any ceremony, and fall on heartily' (II, ii).

Other technical elements of Sterne's style, such as his puns, *double entendres* and rhetorical virtuosity, have always been relished by scholars. Most recently, Pat Rogers has called attention to his continual use of actual proverbs, often unrecognized by modern readers, which reinforce the effect of hearing polite conversation rather than formal prose; though, as Rogers points out, Sterne often seems to introduce proverbs and clichés only in order to mock them or tamper with their meanings.[9] And Iain McGilchrist has speculated suggestively on what he takes to be the predominance of nouns in Sterne's prose – an indication, he thinks, of Sterne's realistic allegiance to the material world that continually invades and puts to rout all Shandyesque theories.[10] McGilchrist, however, overlooks the importance of concrete nouns in virtually all fiction – he does not place passages from Richardson or Defoe beside Sterne for comparison – and it would in any case be possible to argue that Sterne introduces concrete nouns largely for the purpose of transforming them into mischievous ambiguities and images:

There is nothing so awkward, as courting a woman, an' please your honour, whilst she is making sausages——so Tom began a discourse upon them; first gravely,——'as how they were made——with what

meats, herbs and spices'——Then a little gayly——as, 'With what
skins——and if they never burst——Whether the largest were not the
best.' (IX, vii)

But this is only Sterne's routine indecency. Far subtler effects of this
kind emerge from yet more elementary devices of style. Cervantes, for
example, communicates the subjectivity of the world he describes, its
sense of a blurring interaction between reality and fantasy, by means of
the frequent use of such verbs as 'seem', 'appear', 'looked', 'thought',
'believed' and such adverbs as 'seemingly' and 'apparently' (often
formed from word-combinations involving 'paracer' and 'deber de').[11]
And Sterne uses a similar technique to achieve the same end: pervasive
subjunctive constructions, on almost every page, that continually desta-
bilize the world of the narrative. Thus, in the famous chapter describing
Trim's sermon on the death of Bobby, subjunctive expressions roll like
breakers through the whole episode, upending our sense of security,
confirming Trim's message that we may be gone in a moment: 'may in
time to come depend', 'I should have added', 'I wish we were', 'if Trim
had not trusted more to his hat than his head', 'a hat may be dropped',
'Had he flung it, or thrown it, or cast it, or skimmed it, or squirted' . . .
'the effect upon the heart had been lost' (V, vii). It is the actual stylistic
device Walter Shandy describes in his theory of auxiliary verbs. It is a
language that alludes unceasingly to the slipperiness of reality; a language of appearance, conjecture, approximation.

Two further and related aspects of his style can also be mentioned
here. The first is that habit of personification which renders so much
eighteenth-century poetry dry and lifeless to a twentieth-century taste
and which is a surprisingly common feature of Sterne's prose.

To wind up the last scene of thy tragedy, [Eugenius warns Yorick,]
CRUELTY and COWARDICE, twin ruffians, hired and set on by MALICE
in the dark, shall strike together. (I, xii)

FANCY is capricious——WIT must not be searched for——and
PLEASANTRY (good-natured slut as she is) will not come in at a call, was
an empire to be laid at her feet. (IX, xii)

In eighteenth-century critical theory, personification has a double use: to
express passion and even sublimity in a way altogether lost to modern
taste, and also to represent a certain obvious generalizing tendency, a
pleasure in abstraction appropriate to an age of reason.[12] Sterne uses
personifications, however, less as categories of thought than as actual
characters, animated abstractions who tend to gather in groups and to
create action on their own, like the figure of Death who stalks Tristram

surrealistically across the spinning landscape of Volume VII – and in this Sterne resembles no one so much as Blake, likewise a writer of unconstrained, quasi-allegorical personifications, a writer emerging from pre-Romanticism but still strongly bound to eighteenth-century aesthetic values.

Finally, perhaps the most fascinating of all Sterne's stylistic effects appears never to have been discussed at all. Yet few readers can have gone far in *Tristram Shandy* without recognizing that in Sterne we encounter one of the great, incontestable masters of the comic simile. I have in mind, not those wonderful visual images he shows such fertility in inventing ('a number of tall, opake words, one before another, in a right line': III, xx), but the explicit comparisons that pop suddenly around the corner of even the most ordinary syntax:

> others on the contrary, tuck'd up to their very chins, with whips across their mouths, scouring and scampering it away like so many little party-colour'd devils astride a mortgage (I, viii)

> Humph!——said my uncle *Toby*;——tho' not accented as a note of acquiescence,——but as an interjection of that particular species of surprize, when a man, in looking into a drawer, finds more of a thing than he expected. (II, xvii)

> He pick'd up an opinion, Sir, as a man in a state of nature picks up an apple. (III, xxxiv)

> whispering soft——like the last low accents of an expiring saint (VIII, xxv)

There is a wealth of pleasure in such silliness. We can respond to the cleverness of the allusions to Hobbes's state of nature and to Swift's runaway rider 'astride' a mortgage; we like the sly bawdry as 'drawer' turns irresistibly into 'drawers'; or we take simple pleasure in the childlike literalness with which Sterne revitalizes abstractions like mortgages and opinions. In all these cases, it is a pleasure different from the pleasure of logical analogy that we find, for example, in Fielding's urbane mock-heroic or in something like Burke's inspired image of the radical Duke of Bedford: 'whilst the *sans-culotte* carcass-butchers and the philosophers of the shambles are pricking their dotted lines upon his hide, and, like the print of the poor ox that we see in the shop-windows at Charing Cross, alive as he is, and thinking no harm in the world, he is divided into rumps, and sirloins, and briskets'.[13] The ludicrous image of the ox with dotted lines upon his hide serves Burke's satirical purpose, and serves a larger design as well, for characteristically he draws out the analogy until it fills an entire paragraph and then caps the image with a quotation from Pope's *Essay on Man*. But Sterne's similes are not usually satiric, and they never extend into lengthy analogy or elegant design. They are closer to the inspired impudence of Raymond Chandler ('she was as hard to get as a haircut'). Closer still to the zany surrealism of P. G. Wodehouse: 'a slow, pleasant voice, like clotted cream made audible'. This is the comic sense of 'heightened unreality' that W. K. Wimsatt finds in Alexander Pope:

> Nonsense precipitate, like running Lead,
> That slip'd thro' Cracks and Zig-zags of the Head.[14]
>
> As when a dab-chick waddles thro' the copse
> On feet and wings, and flies, and wades, and hops;
> So lab'ring on, with shoulders, hands, and head,
> Wide as a windmill all his figure spread.   (*Dunciad*, bk II, ll. 63–6)

——my father could never subscribe to it by any means; the very idea of so noble, so refined, so immaterial, and so exalted a being as the *Anima*, or even the *Animus*, taking up her residence, and sitting dabbling, like a tad-pole, all day long, both summer, and winter, in a puddle . . . (II, xix)

Wimsatt finds such similes and their related metaphorical figures ('The forests dance, the rivers upward rise,/Whales sport in woods, and dolphins in the skies') characteristic of the English Augustans generally. Richard Lanham sees Sterne's imagery less historically, as game-like, the sheer creating pleasure that children and free spirits take in the nonsensical manipulation of language. Indeed, as his approach suggests, such pleasure in language leads to the creation of a strange but authentic beauty: 'In ev'ry loom our labours shall be seen,/And the fresh vomit run forever green' (*Dunciad*, bk II, ll. 155–6). In Pope this beauty arises in part from a powerful sensitivity to spectacle and colour. In Sterne, it seems to arise from a process of free association, a kind of internal logic of imagery. Tristram, for example, begins a chapter with a reference to Momus' famous complaint that Hephaestus' model of a man lacks a window in his breast, where his desires and secrets can be seen; but he goes on to imagine Momus' device installed in real people, so that to read a man's character one need only have pulled up a chair 'as you would to a dioptrical bee-hive, and look'd in,——view'd the soul stark naked;——observ'd all her motions,——her machinations;——traced all her maggots from their first engendering to their crawling forth', and written down what you had seen (I, xxiii). This may owe something to Pope's fantasy of how literary 'Maggots half-form'd in rhyme exactly meet,/And learn to crawl upon poetic feet' (*Dunciad*, bk I, ll. 61–2) or even to Swift's various restless images of the brain; but the mocking self-revelations of the 'soul stark naked' is an unmistakably Sternian conceit, as is the next sentence, in which Tristram recalls that the planet Mercury is so hot that the 'tenements' of souls there may be nothing else 'but one fine transparent body of clear glass (bating the umbilical knot);——so, that till the inhabitants grow old and tolerably wrinkled, whereby the rays of light, in passing through them, become so monstrously refracted', they can be seen through without effort, and a Mercurian soul might as well 'play the fool out o'doors as in her own house'. And this conceit of wrinkled glass men itself metamorphoses into a wonderful, and not unpreacherly, image of ourselves as we really are:

> But this, as I said above, is not the case of the inhabitants of this earth;——our minds shine not through the body, but are wrapt up here in a dark covering of uncrystalized flesh and blood; so that if we would come to the specifick characters of them, we must go some other way to work.

Patterns and connections can be found here – tenements to houses, for instance – but the general effect is not the conventional metaphorical one of stressing similarities between classes of things ('my love is like a red, red, rose'), the 'common-sense basis' of 'likeness' that Northrop Frye attributes to classical and Augustan taste. Neither is the effect that of literal identification or reality that Frye finds in the metaphors of the age of sensibility: Sterne's glass Mercurians have no real or symbolic resonance whatsoever. I. A. Richards many years ago pointed out that similes and metaphors usually stress disparity and dissimilarity as much as resemblance.[15] In the comparison of self and beehive, body and glass, earthlings and Mercurians, we may only be dealing with a comic version of metaphysical wit, that 'discovery of occult resemblances in things apparently unlike' that Johnson observed in Cowley and his school.[16] But Sterne's concluding image has a moral as well as a comic force: some reference to 1 Corinthians 13:12 ('through a glass darkly') may be at work in a clergyman's prose; the mind and body are contrasted in traditional terms of light and darkness ('shine not'); and the lovely adjective 'uncrystalized' is followed by the almost shocking concrete image of 'flesh and blood'. Wimsatt likewise explains the Augustan delight in fantastic imagery as having a moral purpose:

> The world which the Augustan wit found most amusing and into which he had his deepest visions was an inverted chaotic reality, the unreality of the 'uncreating word' ... The peculiar feat of the Augustan poet was the art of teasing unreality with the redeeming

force of wit – of casting upon a welter of unreal materials a light of order and a perspective vision. (*Hateful Contraries*, p. 158)

It is hard to think of a more chaotic reality (or unreality) than that of *Tristram Shandy*, or of a writer more fascinated with uncreating words than Sterne. Whether he casts light and order on to his unreal materials, however, can only be decided in a broader context of style.

(ii) CHANCE DESIGN

Tristram makes a famous running joke of his disorderly style of composing and the resultant confusion of his book:

> My mother, you must know,——but I have fifty things more necessary to let you know first,——I have a hundred difficulties which I have promised to clear up, and a thousand distresses and domestic misadventures crouding in upon me thick and three-fold, one upon the neck of another,——a cow broke in (to-morrow morning) to my uncle *Toby*'s fortifications, and eat up two ratios and half of dried grass ... (III, xxxviii)

> It is not half an hour ago, when (in the great hurry and precipitation of a poor devil's writing for daily bread) I threw a fair sheet, which I had just finished, and carefully wrote out, slap into the fire, instead of the foul one. (IV, xvii)

> I begin with writing the first sentence——and trusting to Almighty God for the second. (VIII, ii)

To some extent this account must be true: the very speed of appearance – nine volumes between 1760 and 1767, plus the two volumes of *A Sentimental Journey* in 1768 – argues speed of composition. None the less, although no manuscript of *Tristram Shandy* survives, a holograph manuscript of the first volume of *A Sentimental Journey* does exist, and it reveals a writer, not slap-dash and unthinking, but meticulous and attentive to the smallest effects. Wilbur Cross discusses these revisions in some detail, noting expansions of scenes and speeches, numerous cancellations, and a fussy sensitivity to rhythm and repetition; and suggests that, even if Sterne devoted an unusual amount of care to his new novel, it still seems fair to reason that most of the volumes of *Tristram Shandy* were written far less casually than Tristram claims.[17] (Sterne has the habit, not frivolous, of describing his books as his children and their production as his labour pains.)

This apparent disorderliness has attracted critical discussion, explanation and apology from the first. Most readers have agreed that it derives in large part from the disorderliness of literary models like Montaigne and Burton; and it has recently been suggested that it derives as well from the irregularity of form common to satire in general and to the Augustan satirists of Sterne's youth in particular, with their chaotic parodies, imitations and mock-heroics.[18] A still more precise model may occur in Longinus' treatise *On the Sublime*, which Tristram mentions (IV, x) and which praises Demosthenes in terms that suggest his own practice in achieving a 'comic sublime':

> He seems to invert the very order of his discourse, and, what is more, to utter every thing extempore; so that by means of his long Transpositions he drags his readers along, and conducts them through all the intricate mazes of his discourse; frequently arresting his thoughts in the midst of their career, he makes excursions into different subjects, and intermingles several seemingly unnecessary incidents: by this means he gives his audience a kind of anxiety, as if he had lost his subject, and forgotten what he was about; and so strongly engages their concern, that they tremble for, and bear their share in, the dangers of the speaker: at length, after a long ramble, he very pertinently, but unexpectedly, returns to his subject, and raises the surprise and admiration of all by these daring, but happy Transpositions.[19]

The disorder of *Tristram Shandy*, including the disorder of its figurative language, may also be explained in the very different, very speculative linguistic terms advanced by Roman Jakobson, who distinguishes between metaphoric and metonymic ways of writing and argues that one or the other process always predominates: one topic leads to another according to a principle of similarity in the writer's mind, or according to a principle of simple contiguity. And, while romantic literature and poetry in general tends in this scheme towards the metaphorical pole, fiction tends towards the metonymical, using synecdoche to establish character and moving constantly from plot to atmosphere and from characters to setting.[20] Certainly it is fair to say – Tristram himself says it – that *Tristram Shandy* proceeds on the surface from association to association, metonymically, substituting hobbyhorses for full character sketches, moving from squeaky hinges to Toby's fortifications to Tristram's crushed nose in a confusing mish-mash of recollections and impulsive connections. And yet, as almost every reader has perceived, the disorder is only superficial. Underneath these eccentric and subjective associations, the novel is criss-crossed with similarities large and small, laced tight with correspondences. And to these correspondences, stylistic features in a broad definition, it owes its paradoxical effect of manifest disorder and structural unity.

At the simplest level, these correspondences include all the recurring motifs and images that seem to preoccupy Tristram's consciousness: hobbyhorses, for instance, and with them horses of all kinds from Yorick's death's-head nag and Rosinante to the leering stallions of sexual folklore. Other such motifs would certainly include the metaphors of painting and music that Tristram uses to describe his novel; the image of the 'machine' for both the book and certain characters; the motif of 'gravity', in the sense of solemn deportment (a thing Yorick could not abide) and in the sense of the inescapable force that fells hats and window-sashes; the idea of 'birth', present from the first chapter and intruding into the most unlikely contexts (Walter's discourse on analogy was 'as notable and curious a dissertation as ever was engendered in the womb of speculation': II, vii). More subtle motifs of this kind might include the image of 'spirits' that Tristram uses so frequently in Volumes I and II, partially as contrast to 'machine'; the many references to clothes and spinning, which James Work in his edition of the novel suggests grow out of Sterne's knowledge of the Halifax clothing industry; and the numerous allusions to Shakespeare and the Book of Common Prayer. And all of these more or less elementary verbal motifs are attached to the well-known larger recurring themes of the novel, such as impotence, language and writing, false learning, chance and fate, or the flexibility of time.

These are the involuntary orderings and repetitions that anyone writing at length will inevitably achieve. Sterne also achieves structural order on a broader scale. The chapter, for example, is obviously Sterne's basic unit of composition. But the chapters follow long rhythms of organization, as in the numerous digressions, which W. B. Piper has shown usually contain two balanced, parallel sections, logically organized and rising from 'negative-to-positive' statements.[21] And Sterne's largest units of composition, the two-volume sets in which his novel is written and published, shows similar organization. Eric Rothstein has analysed Volume VI in great detail, finding it divided into clear halves, each containing four episodes, and united by a transitional chapter; the second set of four episodes then builds upon the thematic material of the first four, altering rhythm and tone somewhat to represent a 'complement' to them. The other volumes of the novel follow the same kind of 'arithmetic', turning at the centre upon pivotal episodes like the story of the abbess of Andoüillets (VII, xx–xxv) and resolving in the second half the themes of the first half. Rothstein does not argue that *Tristram Shandy* follows an external framework, as *Ulysses*, for example, does – only that Sterne's sense of structure is far less disorderly and subjective than previously thought.[22] And Wayne Booth, in a pioneering article 'Did Sterne complete *Tristam Shandy*?' makes a related and bolder claim: that from the beginning Sterne had in mind to conclude his plot with the story of Toby's courtship.[23] Thus Booth (like Work before him) identifies two major story-lines in the novel – Tristram's birth and subsequent early misfortunes, and Toby and the Widow – which run simultaneously, but dominating the first six and last three volumes respectively. To Booth's and Rothstein's analyses, finally, may be added the fact that underneath the mad digressions and misplaced episodes Sterne has laid a fairly exact track of chronology, from Trim's enlistment in the army in 1689 to Tristram's conception on the night of 1/2 March 1718 to the death of Yorick in 1748, a chronology such as any novelist might have in mind, but surprising in Sterne and all the more impressive in its coherence over nine volumes and seven years of composition.[24]

These critical efforts to prove a calculated disorder in Sterne's book may well appear slight or subjective, however, in the face of the sometimes bewildering experience of actually reading it. Yet, if that exuberant disorderliness cannot finally be tamed to academic systems, it can be defended in another way, a way implied all along by Tristram's philosophy of writing, as an accurate reflection of reality. For as Sterne weaves together in his prose so many seemingly disparate sensations – the play of wit against sentiment, the collision of spiritual and carnal, the falling nouns of the real world – he creates an extraordinary sense of the immediacy and richness of experience. His taste, of course, like the taste of all novelists, is for detail: the luxurious tactility of Toby's new black-plush breeches, the salient angle of the demi-bastion of St Roch where Toby received his wound, the chamber pot-handle on which Walter's knuckles rest. This is the allegiance to the material world that McGilchrist noted in Sterne's concrete nouns. But it is a material world whose reality can be apprehended only piecemeal and in a human perspective, a perspective forever partial, inconsistent and limited by the intangibility of language. When Sterne parodies this most novelistic of traits, therefore, he withdraws to that implausible Rabelaisian precision we have noted earlier, the geometrically exact descriptions of people and things that suggest an objective, non-human order: Trim about to read the sermon at 85½ degrees, Toby's and Widow Wadman's hands criss-crossing in the sentry-box – an 'absurd and alienating realism', in Jean-Jacques Mayoux' suggestive phrase, 'which knows nothing in the world but pure matter' (Traugott, p. 116). It has been suggested that such minuteness of description arises from Sterne's illness and represents a method of defeating, vicariously and for a moment, the rush of time, pinning down the impression made by one instant before it blurs into the next. But Peter Quennell reminds us that Sterne possessed a preternaturally visual personality, which habitually seeks expression in a startling distinctness of image. And Sterne, in any case, is inclined to find the truth of things in surfaces and appearances alone, just as Walter

Shandy can deduce a man's character from the way he enters a room. To
Sterne, 'the inward and the outward were part of the same fabric',
Quennell observes. Any object or gesture, illuminated with sufficient
detail and brilliance, will disclose a meaning. 'The *psyche*, he insists, is no
recluse, locked up out of sight in some inaccessible corner of the body; it
appears continually, flows like an electric current through nerves and
muscles, is manifest in the movements we make and even the clothes we
wear.'[25]

Both his immediacy of detail and parody of order, however, stand in
strong contrast to the great magisterial prose styles generally characteristic of the eighteenth century: Burke's elegance and detail, for example;
Hume's and Gibbon's ironic control; and, above all, Johnson's powerful
universalizing authority. Johnson, indeed appears to understand the
chief virtue of writing itself in a way opposite to Sterne. To Johnson
prose serves as a stabilizing device, a means of resolving the near-chaos of
ordinary experience. Hence a great sentence like the one that opens the
'Preface to Shakespeare', or this shorter example a few pages later,
manages to organize verbs of contrary action into a pattern of vigorous
symmetry: 'The irregular combinations of fanciful invention may delight
a-while, by that novelty of which the common satiety of life sends us all in
quest; but the pleasures of sudden wonder are soon exhausted, and the
mind can only repose on the stability of truth.'[26] Against which the least
mischievous of us might want to set this from Sterne:

> Ptr..r..r..ing——twing——twang——prut——trut——'tis a cursed
> bad fiddle.——Do you know whether my fiddle's in tune or no?—
> —trut..prut..——They should be *fifths*.——'Tis wickedly strung—
> —tr..a.e.i.o.u.–twang. (V, xv)

And yet the truth is that Johnson perceives the essential formlessness of
human experience quite as clearly as Sterne – we have only to think of the
melancholy weariness with which he dismisses his great ordering Dictionary and its impossible attempt to 'fix' the language into place. He
understands very well that, while language stabilizes experience for an
instant, it does so only by falsifying experience, necessarily. The difference – one of temperament clearly, but also of moral value – is that
Johnson is saddened by the irreducible incoherence of our lives, while
Sterne is invigorated by it, embraces it with cheer and with something
approaching a complete faith in its ultimate meaning (or complete
indifference to its ultimate meaninglessness).

Not everyone agrees that Sterne's style communicates such incoherence. A. D. McKillop has written influentially of Sterne's vision of
order, taking the 'Fragment' on subjectivity as a paradigm for *Tristram
Shandy* and finding in both works a picture of the universe 'as a great

multiple system, in which sense and spirit, macrocosm and microcosm, are linked by analogies and correspondences'.[27] His evidence for this picture inheres chiefly in Sterne's frequent tinkerings with novelistic conventions of time and space – conflations or expansions of moments such as the brothers' progress downstairs – and also in Sterne's humorous interest in cause and effect: that obsessive willingness to trace any event back through a convoluted sequence to its remotest point of origin, as the occasion of Tristram's involuntary circumcision leads back to Susannah's laziness, Trim's expediency and Toby's fortifications; and as Tristram's very character is traced back to its first causes, when the homunculus sets out, disordered, on his strenuous journey.

If this is a vision of order, however, it belongs to that odd category of things manifested by their opposite. For to most of us the general effect of these accounts is undoubtedly a delight in confusion, an epiphany, as E. M. Forster thought, of the great god 'Muddle': if Tristram understands the universe as a 'great multiple system' of analogies, it is a clown's idea of system.[28] Analogies in his book – significantly Walter breaks off before he can explain the term 'analogy' to Toby – do not function as they do in earlier literature: as they do in Dante or Spenser, for instance, where divine and political analogies reveal a meaningful universe, organized and purposeful.[29] On the contrary, in a disconcertingly modern way Tristram's analogies parody those older universal systems; they belong to a private world instead of a public, a private system of similitudes communicable and comprehensible only in part: '*Pray my dear*, quoth my mother, *have you not forgot to wind up the clock?*' (I, i)

At the same time, one can say with some confidence that Sterne reveals a genuine instinct for creating a new kind of order, but a disguised order typical of later eighteenth-century writing generally. We see it, for example, once again in those marvellous metaphors and similes that so violently yoke disparate ideas together. It is true that, in the absence of an overdetermined plot such as organizes Chandler's mysteries or Wodehouse's burlesques, these metaphors may contribute even more than otherwise to our sense of stylistic chaos. But in a long 'Preface' (III, xx), originally provoked by one of Toby's ludicrous associations, Tristram defends the function of wit to create order in any way it likes, even an unreal order, which conforms only to our emotions. The immediate occasion for the defence is his recollection of Locke's pronouncement that judgement, which distinguishes between unlike ideas, leads to knowledge, while wit, which seeks out resemblance, leads only to 'Metaphor and Allusion', mere 'pleasantry' (*Essay*, II, xi, 2). '——So, says *Locke*,——so are farting and hickuping say I.' The human mind will wring symmetry out of the least tractable reality, simply to satisfy its appetite for order. Wit and judgement are in fact like the ornamental knobs on the top of a chair, Tristram insists; they balance each other, and

a man (or chair) with only one is 'as miserable a sight as a sow with one ear
... lay your hands upon your hearts, and answer this plain question,
Whether this one single knob which now stands here like a blockhead
by itself, can serve any purpose upon earth, but to put one in mind of the
want of the other'. Sterne is here tweaking Locke's solemnity, as he so
often does. But his real subject is not Locke's rather conventional
concept of the two mental faculties. What he is taking up indirectly is
Locke's view of language, his position that content and image, idea and
metaphor, are separable, that metaphor merely 'ornaments' an ideally
neutral, truth-telling language in which words correspond directly to
single ideas in the user's mind. No more than he believes body and mind
(jerkin and jerkin's lining) to be separate does Sterne see language as
expressive only of idea. His own style, with its mysterious dashes, its
forays into formlessness, its self-conscious and gymnastic rhetoric,
stands entirely opposed to Locke's notion ('The highest stretch of
improvement a single word is capable of,' declares Walter Shandy, 'is a
high metaphor': V, xlii). In Sterne's sense of writing as *motion* – as
two-way conversation, as the 'witty' discovery of metaphor – we feel a
creative act going forward, however obscurely, an emotional process of
self-explanation and clarification that no one word or idea could
accomplish.

There is indeed something thus poetic in Sterne's style, as there is in
Johnson's, both grounded in concrete imagery, both flying outwards to
link, systematically or impulsively, abstraction to experience. But, more
clearly than Johnson, in his reconstitutive wit Sterne is also approaching
the great underlying task of the later eighteenth century, the recovery of
poetic language. For, as Howard Anderson points out, what Sterne's wit

proves, in the end, is the mind's affinity for symbols: he shows that our
minds cling to resemblances that may be more sensuous than rational
and of which we may not even be entirely conscious, but which are
nonetheless a part of a human being's real mental experience.[30]

But it will be left for others to complete this process and to arrive at the
modernist use of symbols in literature. Or, more precisely, to arrive at
the position that the imagination which discovers resemblances and
symbols is not merely equal to reason, but actually superior to it as a
means of grasping reality. Sterne only proves our 'affinity' for symbols –
and, in truth, only our universal affinity for indecent symbols. Nowhere
in *Tristram Shandy* do we encounter any stylistic figure that provokes
thoughts 'too deep for tears' – only sausages, noses, hobbyhorses. If
Sterne scrutinizes as closely as humanly possible gestures like Trim's
pose or objects like Dr Slop's bag, he none the less arrives at no further or
deeper meaning than the appearance itself. Rather than the heightened

apprehension of reality characteristic of Romantic language, Sterne offers the humbler (and funnier) experience of interpretation – the auxiliary unreality of the Augustan wits:

Did my father, mother, uncle, aunt, brothers or sisters, ever see a white bear? What would they give? How would they behave? How would the white bear have behaved? Is he wild? Tame? Terrible? Rough? Smooth?
——Is the white bear worth seeing?——
——Is there no sin in it?——
Is it better than a BLACK ONE? (V, xliii)

NOTES: CHAPTER 4

1 Cyril Connolly, *The Condemned Playground: Essays: 1927–1944* (New York: Macmillan, 1946), p. 24.
2 Virginia Woolf, *The Common Reader: Second Series* (London: Hogarth Press, 1932), p. 79.
3 David Thomson, *Wild Excursions: The Life and Fiction of Laurence Sterne* (London: Weidenfeld & Nicolson, 1972), p. 22. As the Florida edition shows, in the first edition (York) of Volumes I and II, Sterne occasionally used from two to five hyphens instead of dashes. Sterne's varying dash-lengths, moreover, are plainer in the Florida edition than in any other modern reprint. For reasons of economy and simplicity, I have standardized the dash-lengths in my quotations, except in a few obvious instances.
4 Ian Watt, 'The comic syntax of *Tristram Shandy*' in Howard Anderson and John S. Shea (eds), *Studies in Criticism and Aesthetics, 1660–1800: Essays in Honor of Samuel Holt Monk* (Minneapolis, Minn.: University of Minnesota Press, 1967), p. 321.
5 Henry Fielding, *Tom Jones*, ed. Martin C. Battestin and Fredson T. Bowers (London: Oxford University Press, 1975), bk XIV, ch. vi.
6 Louis T. Milic, 'Observations on conversational style', in John H. Middendorf (ed.), *English Writers of the Eighteenth Century* (New York: Columbia University Press, 1971), pp. 279–80.
7 Sermon XII, *The Sermons of Mr Yorick*, in *Works* (Oxford: Basil Blackwell, 1927), Vol. 6, pp. 139–43.
8 Bertrand H. Bronson, *Facets of the Enlightenment: Studies in English Literature and Its Contexts* (Berkeley/Los Angeles, Calif.: University of California Press, 1968), p. 299.
9 Pat Rogers, 'Tristram Shandy's polite conversation', *Essays in Criticism*, vol. 32 (1982), pp. 305–20.
10 Iain McGilchrist, *Against Criticism* (London: Faber, 1982), pp. 139–40.
11 See the interesting discussion by Richard L. Predmore, *The World of Don Quixote* (Cambridge, Mass.: Harvard University Press, 1967), pp. 68–9.
12 Two important discussions of this topic are Bronson, op. cit., pp. 119–52; Earl R. Wasserman, 'The inherent values of eighteenth-century personification', *PMLA*, vol. 65 (1950), pp. 435–63. A longer treatment is Chester F. Chapin, *Personification in Eighteenth-Century English Poetry* (New York: King's Crown Press, 1954).
13 Edmund Burke, *A Letter to a Noble Lord*, in *Writings and Speeches of Edmund Burke* (Boston, Mass.: Little, Brown, 1901), Vol. 5, p. 221.
14 Alexander Pope, *The Dunciad, in Four Books*, ed. James Sutherland, The Twickenham Edition (London: Methuen, 1943; revised 1963), p. 278, bk I, ll. 123–4. I take Wimsatt's phrase from his well-known essay 'The Augustan mode in English poetry',

conveniently reprinted in his *Hateful Contraries: Studies in Literature and Criticism* (Lexington, Ky: University of Kentucky Press, 1965), p. 158.

15 I. A. Richards, *The Philosophy of Rhetoric* (London: Oxford University Press, 1936; reprinted 1965), p. 127.

16 Samuel Johnson, *Lives of the English Poets*, ed. G. B. Hill (Oxford: Clarendon Press, 1905; reprinted New York: Octagon Books, 1967), Vol. 1, p. 20

17 Wilbur L. Cross, *The Life and Times of Laurence Sterne*, 3rd edn (New Haven, Conn.: Yale University Press, 1929), pp. 471–7.

18 Jonathan Lamb, 'The comic sublime and Sterne's fiction', *ELH*, vol. 48 (1981), pp. 110–43.

19 Longinus, *On the Sublime*, trans. W. Smith (London, 1819), pp. 148–9. This point is first discussed in Margaret R. B. Shaw, *Laurence Sterne: The Making of a Humorist, 1713–1762* (London: Richards Press, 1957), pp. 29–32.

20 Roman Jakobson, *Fundamentals of Language* (The Hague: Mouton, 1956), pp. 76–82.

21 William B. Piper, *Laurence Sterne* (New York: Twayne, 1965), pp. 31–46.

22 Eric Rothstein, *Systems of Order and Inquiry in Later Eighteenth-Century Fiction* (Berkeley/Los Angeles, Calif.: University of California Press, 1975), pp. 88–108.

23 Wayne C. Booth, 'Did Sterne complete *Tristram Shandy?*' *MP*, vol. 47 (1951), pp. 172–83. For a rejoinder, see Marcia Allentuck, 'In defense of an unfinished *Tristram Shandy*', in Arthur H. Cash and John M. Stedmond (eds), *The Winged Skull: Papers from the Laurence Sterne Bicentenary Conference at the University of York* (London: Methuen, 1971), pp. 145–55.

24 See, for example, Theodore Baird, 'The time-scheme in *Tristram Shandy* and a source', *PMLA*, vol. 51 (1936), pp. 803–20.

25 Peter Quennell, *Four Portraits: Studies of the Eighteenth Century* (London: Collins, 1945), pp. 158–60.

26 Samuel Johnson, *Johnson on Shakespeare*, ed. Arthur Sherbo (New Haven, Conn.: Yale University Press, 1968), Vol. 1, pp. 61–2.

27 Alan D. McKillop, *The Early Masters of English Fiction* (Lawrence, Kans.: University of Kansas Press, 1956), p. 198.

28 E. M. Forster, *Aspects of the Novel* (New York: Harcourt, 1927), p. 164.

29 A longer discussion of Sterne and analogy can be found in Mark Loveridge, *Laurence Sterne and the Argument about Design* (London: Macmillan, 1982), pp. 38–9, 94–117.

30 Howard Anderson, 'Associationism and wit in *Tristram Shandy*', *Philological Quarterly*, vol. 48 (1969), p. 41.

CHAPTER 5

The Discovery of a Key:
Volumes I and II

One would give a good deal to know if Sterne struck out his famous first chapter at a blow, as Joe Gargery told Pip he wrote his father's epitaph, or if he came to form it in the revisions he undertook during the summer of 1759. For while the first chapter reveals his characteristic mastery of comic style – the arm slung confidently across the shoulder of the reader, the pedantic physiological humour, the inspired Lockian association of Mrs Shandy's question – the rest of Volume I shows unmistakable signs of tentativeness and inconsistency, the tell-tale waverings of a first novel in its first stages; not until chapter xxi, in fact, does he once again assume the voice and authority of a practising novelist.

That tentativeness may have arisen from the simple psychological difficulties experienced by any beginning writer. Or it may have its sources, as R. F. Brissenden has brilliantly argued, in Sterne's uncertainty about precisely what kind of book he thought he wanted to write: a Scriblerian satire against pedantic learning, a local satire against John Burton (Dr Slop) and other Yorkshire figures, or the humorous version of the Grand Tour he once described to John Croft.[1] It is by no means clear that Sterne sat down to write a *novel* at all, a piece of fiction that more or less realistically renders a narrative set in the familiar world. Nor is it clear that those principles of order so often cited by critics – the complex time-scheme and the design to end with Toby's amours – are present in Sterne's mind before the middle of Volume I. Brissenden discusses most of the important evidence: the inconsistency in Toby's character here, 'Mr Toby Shandy' (not Captain) who shows enough worldliness to advise his brother on handling false pregnancies; the promised story of Tristram's travels through Denmark (I, ii); the long self-contained digression on Yorick, written in a more formal, Cervantic style than the other chapters; the rather tearful blandness of Walter's personality in Chapter iii. Only in chapter xxi, as Toby smokes his pipe and engages in 'mute contemplation of a new pair of black-plush-breeches', does Sterne begin to fasten an attentive, loving eye on those selected concrete details that animate all successful fiction; only then does he place Toby in the army and begin an actual scene of dialogue between the brothers, now set against each other like the balance-wheels of a watch (there is in fact but one earlier paragraph of dialogue in the volume, Yorick's death-bed scene). And only then, we can surmise, does he conceive of ending the book, as Wayne Booth holds, with Toby's amours – though in his admiration for Sterne's design Booth seems unaware that a great many novelists begin in precisely that way, by imagining the last scene or episode of their plot and working towards it. In this formal sense, Brissenden is surely right to call *Tristram Shandy* an '*accidental* novel', a story and set of characters that somehow irresistibly came to life under Sterne's hands, even as he was casting about to write a different book.

(i) FIRST CHAPTERS: CLOCK AND BULL STORIES

Three general points can be quickly made about the celebrated first chapter. Sterne's tone, for one thing, modulates through an astonishing range for so short a space, from the rueful complaint with which Tristram begins (his mockingly literal way of beginning at the beginning) to the folksy 'good folks' with which he explains animal spirits, to the four separate voices of the last paragraph: Mr and Mrs Shandy's conjugal exchange and the subsequent commentary from the first row by Tristram and a reader. (We should note as well Walter's wonderfully self-contradictory way of speaking as Tristram describes it, 'making an exclamation, but taking care to moderate his voice at the same time', which perfectly captures his normal civilized explosiveness, 'smiling, though very angry at the same time': III, xxii.)

In the second place, Sterne's much-discussed debt to Locke appears at the very outset of the novel, in Mrs Shandy's unnerving question, '*Pray, my dear . . . have you not forgot to wind up the clock?*' Three chapters later Tristram will explain her 'unhappy association of ideas which have no connection in nature' and refer us to 'the sagacious *Locke*' (silently lifting several phrases from Locke's *Essay*). Meanwhile, the reader not absolutely shocked by the picture of Tristram's parents busy at begetting will surely recoil in surprise from the indecent image of key turning in keyhole that the question creates, the first of innumerable such insinuations. To the reader familiar with the general eighteenth-century admiration for clocks and all clocklike machinery, moreover, the joke takes on additional resonance, as it also does for the reader who thinks of Bergson's notion of comedy as mechanical rigidity imposed upon vital energy. Mrs Shandy's question, in any case, passed instantly into common usage, prompting a witty protest on the part of London 'Clockmakers' that no woman of modesty now dared to refer to a clock at all (*CH*, pp. 67–71). But this famous question actually constitutes Sterne's second use of Locke in chapter i, for in the preceding paragraph he takes without acknowledgement virtually a whole sentence from the same source in the *Essay*: custom starts 'Trains of Motion in the Animal Spirits, which, once set a going, continue on in the same steps they have been used to, which by often treading are worn into a smooth path, and the Motion in it becomes easy, and as it were Natural' (*Essay*, II, xxxiii, 6).[2] The significance of this theft is hard to know: whether Sterne is simply padding out his material nervously; or whether his mind is so suffused with Lockian terminology that he transfers it automatically to the quite different subject of the passage of animal spirits from father to son. But, characteristically, he livens Locke's rather lumpy prose with slang ('hey-go-mad') and metaphor ('smooth as a garden-walk') and adds those adverbs ('again', 'presently') and auxiliary verbs ('shall' be) that transform a generalization into a fragment of narration set in time.

Finally, the reference to the animal spirits leads directly to the account of the HOMUNCULUS in chapter ii, and raises thereby the whole matter of Sterne's fascination with the miniature. It is a fascination he shares with other eighteenth-century writers: when he describes the tiny veins, arteries and ligaments of the homunculus and all its claims to being human, we also think of Pope's Sylphs in *The Rape of the Lock*, Swift's Lilliputians and, above all, Uncle Toby's bowling-green, where Marlborough's European wars are scaled down to a rood and a half of ground. To reduce anything to ludicrous smallness is of course a fundamental technique of satire – it helps explain the presence of so many insects and spaniels in Augustan literature – but such smallness may also have a charm of its own (like the workings of a watch) that appeals to one's sense of aesthetic completeness, as lockets and model railways do.[3] Sterne appears to take a playful delight in such smallness; at the same time it is possible that the miniature represents to him an actual orderliness, a genial power, otherwise unobtainable, over the chaotic circumstances of ordinary life. Certainly the microscopic world of the 'Fragment' exhibits this quality, the manageability of the miniature, as it stands in analogy to the larger world that surrounds it, suggesting a vision of the universe as an endless nest of Chinese boxes. (This may only reflect a kind of literal conciseness, however: Toby's speech to the fly, Tristram says, 'is to serve for parents and governors instead of a whole volume upon the subject': II, xii.) If Sterne thus seems to oppose miniature to muddle for the sake of achieving temporary order, he extends this use of 'smallness' in a curious way throughout the next few chapters; whoever goes through the first third of Volume I marking words like 'little' and 'small' will find that Sterne has extended his original motif of tiny animal spirits into a persistent authorial tic – in contrast to a 'great title or to a great estate' Tristram is a 'small HERO'; the good midwife has 'no small degree of reputation', her world is a 'small circle'; there are 'little family concernments', the reader needs 'a little patience', and so on. Despite its thematic ties, this habit of phrasing is in fact common to many first novels, where it denotes a self-conscious, defensive belittling of the novelist's real ambition that good editors usually catch and red-pencil. Significantly, after a few more chapters the 'little'.phrases disappear and Tristram begins to speak of his father's 'extensive' views.

To these miscellaneous observations, we can add the further point that, although the early chapters do not reveal Sterne's characters in full maturity, they do otherwise introduce many of the stylistic tricks and motifs that are to dominate the rest of the novel. In explaining his mother's association of ideas, for example, and pointing to his father's pocket-book on the table, he is already creating his characteristic effect of an audience of readers gathered around his desk, passing each sheet about as it is written. And, by the middle of the volume, he and the reader are both accustomed to the curiously Beckettian feeling that reading (and perhaps writing) *Tristram Shandy* gives rise to: a spotlight falls on two or three characters for a moment of dialogue and then vanishes as another illuminates the narrator, who speaks at length, then vanishes in his turn when the characters are illuminated once again. Verbal motifs show a similar coherence. R. M. Adams has noted how the *Tale of a Tub* is built around the opposing images of machine and spirit; Sterne's first volume shows the same pattern of imagery, with innumerable references to 'spirit' and 'spirits' and to the 'machinery' of his work and the 'petite canule' (not to mention the obstetric machinery looming in Volume II).[4] In developing the bawdy humour of the early chapters, moreover, Sterne takes yet another motif from the *Tale*: the runaway horse that stands for erotic imagination. Tristram's horse – prefaced by a series of amazing verbal games with 'members' and 'whim-wham' – appears first, of course, as the hobbyhorse and continues the theme of journeying begun by the homunculus and the animal spirits. But, while most readers understand the hobbyhorse as 'obsession' and take Tristram's discussion as a defence of eccentricity (reinforced by the references to fiddling and painting, both hobbies of Sterne's at Sutton), the term 'hobbyhorse' also has a long history of meaning 'loose woman' or 'prostitute', so that the image of riding it presents a far from innocent second meaning. (Tristram makes the most of this ambiguity in chapter xxiv, where he begins with the friction of the 'heated parts of the rider' on the back of the horse and then inexplicably reverses the sexual roles: 'By long journies and much friction, it so happens that the body of the rider is at length fill'd as full of HOBBY-HORSICAL matter as it can hold'.)

Together with the possibilities of this kind of bawdy humour, Sterne appears to be developing the character of Tristram in these early chapters – as hero (though 'small'), as rule-free, as doomed by fortune, as friendly conversationalist with the reader – when suddenly he throws it over to pursue the character of Yorick. The three long chapters that tell his story do not constitute a Shandyesque digression as we will come to know it, but stand instead as a self-contained unit, almost as if they were being drawn from some earlier sketch or story-plan, and inserted into the book rather than growing out of it. Clearly, one attraction is the opportunity Sterne sees to portray himself more directly; for, of his two jesting surrogates, Yorick comes nearer the reality of his situation – even his name, while it reminds us of the jester of infinite jest, also reminds us of 'York', that 'bye corner of the kingdom' where *Tristram Shandy* was begun (I, Dedication to Mr Pitt). There are indeed other ambivalences in Yorick's character: the Cervantic knight grafted on to the Shakespearian fool, the witty minister who will not speak the truth, the meditative rider who stares at the head of his impotent horse and explains that 'brisk trotting and slow argumentation, like wit and judgement, were two incompatible movements.——But that, upon his steed——he could unite and reconcile everything' (I, x). Only when Sterne invents his name in chapter xi does Yorick become something more than a rather stilted effort to portray and reconcile his own contradictions as preacher and wit.

Yorick's name, that is, has scarcely been hit upon before Sterne involves it with two of his most important themes: the importance of names and the treacherous instability of language. For he begins by telling us that Yorick's name has not changed its spelling in nine hundred years, although half of the best surnames in England have so altered that the identities they signify are actually threatened: one day 'no one shall be able to stand up and swear, "That his own great grandfather was the man who did either this or that"'. And he proceeds to transform Yorick's original Cervantic eccentricities and refractoriness into qualities of language itself. Hence, not cold and phlegmatic like a regular Dane, Yorick was on the contrary like an irregular noun, 'as mercurial and sublimated a composition,——as heteroclite a creature in all his declensions' as the English climate could have created – and linked specifically to that mythic Mercury who served the cause of communication as messenger of the gods. But it is ironic that Yorick, whose power over words is considerable, should himself die the victim of words, assailed by all those personifications who invade 'the last scene of thy tragedy, CRUELTY and COWARDICE, twin ruffians, hired and set on by MALICE in the dark' (I, xii). He dies, in fact, in the most literary way possible, with a Cervantic tone and a Shakespearian spirit, as Tristram tells us. The two black pages that follow his epitaph are among Sterne's most famous typographical tricks. From one point of view they can obviously represent a final transformation or instability of language: words changed into mere ink, without meaning. But in their hypnotic suggestiveness they have long served as a kind of critical Rorschach test. Do they stand as a visual pun, a literal *memento mori*? Do they represent an open grave into which we stare? Do they cover some mystical meaning like an opaque blanket, as Tristram will later suggest of his marbled page (III, xxxvi)? Do they spring from the two other occurrences of darkness thus far in the novel – the 'dark entry' of chapter ix, where an author strikes a bargain with a whore, or the tragic 'dark' in which Yorick is attacked? Or are the black pages the typographical equivalents of Hamlet's prop, Yorick's skull, which Hamlet touches, sees and smells. Does Sterne do his best to elicit in us a response no less physical than Hamlet's rising gorge? From this insoluble riddle he returns to Tristram's story, and at once takes up a problem whose solution may constitute his single greatest contribution to the art of the novel.

(ii) THE ENLARGEMENT OF TOBY

Walter's dissertation on names (I, xix) continues the exploration begun with Yorick of the relationship between words and character – the dissertation may be partially indebted to both Locke (III, iv–vi) and Rabelais (IV, lv) – and thus the great theme of language that is to shape so much of the book. Just as significantly, his dissertation represents Sterne's second attempt to create and establish character. And although his account of Yorick had been largely conventional – a physical and psychological description welded into one or two static paragraphs – his account of Walter extends, with numerous interruptions, over four chapters and offers neither physical description nor biography. Robert Alter has suggested that Sterne takes his relish for eccentrics like Walter from the novels of Smollett, whose affection for oddity of character borders on the grotesque. (Alter proposes, in fact, that Toby is modelled on Smollett's Commodore Trunnion in *Peregrine Pickle*, a conjecture not generally accepted.)[5] Yet it is simpler to take Sterne at his word in the matter of literary influence and to see that he has initially sketched Walter in the Cervantic mould, as an eccentric dominated by a single trait: ''Tis known by the name of perseverance in a good cause,——and of obstinacy in a bad one' (I, xvii). But a pressure towards generalization, not to be underestimated in Sterne, leads to a refinement: Walter is a systematic reasoner, and 'like all systematick reasoners, he would move both heaven and earth, and twist and torture every thing in nature to support his hypothesis' (I, xix). In short order, his obstinacy becomes oddity, and his single humour becomes a vast, unpredictable arsenal of 'odd opinions' (I, xix). The explicit criticism of reason that this humour conveys – the implicit criticism of Locke, to many readers – has sometimes been taken as evidence of Sterne's philosophical views, his 'existential' belief that reason of any kind is inadequate to discover meaning in human life or to grasp its reality. Walter, however, embodies nothing of this. He remains for the rest of the book simply one of the great eccentrics in English fiction, exploiting in every speech that comic principle defined by Bergson as the imposition of mechanical system upon an evasive and mocking reality.

But the development of Walter's character leads at once, by a second instance of Cervantic logic, to the development of Toby. Readers have long noted how Sterne's characters form a network of pairings on the model of Don Quixote and Sancho: Tristram–Yorick, Toby–Trim, Walter–Slop. Chief among these is clearly the pairing of Walter and Toby, brothers with arms locked and legs out of step, marching to a comic principle older still than Bergson's, the marriage of opposites that begins in Genesis and includes Hal and Falstaff and Panurge and Pantagruel. As soon as Walter has begun to take on flesh, therefore, Sterne automatically turns to Toby and begins similarly to expand his character. Chapter xxi, after the digression into French practices of baptism, not only introduces those novelistic details mentioned earlier, but also establishes Toby's character on the same 'humorous' basis as Walter's. Here for the first time we learn that Toby is a soldier; but Tristram immediately subordinates that information (promising to elaborate 'hereafter') to Toby's defining humour, his 'extream and unparallel'd modesty of nature'. This trait – perhaps modelled on Parson Adams's innocence in *Joseph Andrews* – Tristram at once proceeds to illustrate with the wonderful account of Walter's perpetual reference to Aunt Dinah's backsliding and Toby's perpetual discomfiture. In a sense, the whole of chapter xxi concerns silence: it begins by interrupting Toby, moves in a digression to the idea of ending all writing whatsoever, then returns to Toby's silencing of Walter with 'Lillabulero' and the whole technique of silencing any argument with a rhetorical flourish. And this surprising thematic unity appears to have its source in Toby's choked modesty or, more precisely, in the initial mechanical opposition of the voluble Walter and the inarticulate Toby. But from this point Tristram takes the momentous step of declaring that he will enlarge further upon Toby's character 'by no mechanical help whatever;——... in a word, I will draw my uncle *Toby*'s character from his HOBBY-HORSE' (I, xxiii).

The implications of this step are so complex and numerous that it may be easiest merely to list them.

(1)   Sterne's intention to portray Toby primarily from his hobbyhorse implies that the way to understand another person is not by means of the reason and the reason's instruments – biography, appearance, analysis – but by means of his irrational parts. It is a method of character description that gives new prominence (like so much else in *Tristram Shandy*) to the role of the irrational in human life generally; and it further implies, though Sterne does not say so, that the reader understands Toby by means of his own irrational, sympathetic projection. The precedent is in Richardson's obsessed

and impassioned characters, but Richardson never announces his methods so self-consciously as Sterne.

(2)   It sets in motion the creation of a character who is defined by his incongruities rather than by his humour. That is, Tristram may begin with the idea of sketching Toby according to his ruling passion of modesty, but that passion quickly breaks apart into elemental contradictions: the kind-hearted soldier, the soldier innocent of women, the pedantic scholar of siegecraft and gore, the mild boy inspired to warfare by reading Homer, the sweet-tempered and relentless anti-Catholic. The significance of this approach lies first in the link it establishes with certain other memorable characters: Falstaff, for instance, is to be the subject of Maurice Morgann's major essay in the next decade, suggesting that he has been 'made up by *Shakespeare* wholly of incongruities' – a genuinely realistic character who could not have been formed by mechanical prescription or stereotype; a 'round' character in E. M. Forster's famous distinction rather than a 'flat' one.[6] And, in the second place, this approach implies that Sterne is content to present his characters (and his book) as less than wholly unified objects: neither book nor person is a 'well-wrought urn', but exhibits those irreconcilable inconsistencies that belong to creatures of mood and time, who are unified by subjective identity instead of by logic. Few writers (and fewer critics) have been able to accept this principle of inescapable formlessness in art, though it clearly springs from the deepest soil of experience; indeed, one of the most common justifications for art begins precisely with the premiss that it bestows order and logic upon disorderly experience; but Sterne appears always capable of living among 'mysteries and riddles' without dismay and without theory (IX, xxii).

(3)   Tristram here arrives at something like a new technique of presenting character, as in place of the conventional paragraph or two of introductory description, he substitutes a fragmentary, haphazard description, scattered throughout the narration. James Swearingen understands this method of interruption and complication as part of Tristram's phenomenology, extending the horizon of his consciousness as far as possible in order to render completely and simultaneously the whole mental world he inhabits.[7] But a less philosophical appreciation is also possible. 'It became very early evident to' Conrad and me, recalls Ford Madox Ford,

> ... that what was the matter with the Novel, and the British novel in particular, was that it went straight forward, whereas in your gradual making acquaintanceship with your fellows you never do go straight forward. You meet an English gentleman at

your golf club. He is beefy, full of health, the moral of the boy from an English Public School of the finest type. You discover, gradually, that he is hopelessly neurasthenic, dishonest in matters of small change, but unexpectedly self-sacrificing, a dreadful liar but a most painfully careful student of lepidoptera and, finally, from the public prints, a bigamist who was once, under another name, hammered on the Stock Exchange.[8]

(4) And, last, Sterne's decision to unfold Toby's character in this way effectively permits character to predominate over plot (though one can hardly claim that Sterne had ever shown much commitment to plot). In this choice, surprisingly enough, he goes against the usual practice of comic narratives, which tend to propel 'flat' characters into the mazes and circuits of the most elaborately structured plots, as Dickens and Wodehouse so classically do. From the writer's point of view, plot in general can best be understood as a mechanism for change – for change from an initial unstable situation to a final stable one. In comic narratives, however, the characters themselves do not change – that is the prerogative of tragedy – they remain eternally dedicated to pigs or to the proposition that something will turn up. Once established, Sterne's comic characters observe this convention and do not alter in any important sense; but they are perhaps inflatable rather than flat; they tend to spread out in space, laterally, gaining a horizontal density of personality yet never turning very deeply inwards. And, in fact, if Sterne's characters show no important change, neither does his plot: after nine volumes we leave the Shandys in mid-conversation, just as we met them, suspended for eternity in the same comic aspic that first enclosed them.

The enlargement of Toby also raises in a new form the issue of Sterne's self-portraiture in *Tristram Shandy*. For Volume II begins with the story of Toby's frustrated efforts to describe to well-wishers precisely how he received his wound at the siege of Namur. 'The many perplexities he was in,' Tristram says in a passage of rich suggestiveness,

arose out of the almost insurmountable difficulties he found in telling his story intelligibly, and giving such clear ideas of the differences and distinctions between the scarp and counterscarp,——the glacis and covered way,——the half-moon and ravelin,——as to make his company fully comprehend where and what he was about. (II, i)

The last phrase might serve as another motto for the book. For if Sterne at times seems impelled by some hidden logic to make Toby the central figure of the story – certainly the central figure of the later volumes – that may be because in this one crucial matter Tristram and Toby so nearly resemble each other, and in turn resemble their author. Toby's difficulty in 'rendering' himself, that is – in making 'his company fully comprehend where and what he was about' – parallels Tristram's difficulty in rendering himself, and they both recall Sterne's insistence that his book be understood as a picture of himself. Indeed, the comparison with which Sterne's next paragraph begins explicitly links Toby's problems and those of 'writers' generally ('Writers themselves are too apt to confound these terms'). Or, to put it another way, Tristram like Toby is wounded, mutilated physically and psychically – 'Through the mediation of the sash window,' Sigurd Burckhardt observes, Toby in fact 'transmits his wound to his nephew' – and recovery in both cases appears to depend upon their telling their stories 'intelligibly', making themselves clear, if not transparent, to their audiences.[9] In both cases, however, the original impulse gives way quickly to the most extravagant expansion of scale – Toby's to the model battlefields of Europe, Tristram's to the scheme of two volumes a year for the rest of his life. And for each this expansion comes about partly because self-explanation grows into a sheer, joyous hobbyhorse, and partly because the stubborn, opaque and temporal nature of language interferes with the task of straightforward narration.

Hence, Volume II moves from Toby's inarticulate eloquence on his sick-bed to the question of Tristram's style in chapter ii, and then to the related subjects of Locke's *Essay* and the innate confusion of all language. Here, in fact, Sterne combines two separate Lockian themes: the origin of our knowledge through the senses, which Sterne illustrates with the homey and obscene metaphor of 'Dolly' fumbling in her pocket for a thimble, and the 'unsteady uses of words', which perplex our knowledge and which Locke preaches against at length in the *Essay* (III, ix–xi). But at this point Tristram's and Toby's characters diverge, as Tristram learns to delight in the unsteadiness and plasticity of words, while Toby proves himself the only true Lockian in the novel, and takes no delight in their slippery impertinences. Just as Locke prescribes, he insists on understanding all words in one sense only, and he clings to the unreasonable Lockian ambition of communicating precisely and clearly with language:

> when thou considers this, thou wilt not wonder at my uncle *Toby*'s perplexities,——thou wilt drop a tear of pity upon his scarp and his counterscarp;——his glacis and his covered-way;——his ravelin and his half-moon: 'Twas not by ideas,——by heaven! his life was put in jeopardy by words. (II, ii)

The result is therefore Cervantic: with as many books on siegecraft as Don Quixote had of chivalry, he falls under the spell of a ruling passion whose symptoms are both mental (mad obsession and frustration) and physical (the wound exacerbated, animal strength wasted).

Toby's solution, though not Tristram's, is to pass beyond language to the primitive origin of language in things themselves, by means of the famous model battlefield on his rood and a half of bowling-green at Shandy. Readers in 1760, of course, would have understood Toby's games otherwise, as a Lilliputian mockery of the Duke of Marlborough and his wars. Moreover, as John Butt notes, 'The quiet and seclusion of Toby's theatre of war would have hit the fancy of Sterne's first readers the more particularly because the first half-dozen books appeared while the Seven Years War was still being fought.'[10] He adds, less plausibly, that Toby's tender nature corresponded to a change in the image of the British soldier over these years, summed up in the legend of Wolfe at Quebec, which transforms a warrior into 'something of a hero of sensibility' – as humane as he was militant. Toby's hobby-horse has long drawn an imposing train of psychological as well as historical interpretations, however, and it is a subject to which we shall return in Chapter 7. Here we can only pause to note that, because they so completely engross him, Toby's games raise in special form the question of reality so often explored in the book – for like Don Quixote he seems to take the illusion as the thing itself. And, although many games imitate the real world as Toby's does (chess, doll's houses, 'Monopoly'), the war games actually incorporate reality day by day, feeding on it like a furnace: Trim and Toby construct their citadels and execute their sieges according to the daily reports in the newspapers; but as they do they shrink to manageable proportions the real world, they disarm its genuine power to threaten and destroy, reducing it (as Sterne's novel reduces his unhappiness) to child's play. And if we remember the poignancy of his *Memoirs* it is easy to see how Sterne would want to render harmless the world that had taken his father. 'The opposite of play', Freud claims, 'is not serious occupation but – reality.'[11]

(iii)   DR SLOP AND TRIM'S SERMON

Dr Slop enters the novel with an ominous metaphor:

> Here a Devil of a rap at the door snapp'd my father's definition (like his tobacco-pipe) in two,——and, at the same time, crushed the head of as notable and curious a dissertation as ever was engendered in the womb of speculation. (II, vii)

The image of the crushed head, of course, prefigures all too accurately his contribution to Tristram's birth. Slop himself, once on stage, constitutes the principal 'local satire' that Sterne retained, and may well also represent what is left of his original conception of the book: the ill-fated birth that accounts for so much of Tristram's oddity. Yorkshire readers would have immediately understood Slop as a satire against Dr John Burton, a political enemy of both Sterne and his uncle Jacques, and a well-known enthusiast for modern obstetrics. As Arthur Cash has shown, however, Sterne alters Burton's character in two notable ways: first, there is no evidence that Burton was a Catholic, as Slop so emphatically is; and, second, he bore no resemblance at all to Tristram's portrait (Cash, pp. 179–80).

> Imagine to yourself a little, squat, uncourtly figure of a Doctor *Slop*, of
> about four feet and a half perpendicular height, with a breadth of back,
> and a sesquipedality of belly, which might have done honour to a
> Serjeant in the Horse-guards. (II, ix)

(Cash records that he was a 'tall well sett Gentlem[n]'.) An imaginary garden with a real toad in it: it is an avowedly Hogarthian description, making full use of the satiric principle that one attacks one's enemies either by blowing them up to ludicrous size or shrinking them to insignificance. (Sterne's compliment to Hogarth in the next paragraph served its purpose, prompting the great artist to offer two illustrations for a new edition.) None the less, Sterne's attack has its factual basis in Burton's two notorious books: *Essay towards a Complete New System of Midwifery* (1751) and *A Letter to William Smellie, MD* (1753), both characterized by a wide and pedantic antiquarianism, the *Letter* a particularly bad-tempered diatribe against the most eminent of contemporary obstetricians. Walter's obstinate championing of Slop, reinforced no doubt by the appeal of his pedantic learning, pits the much-ridiculed figure of the 'male midwife' against traditional midwives like the widow set in business by Yorick; and a certain amount of Slop's lechery – including perhaps Toby's belief that his sister 'does not care to let a man come so near her ****' – can be attributed to the unsavoury reputation these male midwives had recently acquired. Burton's forceps also attract their share of ridicule; for, although forceps were coming into general use in the mid-eighteenth century (they had been invented but kept secret in late seventeenth-century France), his version of the instrument was much inferior to those devised by Smellie and others, and never accepted by the profession. (They are described by one medical historian as 'an ingenious but very unserviceable forceps, working like lobster's claws'.)[12] The other 'instruments of salvation and deliverance' (II, xi) hanging in his green bag are actually, as Cash points out, instruments of death, used to extract dead foetuses from the mother or, like the little squirt, to baptize a foetus about to die. (For once Sterne passes over an opportunity to link his comedy with the theme of mortality.)

Yet, while the episodes of Tristram's birth and subsequent disasters provide the framework for all of Volumes I–IV, Slop himself falls curiously outside their predominant tone, as if he has been transplanted into the present book from an earlier and markedly different version. He is, for one thing, the only completely satirical figure of any importance. Tristram's 'Cervantic' account of his thunderous collision with Obadiah, for example, depends quite literally on that second great principle of satiric attack, cover your enemy with filth:

> He stood like *Hamlet*'s ghost, motionless and speechless, for a full minute and a half, at the parlour door, (*Obadiah* still holding his hand) with all the majesty of mud. His hinder parts, upon which he had received his fall, totally besmear'd,——and in every other part of him, blotched over in such a manner with *Obadiah*'s explosion, that you would have sworn (without mental reservation) that every grain of it had taken effect. (II, x)

('Majesty of mud', from *The Dunciad*, bk II, l. 326, suggests that Pope's mock-heroic games were as much in Sterne's mind at that moment as Shakespeare.) Slop's Catholicism, alluded to in 'without mental reservation', provides a third point of satiric attack, along with his medical theories and his appearance, and his irritable, leering normality likewise makes him an outsider in the Shandy household, where Toby is innocent of sex and Walter annoyed with it:

> you do increase my pleasure very much, [Toby tells Walter] in begetting children for the *Shandy* Family at your time of life.——But, by that, Sir, quoth Dr *Slop*, Mr *Shandy* increases his own.——Not a jot, quoth my father. (II, xii)

With Trim's reappearance in chapter xv, sermon in hand, Sterne's cast of characters is nearly complete – only the Widow Wadman is left to introduce – and we are in a position to see that he has instinctively assembled them according to a traditional comic formula, one as evident in the newest television 'situation' skit as in *A Midsummer Night's Dream* or *The Alchemist*: the characters must move outwards by stages along a psychological scale from near-normality to utter lunacy, like a row of stepping-stones disappearing into the distance. In the genial dementia of Shandy Hall, Trim (or occasionally Slop) stands nearest the normal centre of things, though Trim's first act, it must be admitted, is to stand in so peculiar a way as to challenge Tristram's powers of description:

with his body sway'd, and somewhat bent forwards,——his right-leg
firm under him, sustaining seven-eights of his whole weight,——the
foot of his left-leg, the defect of which was no disadvantage to his
attitude, advanced a little, not laterally, nor forwards, but in a line
betwixt them;——his knee bent, but that not violently,——but so as
to fall within the limits of the line of beauty. (II, xvii)

We have already traced this kind of joke to Rabelais; here we can quickly
add that Sterne, who at one time pursued painting and drawing as
hobbies, may also have been inspired by certain recurring 'expressive'
poses in eighteenth-century painting and in novels, or even by poses
recommended in contemporary conduct manuals, pictures of the correct
posture for communicating passion, reserve, anger, etc. Certainly,
Hogarth was able to illustrate Trim's pose exactly according to Sterne's
specifications. The whole elaborate analysis belongs, in any case, to that
wider conflict of pictorial versus temporal expression that some critics
have seen informing the structure of *Tristram Shandy*, deflecting
Sterne's anxiety about the inexorable forward motion of time and
permitting him to extend characters horizontally, to ignore the time-
bound rules of plot, and to freeze the action for pages together, as here, in
defiance of narrative time.[13]

Despite Trim's eloquent pose, the sermon itself presents difficulties of
interpretation for many readers, who may share the critical reaction of
Sterne's contemporaries against placing a genuine sermon in the ribald
context of his novel – Sterne had actually preached and published it in
1750 – or, worse, making it the occasion of blatant huckstering:

by laying open this story to the world, I gain an opportunity of
informing it,——That in case the character of parson *Yorick*, and this
sample of his sermons is liked,——that there are now in the possession
of the *Shandy* family, as many as will make a handsome volume, at the
world's service,——and much good may they do it. (II, xvii)

Modern scholarship, taking the sermon seriously (not to say gravely), has
passed over the possibility that a nervous first novelist was simply
padding out the material of his second volume. In an influential study,
Arthur Cash has seen it as indicative of Sterne's old-fashioned, Augustan
confidence in the powers of reason to direct our conduct: 'Consult calm
reason and the unchangeable obligations of truth and justice,' it declares.
And this reasonableness, so uncharacteristic of Sterne on the face of it,
Cash traces back to complex discussions of *a priori* and *a posteriori* reason
in Locke and earlier rationalist philosophers ('Sterne is the most philosophic of novelists').[14] The sermon has also been understood more
simply as an interpolated tale, like the story of the Man of the Hill in *Tom*

Jones, a thoroughly conventional device in eighteenth-century fiction, and its explicit lesson therefore complements the hidden moral purpose Sterne sometimes claimed for his novel. But, ironically, the sermon's moral points are, first, that we should rigorously scrutinize our consciences to root out self-deception and complacency, and, second, that we are not really likely to pay attention to the first point: 'Sterne strips bare the pretense', writes J. Paul Hunter, 'that readers will learn anything at all from straightforward moral discourse.'[15] Certainly, none of Trim's listeners learns from the sermon: each reacts only in his hobbyhorsical way, Slop commenting defensively on Catholic doctrine, Walter on rhetorical effects, Toby and Trim on military images. Yet even here he manages to touch and complicate one of those major themes we have discussed several times before (like Johnson's, Sterne's thought is all of a piece; begin anywhere and you are led back to the centre at once): Trim's extravagant over-reaction to the mention of the Inquisition raises the question of illusion and reality in a direct, Cervantic way. For as Trim groans and claps his hands in pity for his brother Tom, a victim of the Inquisition in Portugal, Walter and Slop remind him repeatedly that the sermon is not to be interpreted as real: ''Tis only a description, honest man, quoth *Slop*, there's not a word of truth in it.' Yet, if Trim resembles Don Quixote in interpreting language as always truthful, he is closer still in his literal-mindedness to his master Toby, with whom he shares an absorbing but illusory reality on the bowling-green: never recognizing words to be arbitrary, fictive signs, they grasp them as trustingly and as thoughtlessly as they might a musket or a staff.

From this high point, Sterne reverts in his last chapter to satire of material in Burton's books, recounting Walter's fear of the pressure on a child's skull during labour and the advantages of Caesarean birth (which both Burton and Smellie recommended in extreme cases; Cash points out that the operation in the eighteenth century 'was always fatal' to the mother).[16] And then, with a bright, smug assurance, entirely justified, of having written something irresistible, he defies us to guess what could possibly follow in Volumes III and IV.

NOTES: TO CHAPTER 5

1   R. F. Brissenden, '"Trusting to almighty God": another look at the composition of *Tristram Shandy*', in Arthur H. Cash and John M. Stedmond (eds), *The Winged Skull: Papers from the Laurence Sterne Bicentenary Conference at the University of York* (London: Methuen, 1971), pp. 258–69.

2   I owe this point to Lila V. Graves, 'Locke's changeling and the Shandy bull', *Philological Quarterly*, vol. 60 (1981), pp. 257–64.

3   See Alvin B. Kernan, *The Plot of Satire* (New Haven, Conn.: Yale University Press, 1965), pp. 51–65.

4   Robert M. Adams, *Strains of Discord: Studies in Literary Openness* (Ithaca, NY: Cornell University Press, 1958), pp. 146–57.

5   Robert Alter, *Partial Magic: The Novel as a Self-Conscious Genre* (Berkeley/Los Angeles, Calif.: University of California Press, 1975), pp. 43–4.

6   Maurice Morgann, 'An Essay on the Dramatic Character of Sir John Falstaff', in *Eighteenth-Century Essays on Shakespeare*, ed. D. Nichol Smith, 2nd edn (London: Oxford University Press, 1963), p. 266; quoted and discussed in Iain McGilchrist, *Against Criticism* (London: Faber, 1982), pp. 70, 155–6. For E. M. Forster's discussion, see his *Aspects of the Novel* (New York: Harcourt, 1927), pp. 103–18.

7   James E. Swearingen, *Reflexivity in 'Tristram Shandy': an Essay In Phenomenological Criticism* (New Haven, Conn.: Yale University Press, 1977), pp. 56–64.

8   Ford Madox Ford, *Joseph Conrad: A Personal Remembrance* (London: Duckworth, 1924), p. 129.

9   Sigurd Burckhardt, '*Tristram Shandy*'s law of gravity', *ELH*, vol. 28 (1961), p. 82.

10 John Butt and Geoffrey Carnall, *The Mid-Eighteenth Century*, Vol. 8 of the Oxford History of English Literature (Oxford: Oxford University Press, 1979), p. 441.

11 Sigmund Freud, 'The Relation of the Poet to Day-Dreaming', in *Collected Papers*, trans. Joan Riviere (London: Hogarth Press, 1948), Vol. 4, p. 174.

12 This whole paragraph is drawn from Arthur H. Cash's fascinating essay 'The birth of Tristram Shandy: Sterne and Dr Burton', in R. F. Brissenden (ed.), *Studies in the Eighteenth Century: Papers Presented at the David Nichol Smith Memorial Seminar, Canberra 1966* (Canberra: Australian National University Press, 1968), pp. 133–54.

13 A very good discussion of the relation of pictorial and temporal themes in *Tristram Shandy* can be found in William V. Holtz, *Image and Immortality: A Study of 'Tristram Shandy'* (Providence, RI: Brown University Press, 1970), esp. pp. 123–57. An important illustrated conduct manual is Francis Nivelon, *The Rudiments of Genteel Behavior* (London, 1737).

14 Arthur H. Cash, 'The sermon in *Tristram Shandy*', *ELH*, vol. 31 (1964), p. 416.

15 J. Paul Hunter, 'Response as reformation: *Tristram Shandy* and the art of interruption', *Novel*, vol. 4 (1971), p. 144.

16 Cash, 'The birth of Tristram Shandy', p. 141.

CHAPTER 6

The Indecent and the Sentimental Sublime: *Volumes III–VI*

Though the 'world' of the Shandys is only four miles across, the world of the book itself is spacious and open, as comic worlds tend to be. The first two volumes had already taken us to London and the planet Mercury, among other exotic places. The opening sentence of Volume III transports us at once to Flanders and its 'prodigious armies'. Thereafter, Sterne moves with ease from Shandy Hall to settings like Strasburg and Navarre and back again, until the whole of Europe, including Russia, Lapland and 'all those cold and dreary tracts of the globe' lie at his feet (III, xx). Even in the casual scale of his language – 'to drop my metaphor, which by the bye is a pity,——for I have fetch'd it as far as from the coast of *Guinea*' (III, xii) – he now displays the relaxed assurance of a writer who has achieved sublime, interplanetary control.

This sense of effortless mastery is nowhere more apparent than in the bibliographical facts. Volumes III and IV were published on 28 January 1761, less than a year after the first two volumes; and eleven months later, on 21 December 1761, Volumes V and VI appeared. All four were written at the house in Coxwold ('Shandy Hall') that Sterne rented for his new living, a gift of the Earl of Fauconberg for which he had previously applied without success, now apparently offered in acknowledgement of Sterne's celebrity. As the dates of publication indicate, they were composed at dizzying speed: Volume III was begun in early June and completed by 3 August 1760; Volume IV was completed by 4 November; Volumes V and VI were written between mid-July 1761 and the end of October. And they were written in that characteristic absorption his friends and parishioners had come to expect of Sterne: 'The act of composition was to him a sort of obsession,' Cross observes.

> ... When the fit was on, he could write almost continuously through the day – at will, he used to claim, before meals or after meals, dressed or undressed, clean shaven or in neglected beard ... Sometimes, it is a local tradition, Sterne would issue forth from Shandy Hall at a great rate, and half way down the hill would come to a sudden stop, and then

rush back to his study to note down some fancy before it could escape him.[1]

Despite their speed of composition, these volumes show a certain thematic unity that permits us to discuss them together (Volumes VII and VIII were not to appear until 1765, and after major changes in Sterne's life). Sterne's preoccupation with the instability of language, for example, re-establishes itself at the outset of Volume III, when Walter supplies Dr Slop with the sulphuric curse of Bishop Ernulphus, for use against the clumsy Obadiah. And that special branch of language, names, receives full attention in the blank spaces of the curse, where any name at all can be asserted, and at much greater length in the chain of mistakes that leads to Tristram's christening. Even such matters as the constant renaming of Toby's model town and the demented flexibility of Walter's 'auxiliary verbs' contribute to this same theme of language in flux, skimming lightly over the surface of a restless and not quite pacified reality. Similarly, Sterne's subversion of literary form reappears in these volumes, as he repeats his black-page trick with marbled endpaper (no modern reprints do justice to the vivid colour of the original); or again as he inserts his preface midway through Volume III, just as he had delayed the dedication until chapter vii of Volume I. Self-consciously, too, he omits a chapter in Volume IV, misnumbers pages, and diagrams the whole course of the book to date with snake-like squiggles, declaring over and over in these ways that he writes as spontaneously as humanly possible, without the least inhibition of plan or form. The sexual jokes continue to focus on the themes of impotence – Tristram's involuntary circumcision is the central event – and lechery, most memorably in those long (and overlong) discussions of noses and whiskers that combine genital pride and linguistic embarrassment. And, finally, the great theme of time, central to so many eighteenth-century moralists, reasserts its presence in Sterne's mind at almost every point – in the Lockian account of duration of time that Walter gives Toby (III, xviii), in the failure of the Tristra-paedia to keep pace with Tristram's growth (V, xvi), in the wonderful sentence with which Tristram laments the complexity of being an author: 'a cow broke in (to-morrow morning) to my uncle *Toby's* fortifications, and eat up two ratios and half of dried grass' (III, xxxviii). Most poignantly, perhaps, the theme of passing time appears in Tristram's sudden realization that he is a full year older, but in his narrative has got no further than the first day of his life: 'I shall never overtake myself,' he cries in a phrase that suggests Sterne's whole project of self-discovery and description (IV, xiii).

We could hardly comment in detail on the development at every turn of these important themes, but four episodes can stand as representative of all the others.

(i) NOSES AND WHISKERS

The joke at the centre of 'Slawkenbergius's Tale' resembles Wittgenstein's famous rabbit/duck drawing: the *coup d'œil* sketch that flickers back and forth between two shapes so rapidly that the eye can never hold it to a single meaning. In the same way the stranger's gigantic nose alternates irresistibly between its higher and lower anatomical meanings, a physical analogy transformed into an exhibitionistic simile. Tristram even calls attention to this equivocal linguistic character of the nose and warns us – insincerely – against 'the temptations and suggestions of the devil': 'For by the word *Nose*, throughout all this long chapter of noses, and in every other part of my work, where the word *Nose* occurs,——I declare, by that word I mean a Nose, and nothing more, or less' (III, xxxi). But in reality, to adapt Bergson's example, the joke works the way a child's jack-in-the-box works: no matter how often we mechanically push down the indecent meaning into its box, it springs up again like the toy clown, grinning, irrepressible.[2]

The joke belongs to another context as well: if the ribald play upon sign and meaning is part of Sterne's recurrent general point that language is inherently unstable, the particular sign of the nose derives from Walter Shandy's character. Tristram interrupts the Tale, in fact, to tell us that it is Walter's favourite because it combines his preoccupations with noses and names into a single text. And these preoccupations, we have long understood, are part of Walter's reductively mechanical approach to human nature. It is paradoxical, of course, to speak of anything about that man of extensive views as reductive, but the truth is, each of his theories boils down at last to the idea that human fate is the result of a purely mechanical force operating upon pliable material: the homunculus, the pressure upon our skulls at birth, our noses, our very names determine our characters. Moreover, while a man of such 'unthinking thought' (to use Tom Sharpe's marvellous phrase) will naturally delight in Slawkenbergius' confirmation of his 'system of noses' – even in the face, so to speak, of his son's crushed nose – he will delight still more in the long debate over the 'reality of the nose' that occupies not only barbers and sentinels, but also professors, doctors and astrologers. The medical dispute, in particular, which begins with the question of conception (can a foetus survive in the womb with such a nose?) and ends with the question of death ('is it the stagnation of the blood'?), must appeal to a man of theory like Walter, and all the more because it evidently derives from a passage in Rabelais (II, i). We can even presume that another part of the Tale's appeal lies in the fact that it confirms Walter's view of sex: a necessary inconvenience that inflames women and irritates men. John Stedmond suggests that the whole Tale actually parallels Rabelais' *Tiers Livre*, that apprehensive and farcical

ruth about sexual life conducted by Pantagruel through
f learned society.[3]

he time, it seems never to have been noticed how much the
th the great nose resembles Sterne himself. He arrives in
s a man of extraordinary interest, a man whose great nose is
compared to Tristram's pen ('worn to the stump as it is'), and whose
entrance into the city captures everyone's imagination, just as Tristram
Shandy, book and author, stormed London in 1760:

> ... so many strange things, with equal confidence on all sides, and
> with equal eloquence in all places, were spoken and sworn to con-
> cerning it, that turned the whole stream of all discourse and wonder
> towards it——every soul, good and bad——rich and poor—
> —learned and unlearned——doctor and student——mistress and
> maid——gentle and simple——nun's flesh and woman's flesh in
> *Strasburg* spent their time in hearing tidings about it ...

And Slawkenbergius writes quite as self-consciously as Sterne –
pausing, for example, to name and analyse the dramatic elements of his
book, just as Tristram concludes Volume VI with his explanatory
squiggles (Slawkenbergius, however, prides himself on slavishly
including every classical element 'in the order Aristotle first planted
them'). Likewise the whole confusing sexuality of the Tale suggests
Sterne's characteristic preoccupations. Desire is limited to touching
('I'll know the bottom of it, said the trumpeter's wife, for I will touch it
with my finger before I sleep'); women are voracious, in a masturba-
tory way, consulting their 'placket holes' rather than their husbands;
and men are rendered defensive and impotent by the stranger's
imagined prowess: 'In the hurry and confusion every thing had been in
the night before, the bakers had all forgot to lay their leaven——there
were no butter'd buns to be had for breakfast in all *Strasburg*' ('butter'd
buns' are promiscuous women). That is, in a way peculiar to Sterne,
actual sex is stopped, but arousal is incessant.

James Swearingen has interpreted Slawkenbergius' Tale as a part of
Sterne's general criticism of European life, seeing its digression on
Martin Luther and the ruin of Strasburg as signs of cultural crisis and
drawing a parallel between the declining fortunes of the Shandy family
and the sterility of post-Reformation England.[4] But it is difficult to
credit Sterne with such a vast historical analysis – there is no evidence
of such a view in any of his other writings – when so much of the Tale
so openly concerns no more than his usual themes of language. As he
describes the promised sequel 'Diego and Julia', for instance, which
defies translation, Tristram continues the Slawkenbergian theme of
symbolic interpretation, speculating that words may be understood by

our 'sixth sense', even when they convey no ideas and have no meaning.

> What can he mean by the lambent pupilability of slow, low, dry chat, five notes below the natural tone,——which you know, madam, is little more than a whisper? The moment I pronounced the words, I could perceive an attempt towards a vibration in the strings, about the region of the heart.——The brain made no acknowledgement.——There's often no good understanding betwixt 'em.——I felt as if I understood it——I had no ideas. (IV, i)

The same speculation, moreover, clearly governs the related story of 'whiskers', in which another community is reduced to chaos by a word. And, if simple context appears to determine the meaning of an enigmatic word like 'pupilability', context also determines completely the meaning of 'whiskers'. For, unlike 'nose', whiskers has no certain physical analogy to explain its indecent attraction. The word has a mysterious air; everyone understands it differently, according to the arbitrariness of sex, rank or personality. It leads the Lady Baussiere 'into a wilderness of conceits', distracting her from her Christian duty, but concentrating her attention upon her horse. And, although no one quite agrees on what the word means, they none the less communicate effectively, if irrationally: 'There are some trains of certain ideas', Tristram says, lifting an idea from Locke,

> which leave prints of themselves about our eyes and eye-brows; and there is a consciousness of it, somewhere about the heart, which serves but to make these etchings the stronger——we see, spell, and put them together without a dictionary. (V, i)

But the resulting communication lacks philosophical dignity:

> Ha, ha! he, hee! cried *La Guyol* and *La Sabatiere*, looking close at each others prints——Ho, ho! cried *La Battarelle* and *Maronette*, doing the same:——Whist! cried one——st, st,——said a second——hush, quoth a third——poo, poo, replied a fourth ...

In the end, the ruin of the word has no grander overtones of culture. The word is simply personified, in one of Sterne's more dazzling exercises with that trope, first into a woman ('ruined'), then into a soldier: '*La Fosseuse* had given it a wound, and it was not the better for passing through all these defiles.' After which, the curate d'Estella recalls the story of noses, warns against the ever-present danger of indecent association, and describes the most wonderful of metamorphoses: 'Chastity, by nature the gentlest of all affections——give it but its head——'tis like a ramping and a roaring lion.' And, if it is not enough to have made chastity into a Swiftian galloping horse, Sterne adds soberly that the curate's warning was not understood: 'The word bridled his ass at the tail.'

(ii) PHUTATORIUS AND THE CHESTNUT

Richard Lanham has shown that the long episode of Phutatorius and the hot chestnut – so apparently formless – is in fact organized around the theme of literary decorum. Or, more precisely, literary indecorum.[5]

For Sterne begins the episode by skipping a chapter and thereafter misnumbering all the remaining pages of Volume IV. He explains this first impropriety with a classical metaphor of book as painting – the omitted chapter is 'so much above the stile and manner of any thing else I have been able to paint in this book' that it would unbalance his composition – and then with a metaphor of book as music: 'to write a book is for all the world like humming a song'; but a moment of inspired harmony will by contrast reduce the hum to noise (IV, xxv). From these lofty aesthetic speculations Sterne descends at once to Yorick's particular literary indecorum at the Visitation Dinner, where he has just cut his sermon into slips of paper and handed them about to light pipes. 'If the Sermon is of no better worth than to light pipes with', declares Didius,

> ——'twas certainly, Sir, not good enough to be preached before so learned a body; and if 'twas good enough to be preached before so learned a body——'twas certainly, Sir, too good to light their pipes with afterwards. (IV, xxvi)

Yorick answers this classically symmetrical criticism by proposing an unclassical, indeed a romantic, theory of literary value, using the imagery of bungled birth never far from the surface of Sterne's novel:

> I was delivered of it at the wrong end of me——it came from my head instead of my heart——and it is for the pain it gave me, both in the writing and preaching of it, that I revenge myself of it . . . for my own part, continued *Yorick*, I had rather direct five words point blank to the heart——

But, just as Toby rises automatically to answer, Tristram interrupts to tell us of another interruption – a word he is ashamed to write, an illegal, uncanonical, utterly indecorous word:

> Zounds! ————————————————————————————
> ——————————————————————————————————
> ————————Z——ds! cried *Phutatorius*. (IV, xxvi)

From this point, Tristram's tone and style undergo a striking change. Reporting 'with all imaginable decency' the story of the chestnut, he adopts a mock-formal, absurdly decorous gravity and diction that reminds us of nothing so much as the 'Ithaca' section of Joyce's *Ulysses*. He traces the path of the chestnut in something of the manner Joyce traces the trajectory of Bloom's urination: 'it fell perpendicularly into that particular aperture of *Phutatorius*'s breeches'. He regrets the indecorous noun, 'breeches', 'for which, to the shame and indelicacy of our language be it spoke, there is no chaste word throughout all *Johnson*'s dictionary'. And he comments polysyllabically, pompously on the question of chance in the fall of the chestnut: '——Accident, I call it, in compliance to a received mode of speaking.' The exclamation has of course provoked other philosophical discussions around the table – some wonder if the oath, like the stranger's nose, is 'a real and substantial oath'; the literary-minded wonder if it is 'the exordium to an oration'; and Walter offers a mechanical explanation based on 'the sudden influx of blood, which was driven into the right ventricle of *Phutatorius*'s heart', a very different organ from Yorick's. But Tristram bustles past these issues to take up a new and self-important role: 'all that concerns me as an historian,' he insists solemnly, 'is to represent the matter of fact, and render it credible to the reader'. He has, of course, long ago given up the pretence that he knows what he knows because Toby or his father has told him. Now he declares himself in effect privy to everyone's consciousness and removes us at once to the dark centre of Phutatorius' brain.

The two paragraphs that take place within Phutatorius' consciousness describe very slowly the rapid motions of sensation, and they reveal at the same time Sterne's gift for personifying almost any idea, as here he transforms Phutatorius' brain into a genuine *psychomachia*, literalizing every faculty into a vast, miniature battlefield, where ignorant armies clash by night:

> the soul of *Phutatorius*, together with all his ideas, his thoughts, his attention, his imagination, judgment, resolution, deliberation, ratiocination, memory, fancy, with ten batallions of animal spirits, all tumultuously crouded down, through different defiles and circuits, to the place in danger . . .

At the place of danger 'sallies' of imagination next throw Phutatorius into pain and disorder, 'as it has done the best generals upon earth', with a fantasy (not unknown in *Tristram Shandy*) of castration. Tristram introduces this fantasy with a telling adjective – 'had his imagination continued neuter' – but in an example of Sterne's wordplay at its subtlest and most instinctive swiftly changes that word into a monstrous

homonym: 'a *Newt* or an *Asker*'. The image of the wound made by such a
'detested reptile' and its fastening teeth progresses into the word itself:
'Z——ds', which stands for God's wounds and which, by an irresistible
association of ideas, lifts Sterne to new heights of indecency. All this
Tristram delivers in a dispassionate tone, even pausing to comment
pedantically upon Phutatorius' rhetoric ('the aposiopestick-break') and
its forgivable indecorum.

A question of decorum is, of course, a question of interpretation.
The aftermath of Phutatorius' exclamation illustrates the tendency of
the whole novel, from the first chapter on, to transform everything
into a matter of literary criticism (*'Did ever woman ... interrupt a man
with such a silly question?'*). For, when Yorick picks up the chestnut as
if he had himself dropped it into the breach, the others around the
table interpret the action as Yorick's criticism of Phutatorius' book *de
Concubinis retinendis*: 'a sarcastical fling at his book——the doctrines
of which, they said, had inflamed many an honest man in the same
place'. The chestnut's meaning becomes literary, the book's meaning
becomes physical. Yorick, meanwhile, in his usual fashion declines to
set the story right, so that Phutatorius, misunderstanding, rises from
his chair with a smile, 'saying only——that he would endeavour not to
forget the obligation'. A text that Tristram carefully interprets for us,
separating word from gesture to disclose their contradictory meanings:

> ——The smile was for the company.
> ——The threat was for *Yorick*.

It is characteristic of Sterne's comedy that it contains so much anger
('Unhappy *Tristram*! child of wrath!': IV, xix). But while Phutatorius
wraps his injured part in a cooling page of the second edition of his book –
perhaps the final literary indecorum – the chestnut episode glides away
from further expression of that anger and yields to a new controversy
over whether a mother is related to her child. Like so many other debates
in the book, this one begins with the instability of words – if a baptism in
Latin contains errors in its noun endings, is the sacrament invalid? – and
proceeds to demonstrate on the one hand the extent to which language is
divorced from reality, and on the other hand the extent to which men
mistake it for reality:

> 'Tis a ground and principle in the law, said *Triptolemus*, that things do
> not ascend, but descend in it; and I make no doubt 'tis for this cause,
> that however true it is, that the child may be of the blood or seed of its
> parents——that the parents, nevertheless, are not of the blood and
> seed of it. (IV, xxix)

Lanham observes that the whole long tangled episode also raises the philosophical issue of chance, so much a part of eighteenth-century consciousness generally, so much a part of Tristram's frustrated life in particular. And he rightly says that Sterne does not pursue such issues in a philosophical, but in a comic manner, for the sheer pleasure of working out their absurdities through the doughy, plastic medium of language (Lanham, pp. 112–16). We can add that Sterne's usual way of representing such chance is by the image of falling, flying, shifting objects: the world of *Tristram Shandy* is criss-crossed with hurtling forces – falling chestnuts and window-sashes, descending laws, dropping hats, colliding horses, even wishes: 'nothing is more dangerous, madam, than a wish coming sideways in this unexpected manner upon a man' (III, i). We explain this phenomenon only partially as Sterne's law of 'gravity', whereby everything seeks its lowest (and most physical) meaning, because the invisibility and unpredictability of these forces are stressed quite as much as their downward direction.[6] The effect is a life of random vectors, pulling Tristram and everyone else first towards one fate, and then towards another, mysteriously. 'What is the life of man! Is it not to shift from side to side?——from sorrow to sorrow?' he asks. 'No body, but he who has felt it, can conceive what a plaguing thing it is to have a man's mind torn asunder by two projects of equal strength, both obstinately pulling in a contrary direction at the same time' (IV, xxxi). This is an image related to the ever-present machines of the novel as well. And at the end of Volume IV we see Tristram declaring in a combination of these mechanical figures that he will master the forces of his life, 'counterbalance' the evils that have befallen him. Then with a joyful burst, very different from Walter's explanation of Phutatorius' explosion, he shows how the comic spirit can harness even those random, malicious forces of fate, and by an act of will turn the 'wheel of life':

> True *Shandeism*, think what you will against it, opens the heart and lungs, and like all those affections which partake of its nature, it forces the blood and other vital fluids of the body to run freely thro' its channels, and makes the wheel of life run long and cheerfully round. (IV, xxxii)

(iii) THE DEATH OF BOBBY

Unlike the superficially jumbled account of Phutatorius and the chestnut, this famous episode makes its intended structure clear from the outset: it is to be a deliberate and self-conscious comparison between Walter's and Trim's speeches on the death of Bobby – 'two orators so contrasted by nature and education, haranguing over the same bier' (V, vi). Tristram reminds us of the comparison at several points, has his characters speak of it, and even rounds off the whole story with the observation – familiar in metaphor, unusual in precision – that 'Had this volume been a farce . . . the last chapter, Sir, had finished the first act of it' (V, xv).

That act begins with a preliminary comparison between Walter and Cicero, both eloquent men who substitute their eloquence for philosophy and who respond to the loss of their children with self-consoling speeches. But before he recounts his father's speech Tristram introduces another preliminary comparison: Walter uses language as consolation for Bobby's death just as he has once used it as consolation for an accident of birth. Obadiah, that is, unluckiest of Shandy servants, had taken Walter's favourite Arabian mare to breed a 'pad' (easy-riding horse), but because of his neglect the result is a mule, 'and as ugly a beast of the kind as ever was produced'.

> My mother and my uncle *Toby* expected my father would be the death of *Obadiah*——and that there never would be an end of the disaster.— —See here! you rascal, cried my father, pointing to the mule, what you have done!——It was not me, said *Obadiah*.——How do I know that? replied my father.
>
> Triumph swam in my father's eyes, at the repartee——the *Attic* salt brought water into them——and so *Obadiah* heard no more about it (V, iii)

Two things are thus established by this prologue: first, that the entire episode will proceed by means of calculated, self-reflecting comparisons, nestled one within the other (as 'the death of Obadiah' prefigures the death of Bobby); and, second, that, like the lawyers at the Visitation Dinner, Walter tends to mistake language for reality. Or, rather, he tends to grind reality up in the mill of rhetoric and reconstruct it to his liking. 'Rhetoric', Swearingen observes, is 'the clue' to his whole character.[7] The resulting hodgepodge of meditative fragments on death ('fine sayings') owes something to Montaigne, most to Burton and Bacon; and, though these orotund sayings serve to ease Walter's sorrow, they also serve to confuse poor Toby utterly, who mistakes language for reality in his own way and supposes that quotations from Servius Sulpicius refer to Walter's days as a Turkey merchant. We may take their vaudeville misunderstandings as one further instance of Sterne's adaptation of Lockian themes – the proposition that imperfect words produce imperfect communications – but it is important to note at the same time how Sterne's own theme of linguistic imperfection is at once more superficial and more vastly elegiac. Just as Yorick's name had decayed, just as modern eloquence has decayed:

'What is become, brother *Toby*, of *Nineveh* and *Babylon*, of *Cizicum* and *Mitylenae*? The fairest towns that ever the sun rose upon, are now no more: the names only are left, and those (for many of them are wrong spelt) are falling themselves by piece-meals to decay, and in length of time will be forgotten . . .'

And we should note, too, how Walter's rhetoric can wheel from such grandiloquence and stoop to the most unforgettable kind of novelistic detail: 'There is no terror, brother *Toby*, in its looks, but what it borrows from groans and convulsions——and the blowing of noses, and the wiping away of tears with the bottoms of curtains in a dying man's room.'

At this point, however, although the detail of the curtains has evidently started a new motif of imagery, thoughts of death and sex interpenetrate, as they so often do in Sterne's imagination, and Walter ludicrously builds to a rhetorical climax by describing a sexual one:

'Tis of *Cornelius Gallus*, the praetor——which I dare say, brother *Toby*, you have read.——I dare say I have not, replied my uncle.——He died, said my father, as **************——And if it was with his wife, said my uncle *Toby*——there could be no hurt in it.——That's more than I know——replied my father. (V, iv)

Mrs Shandy, passing outside the parlour, overhears the 'shrill, penetrating' word 'wife' and pauses, there to rest motionless while Tristram describes her position in two rapid similes and then turns his full attention to the second term of his major comparison.

Sterne is curiously fond of the image of a mechanical spring. Partly, of course, he responds to its quality of irrepressible resiliency, jack-in-the-box vitality. And partly he seems to like the idea of complex, over-elaborate machines, ready to fly apart in a confusion of springs and wheels. To explain how Trim comes to make his speech, Tristram first must explain how the servants know of Bobby's death; and for this explanation he offers such an image:

Though in one sense our family was certainly a simple machine, as it consisted of a few wheels; yet there was thus much to be said for it, that these wheels were set in motion by so many different springs, and acted one upon the other from such a variety of strange principles and impulses——that though it was a simple machine, it had all the honour and advantages of a complex one. (V, vi)

Still another simile, comparing the hallway to the '*Dardanells*', carries Tristram to Trim and Walter again: the latter 'proceeding from period to period, by metaphor and allusion' as he speaks, Trim, not at all machine-like, speaking without learning and wit, but naturally and 'to the heart', like Yorick. But Tristram suddenly breaks into a surprising apostrophe, catching at the hint of curtains, picking up again the motif of clothes that is to hold the entire following scene together in a way typical of Sterne's instinctive art. 'O *Trim*! would to heaven thou had'st a better historian!——would!——thy historian had a better pair of breeches!——O ye criticks! will nothing melt you?'

From these otherwise inexplicable breeches, chapter vii begins a surrealistic fanstasy of clothes. When Obadiah has announced Bobby's death, 'A green sattin night-gown of my mother's, which had been twice scoured, was the first idea which *Obadiah*'s exclamation brought into *Susannah*'s head.——Well might *Locke* write a chapter upon the imperfections of words.' Locke had pointed out, of course, that language fails to communicate properly 'when any Word does not excite in the Hearer the same *Idea* which it stands for in the Mind of the Speaker', and prominent among his examples are the colours gold, yellow and white (*Essay*, III, ix, 4). But nothing in Locke's discussion resembles the interior of Susannah's brain, where a procession of Mrs Shandy's wardrobe now rolls by, as if suspended from a ghostly clothes-line:

> her red damask,——her orange-tawny,——her white and yellow lutestrings,——her brown taffata,——her bone-laced caps, her bed-gowns, and comfortable under-petticoats.——Not a rag was left behind.

With the same confidence that he displayed in exfoliating Phutatorius' mind, and dropping for a moment the clothes-line, Tristram goes on to reveal the reaction of the other servants, the 'fat foolish scullion' and Obadiah himself, before Trim enters the kitchen. The comedy of these revelations has been taken solemnly by academic critics: 'The news that Brother Bobby was dead had as many discrete meanings as the hobby-horses the auditors rode,' writes Earl R. Wassermann, enlarging the scene into a vision of impermeable egoism. 'In Tristram's world, meaning had become a function of each person's private, subjective concerns, which alone remained as an interpretive organization.'[8] And certainly Bobby's death provokes at first only self-centred responses like Susannah's: the scullion 'had been all autumn struggling with a dropsy.——He is dead! said *Obadiah*,——he is certainly dead!——so am not I, said the foolish scullion.' But Trim redirects these self-centred responses, lamenting the lost Bobby from his heart – 'Poor creature!——poor boy! poor gentleman!' And when he begins his famous speech he not only reintroduces the clothing motif, he also redefines the scullion's simple egoism as a general human fear:

——He was alive last *Whitsontide*, said the coachman.——*Whitsontide*! alas! cried *Trim*, extending his right arm, and falling instantly into the same attitude in which he read the sermon,——what is *Whitsontide, Jonathan*, (for that was the coachman's name) or *Shrovetide*, or any tide or time past, to this? Are we not here now, continued the corporal (striking the end of his stick perpendicularly upon the floor, so as to give an idea of health and stability)——and are we not——(dropping his hat upon the ground) gone! in a moment!——'Twas infinitely striking!

Trim's speech briefly parodies Walter's earlier lament ('What is become, brother *Toby*, of *Ninevah* and *Babylon*?') and its elegiac themes of waxing time and decaying names. But such parody or recollection is overshadowed by the famous gesture, the eloquent drop of the hat to the ground, and the negative metaphor that follows ('We are not stocks and stones'), which 'melts' the servants into tears (as the critics of the previous chapter had not 'melted'). Trim's simple gesture also raises a question we have associated with him from the moment he took up his oratorical posture in Volume II and began to read the sermon: the superiority of gesture to verbal language. Sterne would have encountered the question long ago, of course, in the Rabelaisian debate between Panurge and the English scholar, conducted entirely with gestures and grimaces (Rabelais, II, xix). But, where Rabelais appears interested only in the slapstick comedy of their contortions and the ingenious obscenity of their gestures, Sterne seems always to regard gesture as a more spontaneous, more sincere way of speaking, and he exploits it for sentimentality rather than for obscenity. Trim's gesture, we should add, does not belong to the category of literalized proverbs or images, like Toby's release of the fly ('at the drop of a hat' is evidently a nineteenth-century American expression). Trim's gesture is instead like those non-verbal expressions with which Sterne punctuates *A Sentimental Journey*, a revelation of the heart at once more natural and more powerful than any spoken word:

A poor tatter'd soul without a shirt on instantly withdrew his claim, by retiring two steps out of the circle, and making a disqualifying bow on his part. Had the whole parterre cried out, *Place aux dames*, with one voice, it would not have conveyed the sentiment of a deference for the sex with half the effect. (*ASJ*, p. 132)

If we are about to protest that the dropping of a hat to convey an image of mortality is an inherently silly thing to do (or say), Tristram intercepts our criticism and insists that all British government – 'possibly the preservation of the whole world' – depends upon our rightly understanding Trim's eloquence. Therefore, reminding us in his familiar motif that

we are 'but men cloathed with bodies, and governed by our imaginations', he repeats Trim's gesture in slow motion, with commentary:

> ——'Are we not here now;'——continued the corporal, 'and are we
> not'——(dropping his hat plumb upon the ground——and pausing,
> before he pronounced the word)——'gone! in a moment?' The
> descent of the hat was as if a heavy lump of clay had been kneaded into
> the crown of it.——Nothing could have expressed the sentiment of
> mortality, of which it was the type and fore-runner, like it,——his
> hand seemed to vanish from under it,——it fell dead,——the corpo-
> ral's eye fix'd upon it, as upon a corps,——and *Susannah* burst into a
> flood of tears.

In this passage and in the short series of paragraphs afterwards that
conclude the chapter, we experience the heaviest barrage of similes in
Tristram Shandy: it is as if the great comparison with which Sterne began
has suddenly engendered many small ones. For we are invited first to
take the hat as a 'sentiment of mortality', to watch it fall 'as if a heavy
lump of clay' propelled it, to see it as a 'type' (in the biblical sense) of our
deaths, and finally to watch it metamorphose under Trim's gaze into a
'corps'.[9] And, having begun, Tristram proceeds to list other possible
similes: the effect would have been lost if Trim had dropped the hat in
any other manner, 'like a goose——like a puppy——like an ass . . . like a
fool,——like a ninny——like a nicompoop'. He appeals to statesmen
whose '*engines* of eloquence' treat the world like a ball of wax, melting,
mollifying and cooling it, and to orators who turn our passions with
another machine, a 'windlass', and finally to whoever drives men 'like
turkeys to market, with a stick and a red clout' – a puzzling simile that
suggests soldiers driven to war (redcoats?) as much as wasted eloquence
and gesture. Despite their frenetic abundance, however, the effect of all
these images is not the 'heightened unreality' we have already described
in Sterne's style, but alternative realities – a novelist suddenly struck by
other ways of saying the same thing, alternatives for Tristram as well as
for Trim.

This sense of improvisation characterizes the whole episode, whose
promising, self-conscious structure is by now left unfinished while
Tristram, as if embarrassed by his own eloquence, rounds out the
clothing motif with indecent jokes on chambermaids, green gowns and
old hats (even the fish-kettle that the scullion cleans may have its double
meaning as pudendum).[10] There is no further contrast between Walter
and Trim, no further outbreak of imagery, except for a brief, suggestive
personification of death in chapter x, and except for this speech at the end
of chapter ix, which has often been taken as Trim's voice, concluding his
oration, but which surely belongs to an intrusive Tristram/Sterne:

————Now I love you for this————and 'tis this delicious mixture within you which makes you dear creatures what you are————and he who hates you for it————all I can say of the matter, is————That he has either a pumkin for his head————or a pippin for his heart,————and whenever he is dissected 'twill be found so.

The expression of affection for his 'creatures', at once bemused and tender – an utterly un-Swiftian dissection – is followed by Susannah's outburst of sympathy for Mrs Shandy – 'I so much pity my mistress.————She will never get the better of it' (V, x) – which fully displaces the egoism of her first reaction. And the servants sit down in a circle to hear Trim tell the pathetic story of Le Fever. In such warmth of heart we see the sentimental affection that many critics read as Sterne's great moral point: by our hearts (and gestures) alone do we free ourselves from the prison of language and establish true community. And in the whole extended episode of comparisons, it may be said, we see what Coleridge first noted as central to Sterne's comic technique: 'in humour the little is made great, and the great little, in order to destroy both, because all is equal in contrast with the infinite' (*CH*, p. 354).

(iv) THE DEATH OF LE FEVER

Sterne thrills the nerves of his readers, wrote Anna Laetitia Barbauld in an earnest nineteenth-century survey of British novelists, 'by light electric touches'. And, altering her metaphor slightly, she adds a comparison that recalls the genealogy of these electric touches: 'He resembles those painters who can give expression to a figure by two or three bold strokes of outline, leaving the imagination to fill up the sketch; the feelings are awakened as really by the story of *Le Fevre*, as by the narrative of Clarissa' (*CH*, p. 332).

We have already noted in an earlier chapter how Le Fever's entrance marks a change of emphasis for *Tristram Shandy*, and a change much applauded by reviewers of Volumes V and VI. 'One of our gentlemen once remarked, in *print* Mr Shandy', intoned Ralph Griffiths in the *Monthly Review*, '————that he thought your excellence lay in the PATHETIC. I think so too. In my opinion, the little story of LE FEVRE has done you more honour than every thing else you have wrote, except your Sermons' (*Letters*, p. 285, n. 3). Pathos, however, refers to the emotional state induced in a spectator or reader by a text; ethos describes the emotional state of the speaker himself and, although everyone testifies to the teary thrill produced in readers by Le Fever's death, no one can be quite sure of the ethos of the speaker who recounts it. Are we in the presence of unaffected grief, such as *Clarissa* inspires and Richardson sincerely felt? Or do we hear the self-conscious, self-mocking voice that arises from the Swiftian rather than the Richardsonian side of Sterne's lineage?

> I wish, said my uncle *Toby*, with a deep sigh,——I wish, *Trim*, I was asleep.
> Your honour, replied the corporal, is too much concerned. (VI, vii)

The evidence for irony lies first in the name Le Fever itself, a personification of an abstraction, a character as bodiless and unreal as brother Bobby, who exists simply as a focal point for emotion. If this is Sterne's way of mocking his own tuberculosis (and perhaps also the fever that killed his father), it is a familiar technique for him, one that we first saw in the mobbed personifications setting upon Yorick in the dark, and one that he will extend brilliantly in the gigantic personification of Death in Volume VII. Further evidence for irony lies in the equivocal portrait of Toby here, at once a hero and a humorist of compassion, for whose every instance of natural goodness of heart Tristram also offers an instance of sublime silliness. When Trim protests, for example, that he had not offered Le Fever money because he had no orders, Toby rebukes him, saying 'Thou didst very right, *Trim*, as a soldier,——but certainly very wrong as a man' (VI, viii). And then a paragraph later, as Trim foretells Le Fever's death, Toby denies it in a scene of Chaplinesque absurdity:

> He will never march, an' please your honour, in this world, said the corporal:——He will march; said my uncle *Toby*, rising up from the side of the bed, with one shoe off:——An' please your honour, said the corporal, he will never march, but to his grave:——He shall march, cried my uncle *Toby*, marching the foot which had a shoe on, though without advancing an inch,——he shall march to his regiment ... A-well-o'day,——do what we can for him, said *Trim*, maintaining his point,——the poor soul will die:——He shall not die, by G——, cried my uncle *Toby*.
> The ACCUSING SPIRIT which flew up to heaven's chancery with the oath, blush'd as he gave it in;——and the RECORDING ANGEL as he wrote it down, dropp'd a tear upon the word, and blotted it out for ever. (VI, viii)

Cross speculated that there may be a source, as yet undiscovered, for the blotted oath.[11] But it is easier to see that Tristram, who had begun this chapter with a contrast between natural and positive law, deftly ends it with a variation and a repetition: Toby's militant charity now reminds us of the contrast between the Old and New Testament laws, the difference between the word (here literally blotted) and the spirit.

Finally, the famous description of the death itself invites an ironical

interpretation. Are we at the mercy of Sterne's manipulation, as
Thackeray would have it? Driven to 'blubber' by hypocritical calculation? Or does Sterne at the end undercut the sentimentality of the scene,
making a joke about that very manipulation?

> Nature instantly ebb'd again,——the film returned to its
> place,——the pulse fluttered——stopp'd——went on——throb'd—
> —stopp'd again——moved——stopp'd—shall I go on?——No. (VI,
> x)

Certainly it is possible to imagine an actor on a stage reducing the whole
moment to slapstick – wriggling, throbbing, flopping, like Falstaff in his
counterfeit death at Shrewsbury. But it is equally possible to hear
Tristram's voice, caught in imitation of Le Fever's last breaths, as
uniformly solemn, gentle even in the last monosyllables. If there is
laughter, it arises from Sterne's irony, his reminder at the unendurable
moment that this death, at least, is only fiction. Such self-regarding
detachment – formerly reserved only for Tristram's unconventional
method of writing – is what finally distinguishes Le Fever's death from
earlier scenes of pathos like Yorick's death and Toby's release of the fly.
And in its 'knowing' sentimentalism we encounter the first hint of a
stylistic habit that is to become the very basis of *A Sentimental Journey*.
   Tristram undercuts this self-conscious melodrama at once, however,
with Yorick's equally self-conscious but light-hearted musical anno-
tations upon his sermons, though in the annotation on the funeral
sermon for Le Fever he finds a typographical equivalent, rooted in time
but free of its restraints, for his own simultaneous presentation and
criticism of the death-bed scene: 'the word was struck through sometime
afterwards (as appears from a different tint of the ink) with a line quite
across it in this manner, ~~BRAVO~~——as if he had retracted, or was
ashamed of the opinion he had once entertained of it' (VI, xi). This
device may well have prompted Sterne to the further typographical
experiments of self-criticism with which he concludes the volume, the
annotated squiggles that represent the plot to date. But before reaching
that playful conclusion, as if still struck by the deeper irony of the
play-soldier Toby at last encountering death, Tristram returns once
more to the theme of real and fictional deaths. Thus, introducing Toby's
apology for his death-dealing profession, he suddenly falls into an
uncharacteristically grave tone and looks forward in dismay 'to that
future and dreaded page' where he must record Toby's death. And while
even here he manages to draw the reader's attention to himself, to his
own familiar difficulties in writing, by far the greater part of his
emotional energy goes selflessly outwards to his 'dear creatures'. The
scene – imagined, recollected and foretold all at once – begins with Trim

laying his sword and scabbard across the coffin, then centres upon Walter, and gives to him a gesture and a wordless speech that matches and overmatches Trim's earlier oration upon death. No silliness, no similes, no system – for once in the novel we hear an unequivocal utterance. And if Tristram reminds us, as he did with Le Fever, that these 'dreaded' pages are only fiction it is a fiction too deeply felt to be false.

⸻But what⸻what is this, to that future and dreaded page, where I look towards the velvet pall, decorated with the military ensigns of thy master⸻the first⸻the foremost of created beings . . . all my father's systems shall be baffled by his sorrows; and, in spight of his philosophy, I shall behold him, as he inspects the lackered plate, twice taking his spectacles from off his nose, to wipe away the dew which nature has shed upon them⸻⸻When I see him cast in the rosemary with an air of disconsolation, which cries through my ears,⸻O *Toby*! in what corner of the world shall I seek thy fellow? (VI, xxv)

'The truly comic', Coleridge reminds us, '*is the blossom of the nettle*' (*CH*, p. 353).

NOTES: CHAPTER 6

1   Wilbur L. Cross, *The Life and Times of Laurence Sterne*, 3rd edn (New Haven, Conn.: Yale University Press, 1929), pp. 253-4.
2   Henri Bergson, *Laughter: An Essay on the Meaning of the Comic*, trans. Cloudesley Brereton and Fred Rothwell (London: Macmillan, 1913), pp. 69–70.
3   John M. Stedmond, *The Comic Art of Laurence Sterne: Convention and Innovation in 'Tristram Shandy' and 'A Sentimental Journey'* (Toronto: University of Toronto Press, 1967), p. 103.
4   James E. Swearingen, *Reflexivity in 'Tristram Shandy': An Essay in Phenomenological Criticism* (New Haven, Conn.: Yale University Press, 1977), pp. 199–203.
5   Richard Lanham, *'Tristram Shandy': The Games of Pleasure* (Berkeley/Los Angeles, Calif: University of California Press, 1973), pp. 106–7.
6   Sigurd Burckhardt, *'Tristram Shandy*'s law of gravity', *ELH*, vol. 28 (1961), pp. 70–88.
7   Swearingen, op. cit., p. 188.
8   Earl R. Wasserman, *The Subtler Language: Critical Readings of Neoclassic and Romantic Poems* (Baltimore, Md: Johns Hopkins University Press, 1959), p. 170.
9   Paul J. Korshin discusses the typological reference in this passage in *Typologies in England, 1650–1820* (Princeton, NJ: Princeton University Press, 1982), pp. 269–70.
10 Eric Rothstein, *Systems of Order and Inquiry in Later Eighteenth-Century Fiction* (Berkeley/Los Angeles, Calif.: University of California Press), p. 94.
11 Cross, op. cit., p. 281.

CHAPTER 7

'Joy of the Worm':
Volumes VII–IX

'I am very ill,' Sterne wrote to his friend Lady Dacre on New Year's Day, 1762, 'having broke a vessel in my lungs ... I believe I shall try if the south of France will not be of service to me' (*Letters*, p. 150).

For several years a crisis had in fact been building in Sterne's health. He had concluded Volume IV of *Tristram Shandy* with the promise to return 'this time twelve-month ... (unless this vile cough kills me in the mean time)'. And his dedication of Volumes V and VI to Lord Spencer had excused them as the best he could produce 'with such bad health as I have'. The decision to go to France therefore arose chiefly from his illness and his dread of another Yorkshire winter, though it may possibly have arisen as well from another kind of coolness, the increasing estrange-ment, noticed by many contemporaries, between Sterne and his wife. With promises of bringing her and their daughter Lydia over to join him later, however, he set out for Paris in January 1762, intending to stay at least several years. France and England were then at war – but the kind of eighteenth-century war that permitted a certain peaceful commerce: he was greeted with wild enthusiasm by the Parisian literati, and he insisted in a letter to David Garrick that 'Tristram was almost as much known here as in London'; yet the truth was that the book had not yet been translated into French (*Letters*, p. 151). What was known in Paris was simply Sterne's celebrity in England. The adulation, in any case, did much for his spirits, and in the midst of dinners, *salons*, audiences he was able to laugh at the occasional rumours of his death reported to him from London. In mid-July, with Elizabeth and Lydia now beside him, he travelled by coach to a rented house in Toulouse.

There is evidence that, after the excitement of Paris, Sterne regarded his disappearance into the French countryside as comparable to his disappearance into the obscurity of the English provinces. A certain restlessness and boredom begin to appear in his correspondence; and as reports of the poor sales – very poor sales – of Volumes V and VI reach him the restlessness turns into a chatty desperation about his future, both literary and financial. There is also evidence that this 'scuffle with death', to adopt one of his phrases, intensified the sentimentalism that had always been present in his book and in his personality (*Letters*, p. 208). 'I laugh 'till I cry,' he had written to Garrick from Paris, 'and in the same tender moments *cry 'till I laugh*' (*Letters*, p. 163). If this is a good description of the new effect he had achieved the previous autumn in the Le Fever episode, it is also an indication of how clear the threat of death had become. 'I Shandy it more than ever,' he had added to Garrick, 'and verily do believe, that by mere Shandeism sublimated by a laughter-loving people, I fence as much against infirmities, as I do by the benefit of air and climate' (*Letters*, p. 163). The reality beneath this hyper-Shandyism becomes explicit in two sobering episodes. First, he suffers at Paris, he tells John Hall-Stevenson, 'the same accident I had at Cambridge, of breaking a vessel in my lungs. It happen'd in the night, and I bled the bed full, and finding in the morning I was likely to bleed to death, I sent immediately for a surgeon' (*Letters*, p. 180). (This is the accident that Tristram describes again in VIII, vi.) And, second, at Toulouse he meets a young Englishman dying of tuberculosis, George Oswald, nurses him on his death-bed, and then attends the autopsy, where it was to be decided whether Oswald had died of the consequences of an old gunshot wound or of consumption. As he describes what he must have known was to be the fate of his own body, Sterne's voice is bleak and objective, without a single Shandian note:

> He was open'd by the Professor of Anatomy in the presence of the attending physician and myself and it appear'd plain the gunshot wound had no connection with his malady, which was entirely in the lungs, the whole of 'em being full of abscesses—the right lobe almost entirely scirrhous and both of 'em adhering to the pleura to the greatest degree that the physician surgeon had ever seen, so that 'twas a miracle how he has lived at all these last 3 months ...[1]

In the midst of these scuffles, he had also begun to write *Tristram Shandy* again. Apparently, however, he wrote *first* our present Volume VIII and only turned to our present Volume VII in the summer or autumn of 1764, when he had left his wife and daughter in France and travelled back to York. Certainly the evidence is that in Toulouse he began the new instalment with the long-promised story of Toby's amours: 'I am now stout and foolish again as a happy man can wish to be—', he tells John Hall-Stevenson in October 1762, 'and am busy playing the fool with my uncle Toby, who I have got soused over head and ears in love' (*Letters*, p. 186). And as late as September 1764 he is telling the same friend that 'I go on, not rapidly, but well enough with my uncle Toby's amour—There is no sitting, and cudgeling ones brains whilst the sun shines bright—'twill be all over in six or seven weeks' (*Letters*, p. 225). Two months later he is writing to his banker in Paris:

You will read as odd a Tour thro' france, as ever was projected or executed by traveller or travell Writer, since the world began—
—tis a laughing good temperd Satyr against Traveling (as puppies travel) . . . (*Letters*, p. 231)

He may have switched to the subject of Volume VII simply because he was working slowly ('cudgeling' his brains) and needed a second volume to satisfy his contract (as in fact the opening paragraph of Volume VII suggests); or he may have decided to put to comic use the notes towards a more serious travel book that he had evidently been collecting throughout his stay in France (see *Letters*, p. 198). The new instalment opens, in any case, with the most extraordinary, the bravest of all Sterne's fantasies.

(i) VOLUME VII: THE 'TEETH OF TIME'

The style of the first third of Volume VII crosses back and forth between hysterical surrealism and exhausted dullness. The opening chapter establishes the first effect, with its Bergmanesque anecdote of 'DEATH' knocking at Tristram's door – wonderfully painted by Thomas Patch in 1766 – and Tristram's Rabelaisian leap towards France: '*Allons!* said I; the post boy gave a crack with his whip——off I went like a cannon, and in half a dozen bounds got into *Dover*' (VII, i). This explosive departure threatens to extend the geography of the novel to its ultimate limits: 'I'll scamper away . . . to the world's end' – a phrase that both Sterne and T. S. Eliot took from Psalm 72 in the Book of Common Prayer, and one that suggests the apocalyptic scale of the confrontation. How can we imagine this knocking 'DEATH' as anything but colossal? The 'crack' of the post boy's whip only intensifies our sense of sudden chaos, and it leads at once to the most disjointed of Sternian sketches – the voices in a ship's cabin, tossed in and out of hearing by the agitated indecision of the wind:

Madam! how is it with you? Undone! undone! un——O! undone! sir——What the first time?——No, 'tis the second, third, sixth, tenth time, sir,——hey-day——what a trampling over head!——hollo! cabin boy! what's the matter——
    'The wind chopp'd about! s'Death!——then I shall meet him full in the face.
    What luck!——'tis chopp'd about again, master——O the devil chop it——
    Captain, quoth she, for heaven's sake, let us get ashore. (VII, ii)

This is imaginative prose of the greatest originality, lashing itself into wounded motion, daring us to fill in its blank dashes, rendering Sterne's usual bawdy insinuations ('undone') in the bizarre context of a howling storm and a baroque flight from a skeletal personification of death. Until Dickens' late experiments in narrative voice, nothing in English fiction will come near the startling brilliance of such a passage. Or this:

> Crack, crack——crack, crack——crack, crack——so this is Paris! quoth I (continuing in the same mood)——and this is Paris!——humph!——Paris! cried I, repeating the name the third time——
> The first, the finest, the most brilliant——
> ——The streets however are nasty;
> But it looks, I suppose, better than it smells——crack, crack——crack, crack——What a fuss thou makest!——as if it concern'd the good people to be inform'd, That a man with pale face, and clad in black, had the honour to be driven into Paris at nine o'clock at night, by a postilion in a tawny yellow jerkin turned up with red calamanco——crack, crack——crack, crack——crack, crack——I wish thy whip——
> ——But 'tis the spirit of thy nation; so crack——crack on. (VII, xvii)

And yet, although its first lines carry us headlong over the city's pavements, whirled through Paris as we are whirled through Tristram's hysteria, the passage soon limps to a mechanical trot: 'Ho! 'tis the time of sallads.——O rare! sallad and soup——soup and sallad——sallad and soup, *encore*——' And, at its worst, the desperate repetition of the postilion's whip becomes merely pert, a cheeky, witless bit of plagiarism, not from Rabelais or Burton, but from a stagecoach guide:

> I wish I was at Abbeville, quoth I, were it only to see how they card and spin——so off we set.
> *de Montreuil a Nampont-poste et demi de Nampont* à Bernay——poste
> de Bernay a Nouvion——poste
> de Nouvion a ABBEVILLE poste
>
> ——but the carders and spinners were all gone to bed. (VII, x)

Sterne cautions in his motto that Volume VII is not a digression from his work, 'but is the work itself'. It is hard to see how that is true of the story, which takes place far from Shandy Hall and its inhabitants, but it is easier to see that the remarkable stylistic traits of the volume are really those of the rest of the book writ large. Or, rather, speeded up, like trick photography. In its hectic desperation we only encounter, at the highest pitch, the same restlessness and desperation that more subtly underlie his 'normal' prose.

We encounter a new theme as well in Volume VII, for the satire in the early chapters against travel writers – a holdover from Sterne's original plan perhaps – leads by stages to a general satiric opposition of form and energy, measurement and vitality. Thus, when he has arrived in Calais, Tristram drops for a moment the fantasy of a flight from death in order to parody guidebooks and pedantic tourists, especially those who report and calculate the dimensions of every monument. The altar of the church at Calais stands nearly sixty feet high; there are 420 distinct families in the suburbs; the town square actually extends forty feet longer from east to west and, strictly speaking, ought not to be called a square. As Death pounds after him, a stage or two behind, he enters Montreuil and there pauses again to mock mathematics and to study a principle of life: the innkeeper's handsome daughter, who had been eighteen months in Amiens and six in Paris, who drops a dozen loops in her knitting while Tristram stares, and who, despite the precision of these numbers, cannot be rendered except by an artist. Tristram would draw her in all her proportions for us. '――But your worships chuse rather that I give you the length, breadth, and perpendicular height of the great parish church' (VII, ix).

Such petrifactions will continue in their present form for fifty years, he adds, 'if the belief in *Christ* continues so long'.

――but he who measures thee, *Janatone*, must do it now――thou carriest the principles of change within thy frame; and considering the chances of a transitory life, I could not answer for thee a moment; e'er twice twelve months are pass'd and gone, thou mayest grow out like a pumkin, and lose thy shapes――or, thou mayest go off like a flower, and lose thy beauty――nay, thou mayest go off like a hussy――and lose thyself. (VII, ix)

There is a discernible tension here and elsewhere in the volume between Christian and pagan values – Tristram will praise Jupiter and other heathen gods and will end the volume with a pagan dance – but this derives chiefly from Sterne's own anti-Catholic prejudices, jolted to the surface as he tours France. The major tension is obviously still between vitality and measurement, presented as absolutely as Blakian contraries. Yet into this tension, we see, Sterne's pervasive theme of time has now entered. For time represents a deadly measurement, an implacable mathematical form that must be evaded, and the changes that Tristram imagines taking place, in time, in Janatone's 'frame' as in George Oswald's, only parallel the changes Sterne himself has felt and feared since the onslaught of illness had driven him abroad. She carries the 'principles' of her own mortality. She will 'go off like a flower'. But Tristram adds in a few pages more that he, too, is rushing through 'jovial times' – 'I who must be cut short in the midst of my days, and taste no more of 'em than what I borrow from my imagination' (VII, xiv). From this point of view those lists of traveller's 'debts' paid and collected, streets in Paris and stagecoach distances in the country are more than Rabelaisian padding: they belong to the rigid order of calculation and computation that suddenly threatens to cut Tristram short in the midst of his days. And likewise from this point of view the famous speculation about novelistic time belongs to wish-fulfilment as much as to literary theory: Tristram manipulates and masters time, actually toys with time, as no one ever can, dividing himself into parts and slipping away before its grip can close around him and deliver him up to that grim ally pacing two stages back:

> I have brought myself into such a situation, as no traveller ever stood before me; for I am this moment walking across the market-place of Auxerre with my father and my uncle Toby, in our way back to dinner——and I am this moment also entering Lyons with my post-chaise broke into a thousand pieces——and I am moreover this moment in a handsome pavillion built by Pringello, upon the banks of the Garonne . . . (VII, xxviii)

Yet, if the closeness of death, as Martin Price observes, is clearly the cause of Tristram's new commitment in Volume VII to what is 'intensely and authentically alive', that intensity frequently gives the impression of being willed, deliberately summoned to repel the cold authority of numbers and forms.[2] And too often the will falters, vitality flags. Hence the wild prose sometimes sinks into exhaustion; hence, too, Sterne's more familiar themes darken under the pressure of his illness. The theme of impotence, for example, comically presented to this point in Walter's irritation at lust and in Tristram's involuntary circumcision, now grows poignantly confessional. Tristram moves from a calculation of the value of his post-chaise to his 'usual method of book-keeping, at least with the disasters of life': '——Do, my dear Jenny, tell the world for me, how I behaved under one, the most oppressive of its kind which could befall me as a man, proud, as he ought to be of his manhood——' (VII, xxix). And he closes with a flurry of numbers and quantities that delimit and ration his vitality:

> ——I'll go into Wales for six weeks, and drink goat's-whey——and I'll gain seven years longer life for the accident. For which reason I think myself inexcusable, for blaming Fortune so often as I have done, for pelting me all my life long, like an ungracious duchess, as I call'd

her, with so many small evils: surely if I have any cause to be angry with her, 'tis that she has not sent me great ones——a score of good cursed, bouncing losses, would have been as good as a pension to me.

——One of a hundred a year, or so, is all I wish——I would not be at the plague of paying land tax for a larger.

In the same way, Lippius' clock, associated like all clocks in the novel with Mrs Shandy's question, now decays and finally stops, to Tristram's puzzlement: 'of all things in the world, I understand the least of mechanism' (VII, xxx).

When sexuality does not deteriorate into mechanical impotence, it none the less fails in other ways. The two lovers Amanda and Amandus 'both drop down dead for joy' (VII, xxxi). The tomb of the abbey of St Germain, which Toby, Trim and Walter visit, contains the remains of grammatically putative lovers, St Maximus and St Maxima, who came to touch his bones: 'And what did she get by it? said my uncle Toby——What does any woman get by it? said my father——MARTYRDOME; replied the young Benedictine' (VII, xxvii). Even the obscurely salacious abbess of Andouïllets (little sausages) suffers inexpressible frustrations from a 'stiff joint' and a 'white swelling' (pregnancy?) and falls into a disrepair that can only be relieved by the hot baths of Bourbon. As every reader quickly understands, however, Sterne's indecency in this episode is general and illogical. The innumerable insinuations do not add up to a coherent image or conceit, as in a metaphysical poem. The hilarious conclusion, moreover, once again pits form against vitality, words against meaning – its ultimate source may be the splitting of syllables in Swift's *Tale* (pp. 83–4) – as the nuns attempt to evade sin and unwittingly enact thereby a scene of breathless copulation:

Abbess, Bou- bou- bou- bou- bou
Margarita, ——ger, ger, ger, ger, ger,.
    Quicker still, cried Margarita.
Fou, fou, fou, fou, fou, fou, fou, fou, fou.
    Quicker still, cried Margarita.
Bou, bou, bou, bou, bou, bou, bou, bou, bou.
    Quicker still——God preserve me! said the abbess . . . (VII, xxv)[3]

It is worth adding that, while this elaborate joke mocks Catholicism and rigid scholastic ideas of interpretation, it also replicates in miniature the larger theme of motion and progression that has dominated the volume from the first: they are trying to make their mule move, trying to set themselves in motion just as Tristram is. Usually, of course, the motion that interests Sterne is internal, mental rather than physical, vitality located in the mind and far from the intractability of forms and numbers.

Thus the whirlwind travelogue of France begins with 'realistic' street
names and measurements, but grows progressively more subjective,
until Tristram finally declares that as a tourist he prefers a dull, extensive
plain to anything, for his imagination can always transform the plain into
a richer unreality: 'I was always in company', he says of his slow
procession across the rural south of France, 'and with great variety too;
and as my mule loved society as much as myself, and had some proposals
always on his part to offer to every beast he met——I am confident we
could have passed through Pall-Mall or St. James's-Street for a month
together, with fewer adventures——and seen less of human nature' (VII,
xliii). And, as he says this, miraculously another transformation occurs,
whether by chance or by a willed imagination we never learn: a beautiful
peasant girl leads him from his mule (which had just 'made a dead point')
into a pagan dance, where sexuality revives ('They are running at the ring
of pleasure'), social forms collapse and time yields: 'Tie me up this tress
instantly, said Nannette, putting a piece of string into my hand——It
taught me to forget I was a stranger——The whole knot fell
down——We had been seven years acquainted.' A fantasy of life drives
away a fantasy of death with a gesture and a word:

> VIVA LA JOIA!
> FIDON LA TRISTESSA!

The frenzied motion of the prose style has become the harmonious
motion of the dance, and the dance itself becomes the surrealistic
counterpart of those hectic 'bounds' with which his whole flight had
begun:

> Then 'tis time to dance off, quoth I; so changing only partners and
> tunes, I danced it away from Lunel to Montpellier——from thence to
> Pescnas, Beziers——I danced it along through *Narbonne*, Carcasson,
> and Castle Naudairy, till at last I danced myself into Perdrillo's
> pavillion ...

(ii)   IN WHICH NOTHING IS CONCLUDED

Despite the fact that they were written almost two years apart, Volumes
VIII and IX display a remarkably symmetrical structure, for in them the
main love-story of Toby and the Widow Wadman is paralleled by no
fewer than six other romances, all of which serve as comic reflection or
commentary on Toby's siege.

There is, for example, the parallel relationship of Walter and Mrs
Shandy ('romance' will be too strong a word), who stroll past the
Widow's house as Toby and Trim approach it, studying the scene with

something of the complacent voyeurism known to every married couple. Mrs Shandy, moreover, although she wishes 'to look through the key-hole out of *curiosity*', is now described to us as a woman of temperate, indeed unheated sexuality, like Toby in the density of her innocence (VIII, xxxv); her eye is the very opposite of Mrs Wadman's, which Tristram compares to a cannon: hers is 'a thin, blue, chill, pellucid chrystal with all its humours so at rest, the least mote or speck of desire might have been seen at the bottom of it, had it existed——it did not' (IX, i). At the same time, Walter functions more than ever as Toby's opposite, the Man of Irritation rather than the Man of Feeling. He invariably calls the tender passions by the term 'ass' (which Tristram unconvincingly distinguishes from hobbyhorse); and when he comes to write a letter of advice to Toby on courting a woman he recommends evacuations and purges before seeing the beloved, as well as a number of stomach-palling refrigerant herbs. 'Love,' he tells the company assembled in the parlour, appropriating and grossly perverting Toby's military imagery, 'is not so much a SENTIMENT as a SITUATION, into which a man enters, as my brother Toby would do, into a *corps*' (VIII, xxxiv).

Likewise, there are the two parallel courtships in which Trim plays a part, with the sympathetic Beguine and the pliable Bridget, and the courtship of his brother Tom and the widow in Lisbon, conducted according to the semiotics of sausages. And there are finally the encounter between Tristram and Maria and the final (perhaps climactic) encounter between Walter Shandy's bull and Obadiah's cow. Like the seventh volume, which has the story of the abbess of Andouïllets at its centre, each of these volumes has a pivotal counter-affair to Toby's at its centre, reflecting and revising a major theme: the Beguine in Volume VIII also pursues a courtship centred upon a soldier's wound, and Maria in Volume IX sees Tristram's sentimental eroticism collapse into goatish lust.

The two volumes similarly display a striking coherence of imagery and motif, unifying them to an unusual extent. We read, for example, at the beginning of Volume VIII of Tristram's increased frustration in writing ('I declare, I do not recollect any one opinion or passage of my life, where my understanding was more at a loss to make ends meet, and torture the chapter I had been writing, to the service of the chapter following it, than in the present case': VIII, vi); and this is no doubt a truthful reflection of his difficulties in Toulouse, where the volume was probably begun, and the slowness of composition he complained of when he had returned to England. He explains at other points that he has fallen 'into a cold unmetaphorical vein of infamous writing' (IX, xiii), for which his usual remedy is shaving; he leaves two chapters blank in Volume IX – the contraries of his blank pages in Volume I – and returns to write them later; in VIII, xix, he seems to mock Imlac's speech in *Rasselas* on the

qualifications of a poet, offering a satanic paean to the universal knowledge of a soldier; he later tells Jenny that he writes more and more
quickly, as he feels the rush of time about him; and he confesses his 'want
of powers' as he describes Toby's courtship, so that he must pause for a
brief invocation to the spirit of humour that guided Cervantes (IX, xxiv).
And all these authorial frustrations find their parallels in the story itself,
as Trim tries over and over to tell the story of the King of Bohemia or,
most obviously, the Widow tries to make Toby tell the true story of his
wound.

Some motifs appear only briefly, like the theme of 'preservation',
which takes its beginning in Tristram's complaints of ill-health and runs
for a few chapters, concluding first in the marvellous Miltonic image of
Toby subjecting the 'vast empire of time and all its abysses at his feet'
(VIII, xix) and finally in the glance Tristram steals at 'Posterity', asking
rhetorically 'what has this book done more than the Legation of Moses,
or the Tale of a Tub, that it may not swim down the gutter of Time along
with them' (IX, viii)? The theme of liberty, touched upon briefly in the
contrast between France and England in volume VII, now returns, not
only in the humorous context of marriage bonds – Trim flourishes his
stick across the page to demonstrate (IX, iv) – but also in the touching
discussion of Negro slavery two chapters later. (The subject first arose in
a letter to Sterne from a freed slave named Ignatius Sancho, who
suggested that he treat it in a future volume with his inimitable sensibility: *Letters*, pp. 282–3. The result is a tribute both to the generosity of
Sterne's spirit and the flexibility of his novel.) A more extended and
sentimental treatment of political liberty will appear in Volume II of *A
Sentimental Journey*, especially the episode of the caged starling, suggesting how much his stay in France had impressed the theme upon him.

Other motifs run through both volumes from first to last. The imagery
of clothing, for example, intermittent in earlier volumes, now takes on
considerable importance, perhaps reflecting the renewed influence of
Swift, whose *Tale* Sterne explicitly mentions for the first time and whose
Journal to Stella had just appeared; perhaps simply reflecting Sterne's
interest in the more general theme of clothing that serves so much
eighteenth-century literature as an image of what is at once expressive
and mute, human and artificial. Certainly, Tristram begins Volume VIII
by referring to 'slits in petticoats', especially seductive if 'unsew'd up'; he
speaks of Mrs Wadman's inhibiting nightshift, his own furred cap,
Trim's Montero cap and, most elaborately, Toby's courting costume –
crumpled wig, ill-fitting coat, thin scarlet breeches 'unripp'd by the
taylor between the legs' (IX, ii) – and he describes in detail his own
writing costume, 'a purple jerkin and yellow pair of slippers' (IX, i), as
well as that of the Archbishop of Benevento (a severe and priestly
purple). With this motif he also establishes another of those sympathetic

links between himself and Toby, as he holds up his own breeches, likewise piteously 'rent' (IX, xxiv). And he repeats with a variation his conviction that mind and body are inseparably joined like jerkin and jerkin's lining: 'A man cannot dress, but his ideas get cloath'd at the same time' (IX, xiii). Inevitably, Sterne's controlling theme of the arbitrary character of language appears through both volumes, too, in a renewed intensity of sexual innuendo ('By all that is hirsute and gashly! I cry, taking off my furr'd cap': VIII, xi), in the failed communication of so many lovers, in the act of interpretation that accompanies every utterance: 'Now there are such an infinitude of notes, tunes, cants, chants, airs, looks, and accents with which the word *fiddlestick* may be pronounced . . .' (IX, xxv). The Widow Wadman even puts into practice, unknowingly, Walter's theory of auxiliary verbs, as she conjugates desire from blush to lust:

> '*L—d! I cannot look at it——*
> *What would the world say if I look'd at it?*
> *I should drop down, if I look'd at it——*
> *I wish I could look at it——*
> *There can be no sin in looking at it.*
> *——I will look at it.*' (IX, xx)

(Sigurd Burckhardt claims, with more wit than persuasion, that Sterne means us to recall the 'white bare' of Walter's example.)[4]

Finally, the 'want of powers' Tristram bemoans in regard to his writing has its counterpart in the frequent references to sexual impotence that characterize both volumes. This is by no means a new theme – we have just encountered it at its most poignant in Volume VII – but it reappears now in the story of the bull, in the convoluted analogy concerning men who carry poles ('weavers, gardeners, and gladiators': VIII, v), in Walter's embarrassment at discovering that it is the first Sunday of the month, and in numerous references to male size:

> It is a great pity——but 'tis certain from every day's observation of man, that he may be set on fire like a candle, at either end——provided there is a sufficient wick standing out; if there is not——there's an end of the affair; and if there is——by lighting it at the bottom, as the flame in that case has the misfortune generally to put out itself——there's an end of the affair again. (VIII, xv)

But most of all the question of impotence occurs in the Widow's curiosity about Toby's wound, which subverts the conventional image we have of a soldier's prowess and reminds us once more of the fundamental softness of Toby's character. Tristram's own answer to the Widow's question is so roundabout and evasive that many readers have not understood his declaration that Toby was in all respects fit for marriage; and an unfortunate misprint in Work's edition – 'defended' for 'defeated' – has prolonged the confusion: 'The DONATION was not defeated by my uncle Toby's wound' (IX, xxii). In any case, hardly has Tristram made his announcement than he remarks that 'this last article was somewhat apocryphal' and reverts to his jokes about empty bottles and trunk-hose.

But the greatest coherence in these two volumes comes obviously from the dominant character of Toby. His public, of course, had declared at once for the sentimental soldier, and Sterne himself had confessed as early as 1761 that 'so much am I delighted with my uncle Toby's imaginary character, that I am become an enthusiast' (*Letters*, p. 143). By the time he comes to write Volumes VIII and IX, his enthusiasm has placed Toby at the literal and figurative heart of the book and led Tristram to declare (misleadingly, perhaps) that he has 'all along been hastening towards this part of it . . . well knowing it to be the choicest morsel of what I had to offer to the world' (IX, xxiv). As Toby assumes his central role, however, and begins to collide with the outside world of the Widow, we are in a position to identify one further part of his appeal to both reader and author. Beyond his sentimental saintliness, that is, and his wonderful hobbyhorse of siegecraft, we now see Toby's character as representing a unique success, and a success in the very struggle that Tristram has all along been losing: more than any other character in the novel, he has achieved a sense of the real.

His games, of course, permit that success. As we have already noted, Toby's engrossment in them has managed to block out all knowledge of what we ordinarily call reality – the nature of men and women, the destructive horror of war – and it has also blinkered the single medium by which we usually apprehend such reality, so that for him language has meaning only so far as it concerns siegecraft: on nearly all other subjects his mind goes suddenly opaque, his lips pucker into 'Lillabulero'. Yet paradoxically this is an all-absorbing unreality: for Toby it is a world. 'Something in which the individual can become unselfconsciously engrossed', observes Erving Goffman, 'is something that can become real to him.' Furthermore, its hold on him is actually strengthened by the increasing importance of Trim in these last volumes; for, as Goffman adds, '*Joint* engrossment in something with others reinforces the reality carved out by the individual's attention'. Trim not only shares Toby's games completely – co-operating perfectly to extend them to the Widow – but also performs his part with an unending courtesy that seems to validate their reality. Whether they debate the placement of toy cannon, reminisce about past campaigns or collaborate on a love-story, Trim participates with such deference, such delicacy of etiquette, like two breaths drawn in unison, that Toby's world expands for a moment in imperial fantasy, and all but the most obstinate observer smiles in suspended disbelief ('Now what can their two noodles be about? cried my father to my mother': IX, viii). It is to such 'flimsy rules' of courtesy, Goffman insists,

> and not to the unshaking character of the external world, that we owe our unshaking sense of realities. To be at ease in a situation is to be properly subject to these rules, entranced by the meanings they generate and stabilize; to be ill at ease means that one is ungrasped by immediate reality and that one loosens the grasp others have of it. To be awkward or unkempt, to talk or move wrongly, is to be a dangerous giant, a destroyer of worlds.[5]

And, if these sociological concepts explain something about the source of Toby's attractive ease and benevolence, they also suggest why such ease and benevolence escape Walter – who is a born destroyer of worlds – and even Tristram, whose repeated attempts to draw your worships into his conversation are all inevitably one-sided, unvalidating. His absorption in his hobbyhorse, after all, the world of his book, is never so complete as Toby's; and his sense of language is more treacherous, his wounds more recent. Virtually alone in the annals of fiction, Toby is an artist without an ego.

If we return to literary categories, however, it is easy to see that Toby so dominates the final volumes because Sterne has now wrought him into by far the most endearingly Quixotic figure in the novel: humorously 'mad' like the Don in his obsession with siegecraft; but strikingly sane, like the Don, in his compassionate fellow-feeling. It may well be, as Lanham suggests, that Sterne is showing us how such purity of feeling can be bought only at the cost of obsession, for it is true that Toby's remarkable ability to love his fellow-creatures depends ironically upon his games of war, which drain away from consciousness all traces of natural aggression (a term that includes sexual love).[6] But his moral point, if it is there at all, appears firmly subordinated to Tristram's sheer delight in manipulating the contradictions of Toby's character, in pulling the two sides back and forth like the bellows of a concertina. The analogy between soldiering and courtship at the very centre of Sterne's joke is continually stated, reversed and mocked as the soldier Toby, in the very process of describing a siege, finds himself besieged and sapped:

> When the attack was advanced to this point;——the world will naturally enter into the reasons of Mrs Wadman's next stroke of generalship——which was, to take my uncle Toby's tobacco-pipe out of his hand as soon as she possibly could; which, under one pretence or other, but generally that of pointing more distinctly at some redoubt or

breast-work in the map, she would effect before my uncle Toby (poor soul!) had well march'd above half a dozen toises with it. (VIII, xvi)

And, abstractly put, this is simply the comedy of sublimation that we have already mentioned in our discussion of Swift, the 'interchange-ability of sex and war' that Burckhardt calls the 'chief structural meta-phor of the novel'.[7]

What Burckhardt is pointing towards will be better understood as the interchangeability of sex and words – an indecent, waggish metaphorical comedy not to be compared finally with Swift's continual discoveries of corruption in both sex and language and his intensity of revulsion from it. Yet even waggery has its profounder implications and can incorpo-rate, with Sternian grace, the most corrosively serious of Swiftian themes. Such implications emerge plainly in one last (and lesser) paral-lelism: the three love-affairs that centre upon the single event of a woman's reaching forward to touch her lover's ... 'it'. For this event is obviously the whole joke behind Trim's long story of the Beguine (a joke Diderot was to appropriate in *Jacques le fataliste*): 'The more she rubb'd, and the longer strokes she took——the more the fire kindled in my veins——till at length, by two or three strokes longer than the rest——my passion rose to the highest pitch——I seiz'd her hand——' (VIII, xxii). It is also the cause of the Widow Wadman's blushes when Toby offers to show where he was wounded: 'You shall lay your finger upon the place——said my uncle Toby' (IX, xx). And it is shamelessly the means by which Trim's brother Tom captures the Jew's widow's heart as he helps her to make sausages:

First, by taking hold of the ring of the sausage whilst she stroked the forced meat down with her hand——then by cutting the strings into proper lengths, and holding them in his hand, whilst she took them out one by one——then, by putting them across her mouth, that she might take them out as she wanted them——and so on from little to more, till at last he adventured to tie the sausage himself, whilst she held the snout. (IX, vii)

In these episodes language always replaces sexual action, whether from the beginning, as in Tom's *double entendres*, or just at the last moment, as in Toby's order for the map or his conclusion to Trim's story of the Beguine's ascending hand: 'And then, thou clapped'st it to thy lips, Trim, said my uncle Toby——and madest a speech' (VIII, xxii). We have already observed how such verbal laying on of hands, teasing and disembodied, seems evidently central to Sterne's own tremulous sexual-ity and how it figures throughout *Tristram Shandy* and *A Sentimental Journey* as well. But after so many noses, whiskers and cabbages, so many frustrations and teases, perhaps we can conclude by saying that in these last instances of touching we see more clearly than ever that, while sex and language represent ways of communication for Sterne, both of them are flawed in the very nature of things: by the imperfection of words, as Locke has it, and by the imperfections of the failing masculine body. (Paradoxically, only a desexualized and inarticulate person like Toby can achieve genuine, if limited communication, as he does with Trim and Le Fever.) The sexual impotence that hovers over the Shandy males 'like a shadow', in Robert Alter's phrase, therefore takes on a deeply permanent serious meaning: it is an image of the greater and bleaker incapacity for connection that has accompanied Tristram in all his bouts with death and chance. The very 'precariousness . . . of that sexual connection itself,' Alter says, 'its fleetingness and concomitant disappointments, are emblems of the frailty and brevity of human life, with its astonishing variety of frustrations and illusory fulfillments'.[8] In such a context Walter's protest against sexuality and on behalf of human dignity has a certain unexpected force, as for once he transforms theory into idealism:

> That provision should be made for continuing the race of so great, so exalted and godlike a Being as man——I am far from denying——but philosophy speaks freely of every thing; and therefore I still think and do maintain it to be a pity, that it should be done by means of a passion which bends down the faculties, and turns all the wisdom, contemplations, and operations of the soul backwards——a passion, my dear, continued my father, addressing himself to my mother, which couples and equals wise men with fools, and makes us come out of caverns and hiding-places more like satyrs and four-footed beasts than men. (IX, xxxiii)

The subject to which we have thus returned is, of course, the nature of human nature, that abiding eighteenth-century preoccupation. If Sterne's were a tragic vision, we might expect that his characters would have assembled at the end of Volume IX to face some grimmer infertility than that of Walter's bull, and some deeper insight than that their lives amount to no more than a cock and bull story. Tragic action, as Maynard Mack has beautifully said, follows a 'curve of self-discovery' and represents life in the form of experience and consequences. But comic action, he adds, follows a 'curve of self-exposure' – a dangerous phrase to place near Sterne's hands, I know – and represents life in the form of spectacle.[9] It is probably idle to ask if Sterne did indeed finish *Tristram Shandy*. Common sense tells us that, although he may well have aimed first at concluding with Toby's amours, he might easily have continued in later years with new instalments, new variations on his infinitely adaptable themes: human nature was not likely in the meantime to alter its gleeful and impervious absurdity, its dependence upon language for an apprehension of reality or its imprisonment within a high-handed, long-nosed body. At any point he could have unfrozen the last frame of the novel and set his characters bobbing and talking again across the vast abysses of Walter's drawing-room. What he could not have done was to have rendered them rational and tragic.

The last fifteen months of Sterne's life were marked by periods of wretched weakness of health, with some briefer, hopeful remissions: 'I am ill—very ill—Yet I feel my Existence Strongly, and something like revelation along with it, which tells, I shall not dye—but live ... (*Letters*, p. 416). Volume IX of *Tristram Shandy* appeared in January of 1767 to generally tepid reviews, most commentators remonstrating that the Shandian jokes had by now gone on far too long and become flat and stale. Sterne seems to have shrugged them off, however, losing himself first in the feverish affair with Eliza and then, through the autumn, in the writing of *A Sentimental Journey*, which was published in two small volumes on 27 February 1768. This new venture was greeted by warm applause for its delicacy and originality, even from many of those who had disliked *Tristram Shandy*. But Sterne lived to enjoy the applause for barely three weeks. At four o'clock in the afternoon on 18 March 1768, a young footman in London named John MacDonald, sent to inquire after his health, witnessed the last, and not the least dramatic, of Sterne's confrontations with the skeletal personification of Time who had all along been turning the pages almost as fast as he could write them. 'The mistress opened the door; I inquired how he did. She told me to go up to the nurse. I went into the room, and he was just a-dying. I waited ten minutes; but in five he said, "*Now it is come.*" He put up his hand as if to stop a blow, and died in a minute.'[10]

NOTES: CHAPTER 7

1 Archibald B. Shepperson, 'Yorick as ministering angel', *Virginia Quarterly Review*, vol. 30 (1954), pp. 54–66.
2 Martin Price, *To the Palace of Wisdom: Studies in Order and Energy from Dryden to Blake* (Garden City, NY: Doubleday, 1964), p. 339.
3 Richard A. Lanham offers an excellent analysis of this whole passage in '*Tristram Shandy*': *The Games of Pleasure* (Berkeley/Los Angeles, Calif.: University of California Press, 1973), pp. 116–24.
4 Sigurd Burckhardt, '*Tristram Shandy*'s law of gravity', *ELH*, vol. 28 (1961), p. 84.
5 Erving Goffman, *Encounters: Two Studies in the Sociology of Interaction* (Indianapolis, Ind.: Bobbs-Merrill, 1961), pp. 80–1.
6 Lanham, op.cit., pp. 78–88.
7 Burckhardt, op.cit., p.82.
8 Robert Alter, '*Tristram Shandy* and the game of love', *American Scholar*, vol. 37 (1968), pp. 322–3.
9 Maynard Mack, 'Introduction to *Joseph Andrews* by Henry Fielding', in his *Col-*

lected in Himself: Essays Critical, Biographical, and Bibliographical on Pope and Some of His Contemporaries (Newark, Del.: University of Delaware Press, 1982), p. 34.

10   John MacDonald, *Memoirs of an Eighteenth-Century Footman, 1745–1779* (London: George Routledge, 1927), p. 92.

CHAPTER 8

Critical History

It is tempting to offer a pseudo-Shandian account of Sterne's critical history: snake-like squiggles to describe the peaks and valleys of reputation; black pages for the great Victorian disapproval; entirely blank – or perhaps mottled – pages where twentieth-century academics sketch philosophic doodles. For *Tristram Shandy* from the start has endured the most contradictory and bewildering of fortunes: by turns denounced and acclaimed, spurned and outrageously copied, its author sometimes England's second Rabelais, the predecessor of Joyce and Woolf, sometimes merely, in Bishop Warburton's trenchant phrase, 'the idol of the higher mob' (*CH*, p. 205). Despite the vehement complexity of response, however, it is fair to say that Sterne's contemporaries defined at the novel's first appearance virtually all of the issues that were to dominate later discussion. Until the rise of modern academic criticism in the early twentieth century, the major questions each generation of readers addressed all concerned in one guise or another Sterne's indecency, his originality or his sentiment.

(i) CONTEMPORARY

'Oh *Sterne*! thou art scabby,' exclaimed an anonymous pamphleteer in 1760, 'and such is the leprosy of thy mind that it is not to be cured like the leprosy of the body, by dipping nine times in the river Jordan. Thy prophane history of *Tristram Shandy* is as it were anti-gospel, and seems to have been penned by the hand of Antichrist himself' (*CH*, p. 100). An extreme and stupid attack, but it communicates vividly the kind of censure Sterne incurred from those of his contemporaries who took offence at the salacious joking of his novel and even more at the fact that it was actually 'penned', not by the Antichrist, but by a clergyman. Lady Bradshaigh, for example, seemed to swell in disapproval as she described the book to Samuel Richardson (who in turn dismissed it as 'execrable'): 'Upon the whole, I think the performance, mean, *dirty Wit*. I may add *scandalous*, considering the *Man*' (*CH*, p. 90). Others like Samuel Johnson and Horace Walpole stayed aloof from the book, critical of its indecency but ultimately bored by what they saw as its tediousness and predictability. In a number of *The Citizen of the World* in 1760 (Letter liii), alluding clearly to the vogue of *Tristram Shandy*, Oliver Goldsmith combined both criticisms in a lengthy attack upon bawdry and mechanical pertness in comic writing.

Against these, of course, can be set the genuine enthusiasm that greeted Sterne's early volumes and raised him to such heights of celebrity. Many reviewers then not only praised Sterne for his humour, but also expressed a certain pride in tracing the lineage of an English wit back to Rabelais and Cervantes, acknowledged at once as Sterne's models and peers. Other reviewers tended to stress Sterne's absolute originality and could even point to the tribute of imitation already paid *him* in such opportunistic volumes as *The Life and Opinions of Miss Sukey Shandy* (1760), *Jeremiah Kunastrokius* (1760), *Christopher Wagstaff* (1762) and even *Yorick's Meditations* (1760). Of such enthusiasts, moreover, a growing number found his originality to lie less in his wild, digressive humour than in his delicacy and pathos, particularly after the story of Le Fever and the expansion of Toby's role. Indeed, this sentimentality – this power to penetrate the human heart, as it was usually phrased – was frequently taken as the sign of Sterne's real seriousness of purpose, and led many readers to agree completely with his own insistence that his novel was a moral work: 'The writings of Sterne, particularly,' Thomas Jefferson implausibly told a friend, 'form the best course of morality that ever was written' (*CH*, p. 216). Still other readers appeared unaffected by the softening moral effect of Sterne's sentiment and identified the novel instead as primarily a satire, even as a Juvenalian satire. Sterne's response to such variety of criticism is to be found partly in the successive volumes of the novel itself, where he upbraids his reviewers with no little asperity, and partly in his letters, where he defends himself more earnestly to friendly critics like Warburton. His longest defence comes near the end of his life, in a much-quoted reply to an admiring American correspondent who had sent him a walking-stick as a gift: 'Your walking-stick is in no sense more *shandaic*', he tells Dr John Eustace,

> than in that of its having *more handles than one*——The parallel breaks only in this, that in using the stick, every one will take the handle which suits his convenience. In *Tristram Shandy*, the handle is taken which suits their passions, their ignorance or sensibility. There is so little true feeling in the *herd* of the *world*, that I wish I could have got an act of parliament, when the books first appear'd, 'that none but wise men should look into them.' It is too much to write books and find heads to understand them. (*Letters*, p. 411)

Continental readers of the eighteenth century showed the same disposition to take the handle that suited their convenience. Although the French had lionized Sterne when he visited Paris in 1762, afterwards the anonymous reviewers of *Tristram Shandy* in the literary journals tended to be censorious of his ribaldry and baffled by his flights of humour, which they declared typically and mysteriously English. Voltaire and Diderot, however, often praised his wit and his morality, and Diderot openly copied episodes from *Tristram Shandy* at the opening and close of his own novel *Jacques le fataliste*, evidently finding in both Richardson and Sterne kindred spirits of emotional liberation. At the end of the century Madame de Staël praised Sterne for what she took to be his very English humour and allowed that probably no translation could do his jokes justice. At the end of the century as well, Jean Baptiste Suard's *Memoirs* disclosed the interesting and perhaps truthful testimony, gathered in a personal interview, that Sterne thought he owed his originality to his special sensibility, to his daily reading of the Bible and finally

> to the study of Locke, which he had begun in his youth and which he continued all during his life, to that philosophy which those who are able to recognize it explicitly and implicitly will discover or sense in all his pages, in all his lines, in the choice of all his expressions ... (*CH*, p. 414)

Meanwhile, German readers received their first translation of *Tristram Shandy* in 1765 and responded perhaps even more enthusiastically than the *philosophes* to Sterne's sentimental irrationalism. Certainly, Goethe was to praise and quote *Tristram Shandy* all his life; other figures such as Jean Paul Richter and even Hegel would also praise Sterne's ability to mix tears and laughter and would use him as a starting-point for their own serious (not to say Germanic) philosophies of humour.

At the end of the eighteenth century in England, the question of Sterne's originality was raised in a new way, as we have already seen, by John Ferriar, whose *Illustrations of Sterne* grew so much more critical from the first to the second edition that he was understood by most readers as accusing Sterne of wholesale plagiarism. Other scholars were stimulated to find additional parallels and borrowings to add to Ferriar's indictment, until by the turn of the century, as one correspondent put it in the *Gentleman's Magazine*, Sterne's 'far-famed originality and wit have shrunk from the test of enquiry; and the sorry reputation of a servile imitator is almost all that remains of that once celebrated author' (*CH*, p. 314). And Alan B. Howes notes that at this point the charges of plagiarism combined with the rising Evangelical movement – naturally disapproving of Sterne's lighthearted indecencies and his irregular life – to bring *Tristram Shandy*'s reputation to its lowest ebb.[1]

(ii) NINETEENTH-CENTURY

The Romantic revaluation begins with Samuel Taylor Coleridge, whose 1818 lecture on 'Wit and Humour' for the Philosophical Society in London treats Sterne with profound (if occasionally mystifying) seriousness. Coleridge disliked *A Sentimental Journey* and Sterne's sentimentalism generally, but the earlier volumes of *Tristram Shandy* pleased him enormously and provoked him to speculate in his lecture on the universals of comic theory. He insists, for example, that

> you cannot conceive a humorous man who does not give some disproportionate *generality*, universality, to his hobbyhorse, as Mr Shandy; or at least [there is] an absence of any interest but what arises from the humor itself, as in Uncle Toby. There is *the idea* of the soul in its undefined capacity and dignity that gives the sting to any absorption of it by any one pursuit, and this not as a member of society for any particular, however mistaken, interest, but as a man. Hence in humor the little is made great, and the great little, in order to destroy both, because all is equal in contrast with the infinite.

He adds that our tender feelings, even respect, for another man's hobbyhorse, however ludicrous, have their source in our 'Acknowledgement of the hollowness and farce of the world, and its disproportion to the godlike within us'. Finally, his disapproval of Sterne's immodesty of humour, which we have already quoted in Chapter 2, is less severe and more thoughtful than the denunciations of polite morality; and his response to Sterne's chaotic text actually challenges for the first time the whole notion that *Tristram Shandy* is a formless book: 'the digressive spirit [is] not wantonness, but the *very form* of his genius. The connection is given by the continuity of the characters' (*CH*, pp. 353–6).

In the following year William Hazlitt gave a series of lectures on the English Comic Writers, during which he treated Sterne with a similar (if less oracular) respect. Like Coleridge, he made relatively little of Sterne's supposed indecencies, concentrating instead on the sentimental tenderness that Coleridge had found so unappealing. The story of Le Fever, for example, he called 'perhaps the finest in English'; likewise, 'My Uncle Toby is one of the finest compliments ever paid to human nature'. His appreciation of Sterne's delicacy leads him to reject the familiar charge of hard-heartedness towards his wife and mother – 'The true, original master-touches that go to the heart, must come from it' – and to connect him with the sentimental tradition in English literature that Richardson had inaugurated:

His characters are intellectual and inventive, like Richardson's; but totally opposite in the execution. The one are made out by continuity, and patient repetition of touches: the others, by glancing transitions and graceful apposition. His style is equally different from Richardson's: it is at times the most rapid, the most happy, the most idiomatic of any that is to be found. It is the pure essence of English conversational style. (*CH*, pp. 359–63)

Sir Walter Scott, who wrote a biographical preface for Ballantyne's series of standard novelists in 1823, also praised Sterne's sentimentality; the bawdry he regarded as an offence against taste rather than against morals. Ferriar's attack on Sterne's originality struck him as convincing – he added his own perception that the source of Mr Shandy's character was to be found in *Martinus Scriblerus* – but these defects seemed finally unimportant in view of Sterne's 'exquisite' reworkings of his sources. 'In the power of approaching and touching the finer feelings of the heart,' Scott wrote, 'he has never been excelled, if indeed he has ever been equalled; and may be at once recorded as one of the most affected, and one of the most simple writers, – as one of the greatest plagiarists, and one of the most original geniuses, whom England has produced' (*CH*, p. 374).

The Victorian idea of the eighteenth century has never been fully studied. Thackeray's venomous disapproval of Sterne, so typical of Victorian pieties, was shared by such novelists as Trollope and Charlotte Brontë and by some critics such as John Cordy Jeaffreson, who described Sterne as a 'vain, wicked, sensual old dandy', denounced his plagiarisms, and summarized his health in the last years as 'exhausted by pulmonary disease, and also a loathsome affection (the consequence of vicious pleasures)'.[2] But these scathing dismissals were more than balanced by the appreciations of two extremely popular novelists – Bulwer-Lytton and Dickens – and by a growing number of critics and literary historians who dismissed or mitigated charges against his character. Dickens in particular valued Sterne, naming him with Fielding and Smollett as among his favourite authors and alluding to both *Tristram Shandy* and *A Sentimental Journey* in his own novels. (According to his letters, when he was about to begin the actual writing of *Dombey and Son*, he took up *Tristram Shandy* in a superstitious moment and opened it at random to the words 'What a work it is likely to turn out! Let us begin it!')[3] Those critics who approved of Sterne still pointed first to his redeeming sentimentality – and Walter Bagehot noted that Thackeray's attack was in certain respects self-portrait and self-criticism – but they also drew on new biographical materials that tended to soften his reputation from 'rake' to simple 'flirt'. In 1864, Percy Fitzgerald published the first full-length biography of Sterne, a generally impartial survey of the life with little attempt at literary criticism; afterwards Sir Sidney Lee gave a sympathetic and influential account of Sterne's life in the *Dictionary of National Biography*. Other notable Victorian students of the eighteenth century such as Sir Leslie Stephen and George Saintsbury left no extended studies of Sterne, but in shorter pieces wove the familiar variations on his plagiarism, indecency and sentiment. All of them, as Alan Howes points out, combined a pursed-lip disapproval of eighteenth-century coarseness and indecorum and a fascination with that same coarseness and the evident freedom – of morals, of standards – that it implied (*Yorick and the Critics*, p. 171).

(iii) TWENTIETH-CENTURY

The modern study of *Tristram Shandy* begins with the scholarly evidence assembled in four publications. Sterne's complete *Works* were edited by Wilbur L. Cross in 1904, a twelve-volume set that included a reprint of Fitzgerald's *Life* (rather briskly annotated and corrected by Cross) and introductions and commentary for each volume. In 1909, Cross published his own biography of Sterne, *The Life and Times of Laurence Sterne*, revised in 1925 and again in 1929, a large and sympathetic account that remains the standard complete life. Sterne's *Letters* appeared in 1935, edited by Cross's student Lewis Perry Curtis, likewise still the standard text. Finally, James Work's edition of the novel in 1940 for the Odyssey Press, while presenting copious annotation and a long and useful introduction, as a relatively inexpensive university text also served the further purpose of making Sterne available, often for the first time, to a wide audience of college students and their instructors.

These works facilitated, indeed stimulated research into some of the traditional areas of Sterne criticism: the discovery of additional 'sources' and parallels, for example, which to the twentieth-century reader, reared on Joyce and Nabokov, sometimes had the paradoxical effect of causing *Tristram Shandy* to seem all the more complex and creative. Thanks to such scholarly work, biographical questions such as Sterne's behaviour towards his mother and wife were now subject to more judicious (and tolerant) interpretations. And the Yorkshire background of the novel (its 'local satire') has been greatly enlarged, especially by Curtis in *The Politics of Laurence Sterne* (1929).

At the same time, critical appreciation of Sterne's literary artistry has grown more intense and searching as the study of his works has become more systematic. Evidence of his craft, for example, was presented not only in Wayne Booth's essay on the 'completion' of *Tristram Shandy*, but also in the various articles on 'time' in the novel by Theodore Baird (1936), Benjamin Lehman (Traugott, pp. 21–33) and Jean-Jacques Mayoux (in *The Winged Skull*, pp. 3–22), all pointing towards the existence of a time-scheme and Sterne's self-conscious manipulation of it. Many modern fiction writers, notably Virginia Woolf and V. S. Pritchett, have written distinguished essays in praise of Sterne's art (in particular, his style); and a poet, Edwin Muir, has also written a beautifully sensitive account of Sterne's methods. Some remnants of Victorian censoriousness can be discovered in modern criticism – F. R. Leavis notoriously spoke of Sterne's 'irresponsible (and nasty) trifling' – but two powerful essays by Robert Alter (1968) and Mayoux (Traugott, pp. 108–25) have greatly advanced our understanding of Sterne's sexuality, stressing its seriousness as a moral emblem rather than as a compulsive 'trifling'.[4] The danger, in fact, has been that Sterne's seriousness might be overstressed. In *Laurence Sterne as Satirist* (1970), Melvyn New depicts Sterne as a conservative Anglican moralist in the tradition of Swift, satirizing the prevailing tendency of human nature wilfully to abuse reason. In his view, Tristram himself is the object of Sterne's satire, particularly Tristram's sentimentalism in so far as it is split from reason and religion. New's position has been attacked by many reviewers as reductive and one-sided; an entirely different point of view, insisting on Sterne's incorrigible flippancy and good-humour, can be found in E. N. Dilworth's *Unsentimental Journey of Laurence Sterne* (1948), a book in its own way even more overstated than New's, and in Rufus Putney's 'Laurence Sterne, apostle of laughter' (1949).

The fullest general study of Sterne's art to date has been written by Henri Fluchère (1961), a comprehensive biographical and critical analysis (with an excellent bibliography). Fluchère's book has no controlling argument or point of view, but offers an exhaustive discussion of themes, structure and style; he sees Sterne as finally arriving at a kind of 'pantagruélisme', celebrating the complexity of life, and the goodness of human nature. For a compact presentation of the major critical issues, however, most students will probably want to begin with the chapter on Sterne in Alan D. McKillop's *The Early Masters of English Fiction* (1956). Other good general studies are listed in the Bibliography below and in Lodwick Hartley's two excellent annotated bibliographies, *Laurence Sterne in the Twentieth Century* (1966) and *Laurence Sterne . . . 1965–1977* (1978). Here, it may be useful to conclude by describing certain new critical directions recently taken: for, although Sterne's originality, character and sentimentality have continued to be central subjects of critical debate, just as they were in earlier periods, twentieth-century readers have opened up at least two new areas of persistent and important discussion.

The first such area may be called '*Tristram Shandy* and the theory of the novel' and has its origin in the Russian Formalist group, writing in the early years of the Soviet regime. Viktor Shklovsky and A. A. Mendilow both published studies of *Tristram Shandy* shaped by their general aesthetic commitment to questions of form in literature rather than of 'content'. Hence Shklovsky, as we have already noted, saw Sterne working deliberately to make his readers aware of the artificial nature of novelistic form, its impersonal conventions and laws; Sterne therefore parodies the conventions of ordinary fiction – disrupting 'consecutiveness', mocking plot, character development and time-schemes – to bring to the surface and explode before our eyes, like an architectural drawing, the devices that underlie every fiction, perhaps every narrative (Traugott, pp. 66–89). Similarly, Mendilow insisted that Sterne, conscious that literary conventions are only illusions of reality, sets out 'to give as true a picture as possible of real human beings as they are in themselves, not as they imagine themselves to be, nor as others judge them to be by their actions and outward behavior alone. This meant the shifting of emphasis from the external to the internal event, from the patterned plot artificially conceived and imposed on the characters, to the free evocation of the fluid, ever-changing process of being' (Traugott, p. 90).

Among the most important of subsequent attempts to relate *Tristram Shandy* to the theory of the novel are Northrop Frye's idea in *Anatomy of Criticism* (1957) of an 'anatomy', which accounts for its formlessness, not by reference to Sterne's intentions, but by a classification that includes many other formless and unclassifiable works; and Wayne Booth's argument in *The Rhetoric of Fiction* (1961) that Tristram represents an 'unreliable' and self-conscious narrator whose disruptive presence is actually one kind of novel's chief point of coherence. More recently, Robert Alter has incorporated *Tristram Shandy* into his view that the novel itself – not simply the narrator – can be understood as self-conscious, flaunting its ' "naïve" narrative devices, rescuing their usability by exposing their contrivance, working them into a highly patterned narration which reminds us that all representations of reality are, necessarily, stylizations' (*Partial Magic*, p. 30). In making this argument, Alter is not in fact disagreeing with the general point brought forward earlier by Ian Watt in *The Rise of the Novel* (1957), that the novel arises out of and excels in representations of ordinary life; to Alter, however, as to the Russian Formalists, Sterne seems completely aware that such mimesis is, after all, impossible to achieve through language – 'he surrounds the "reality" of the little Shandy world with the constant swirl and eddy of another reality – his mind's and ours' (*Partial Magic*, p. 55). Sterne's very self-consciousness, in other words, carries us in the direction that the novel is theoretically bound to take: towards a 'preverbal and metalinguistic' reality that is none the less communicated by words – words skewered, distorted and manipulated as in Tristram's hands, or afterwards in the hands of Joyce, Woolf and Nabokov. And this whole notion of fiction impinging upon – even absorbing – reality is given a further turn by Walter L. Reed, whose *An Exemplary History of the Novel* (1981) proposes that

> the novel is the literary genre which give the greatest weight to those human fictions – economic, political, psychological, social, scientific, even mythical – which lie beyond the boundaries of the prevailing literary canon. Literary paradigms are not simply modified in the novel, they are confronted by paradigms from other areas of culture. (p. 5)

Thus Reed extends the theory of the novel to include a theory of semiotics as well, and understands the wild disunities of *Tristram Shandy* as a 'protocol of displacement' that begins with *Don Quixote*. Such discussions about Sterne's place in the theory of the novel are bound to continue, especially in the light of the growing influence of literary theoreticians like Roland Barthes and Jacques Derrida; but one of the most valuable of all recent discussions of *Tristram Shandy*, the long chapter in Iain McGilchrist's *Against Criticism* (1982), argues with great sensitivity that no criticism, and certainly no theory, can succeed by imposing abstractions and analysis upon the quicksilver experience of reading.

The second important new trend may be called '*Tristram Shandy* as a philosophic text' and has its beginning in John Traugott's study *Tristram Shandy's World: Sterne's Philosophical Rhetoric* (1954). It is true, of course, that in *John Locke and English Literature of the Eighteenth Century* (1936) Kenneth MacLean had linked Sterne with Locke's association of ideas in a serious (though misleading) way, and other commentators like Cross had also discussed the novel in the same philosophic context – indeed, the whole question of Sterne's morality and moral teaching had once been understood in the widest sense as philosophical. But Traugott's book, intensely felt and elliptically written, begins with the assertion that Sterne 'was a rhetorician and not a "novelist"' and proceeds to see the book as a dramatization of the 'dilemma of Locke's rationalism': his philosophical 'failure to find a convincing relation between two worlds, real and ideal' (p. 6) – i.e., the world of physical experience and the world of mental consciousness. Sterne closes the gap between these two worlds, however, and breaks down the 'isolation' of the Lockian 'mind' – its imprisonment in subjectivity – by means of sentiment and sympathy, particularly the sympathy that unites the otherwise non-communicating Shandy brothers; thus, in Shandyism he carries Lockian rationalism to absurd limits, satirizing its solemnity and narrowness, and shows how human beings none the less communicate and think in non-rational and indeterminate ways. The second part of the book argues that the whole enterprise is under the control of Tristram the 'facetious rhetorician' (p. 83) and suggests links between Sterne as novelist and as preacher.

Traugott's approach has been controversial – many readers are not prepared to reject Sterne as a novelist or to agree that from the specialized literary perspective of the history of the novel *Tristram Shandy* is a 'sad case of arrested development' (p. xiii) – and some reviewers have questioned the accuracy of Traugott's reading of Locke as well. But other critics have gone on to pursue vigorously the idea of the book as a philosophic argument or an episode in the history of ideas, notably Ernest Tuveson in an essay on 'Locke and Sterne' (1962), Ernest H. Lockridge in 'A view of the sentimental absurd: Sterne and Camus' (1964), which reinterprets Sterne in the context of Camus' *Myth of Sisyphus*, and Helen Moglen in *The Philosophical Irony of Laurence Sterne* (1975). Moglen's book is a rather solemn re-examination of the influence of Locke upon Sterne, insisting that *Tristram Shandy* be read 'as a history of the human mind in its particular and universal manifestations' and that what chiefly interested Sterne was Locke's perception of the 'unsteady bridge . . . between two alternatives: the analytic function of reason and man's domination by his senses' (p. 10). A better-balanced, wider-ranging discussion of Sterne in the context of eighteenth-century philosophy will be found in A. D. Nuttall's *A Common Sky*, which he describes as a book 'about solipsistic fear: that is, the fear that the external world of trees, tables, bricks and mortar may not exist at all' (p. 11). Carried to an extreme, Nuttall observes, Locke's epistemology could produce such solipsism; but

> Sterne rather confines himself to the less radical position whereby the minds of other people are inaccessible to us, though their bodies are not. What is presupposed by such a picture is, of course, a Cartesian dualism of mind and body. *Tristram Shandy* stands as a marvellously rich and detailed embodiment of the Cartesian view – mediated by Locke – that the mind is a mysterious, fugitive, invisible substance, interpenetrating and acting upon the extended world of matter. The sense of duality is in one respect stronger in Sterne than in Descartes, for in *Tristram Shandy* the power of the mind to govern the animal spirits and so to move the body is comically diminished. We receive a vivid sense of the imprisoned souls of the Shandys, eccentric ghosts, fluttering inside mechanically determined machines. This is the philosophy of the age and it is also the philosophy of *Tristram Shandy*. (pp. 82–3)

Nuttall's discussion includes shrewd accounts of Sterne's relationship to Hume and Shaftesbury as well.

The most difficult – and most rewarding – study to date of Sterne's philosophical dimension is, as we have already seen, James Swearingen's *Reflexivity in 'Tristram Shandy'* (1977), which treats the book as a 'phenomenology' in the precise sense used by the twentieth-century philosopher Edmund Husserl and which, among other accomplishments, links *Tristram Shandy* to the general question of 'personal identity' – a Lockian term and concept – that has preoccupied many recent studies of eighteenth-century literature. Swearingen's chapters all concern such traditional topics as time, language, style and character, but his idiom is rigorously technical and difficult – not a book for beginners; his last chapter, 'Tristram's sorrow: the crisis of European life', reverts to non-philosophical, historical generalizations, but at that point in fact the book weakens considerably. Readers interested in the 'tragic' character of Tristram (and Sterne) and its eighteenth-century context will do better to consult the concise and eloquent chapter in W. B. C. Watkins's *Perilous Balance: The Tragic Genius of Swift, Johnson, Sterne* (1939).

Finally, Richard A. Lanham's lively *'Tristram Shandy': The Games of Pleasure* (1973) draws upon modern games theory (developed chiefly by Caillois and Huizinga) to describe Sterne's manipulations of rhetoric. His universe, Lanham argues, is populated, not with philosophers, but with pleasure-seekers; Tristram's whole performance is self-indulgent and self-serving, and like all games has as its only objective the production of pleasure. Lanham's sense of sheer mischievous delight in the novel is therefore openly subversive of the philosophical dignity thrust upon Sterne by other critics. For him, Walter Shandy is the 'antitype' of a philosopher and a key to Sterne's general conception of human nature as *poseur*: addicted to the pleasure principle, delighting in the game of philosophy (and literature) for its own sake rather than for any sense of ultimate reality or identity that it may give.

> The novel thus philosophizes the relation of humor to wit, and of both to satisfaction. It provides a pleasure equation of mutual tolerance for the private life. But it philosophizes little else. It does not tell us that, if we ponder role-playing long enough, we shall find a role that is really us. It does not find motive unfathomable. It supplies pleasure at the bottom and proves its valence. It does not tell us how to endure time and chance but how to play games with them, capitalize on them, make them our own. (pp. 166–7)

Here Lanham perhaps comes closest to the spirit in which a grinning Sterne informed a correspondent: '*Tristram Shandy*, my friend, was made and formed to baffle all criticism—and I will venture to rest the book on this ground,—that it is either above the power or beneath the attention of any critic or hyper-critic whatsoever.'[5]

NOTES: CHAPTER 8

1   Alan B. Howes (ed.), *Yorick and the Critics: Sterne's Reputation in England, 1760–1868* (New Haven, Conn.: Yale University Press, 1958), p. 110. I am deeply indebted to this work and to Howe's exemplary *Critical Heritage* volume (1974) throughout this section.

2   Howes, *Yorick and the Critics*, pp. 150–1.

3   ibid., p. 140.

4   F. R. Leavis, *The Great Tradition* (London: Chatto & Windus, 1948), p. 2.

5   Quoted in Helen Moglen, *The Philosophical Irony of Laurence Sterne* (Gainesville, Fla: University Presses of Florida, 1975), p. 6.

SELECTED BIBLIOGRAPHY

(1) EDITIONS OF *TRISTRAM SHANDY*

The standard scholarly edition is now that edited by Melvyn New and Joan New (Gainesville, Fla: University Presses of Florida, 1978). In addition to the two volumes of text and textual annotation already published, a volume of critical annotation is in preparation.

Other good editions are by James A. Work (New York: Odyssey Press, 1940), long the standard text; by Ian Watt (Boston: Houghton Mifflin, 1965), with excellent notes and a memorable introduction; by Howard Anderson (New York: Norton, 1980), with a collection of critical essays following the text; and by Ian Campbell Ross for The World's Classics (Oxford: Oxford University Press, 1983).

(2) OTHER WORKS BY STERNE

New, Melvyn (ed.), 'Sterne's Rabelaisian fragment: a text from the holograph manuscript', *PMLA*, vol. 88 (1972), pp. 1083–92.
Stapfer, Paul (ed.), 'Fragment', in *Laurence Sterne: sa personne et ses ouvrages* (Paris, 1870), pp. xvi–xlix.
Monkman, Kenneth (ed.), *A Political Romance* (Menston: Scolar Press, 1971).
Stout, Gardner D., Jnr (ed.), *A Sentimental Journey through France and Italy, by Mr Yorick* (Berkeley/Los Angeles, Calif.: University of California Press, 1967).
Jack, Ian (ed.), *A Sentimental Journey; To Which Are Added, 'The Journal to Eliza', and 'A Political Romance'* (London: Oxford University Press, 1968).
David, Marjorie (ed.), *The Sermons of Mr Yorick* (London: Carcanet Press, 1973). A selection.
Cross, Wilbur L. (ed.), *Works and Life*, 12 vols (New York: J. F. Taylor, 1904). Includes Fitzgerald's *Life* and annotation and commentary for each volume.
Works, 7 vols (Oxford: Basil Blackwell, 1926–7).

(3) BIOGRAPHY AND LETTERS

The standard complete life is still Wilbur L. Cross, *The Life and Times of Laurence Sterne*, a cheerful, enthusiastic portrait of Sterne as carefree humorist, but a book occasionally mechanical in its assembly of facts. This is being replaced as a scholarly source by Arthur H. Cash, *Laurence Sterne: The Early and Middle Years* (London: Methuen, 1975), with a second volume promised. Cash has not greatly altered our idea of the outlines of Sterne's life, but he has corrected numerous minor errors in Cross and has expanded remarkably our knowledge of the background of Sterne's life, his financial and ecclesiastical affairs in Yorkshire and his troubled relationships within his family; unlike Cross, Cash deliberately offers little in the way of critical comment on Sterne's writings. An outstanding shorter biography is David Thomson, *Wild Excursions: The Life and Fiction of Laurence Sterne* (London: Weidenfeld & Nicolson, 1972), which is particularly good on Sterne's personality.

And an important specialized biography is Lewis P. Curtis, *The Politics of*

Laurence Sterne (Oxford: Oxford University Press, 1929). Other useful biographies include Lodwick Hartley, *This is Lorence: A Narrative of the Reverend Laurence Sterne* (Chapel Hill, NC: University of North Carolina Press, 1943), revised and reissued by the same publisher as *Laurence Sterne: A Biographical Essay* (1968), and Margaret R. B. Shaw, *Laurence Sterne: The Making of a Humorist, 1713–1762* (London: Richards Press, 1957), a somewhat tendentious book. Finally, there is a good biographical section in Henri Fluchère, *Laurence Sterne, de l'homme à l'œuvre* (Paris: Gallimard, 1961); the critical section of the book was translated and abridged by Barbara Bray and published as *Laurence Sterne: From Tristram to Yorick: An Interpretation of 'Tristram Shandy'* (London: Oxford University Press, 1965). Additional biographical material can be found in the following:

Croft, John, 'Anecdotes of Sterne', in W. A. S. Hewins (ed.), *The Whitefoord Papers* (Oxford, 1898), pp. 225–32.
Kuist, James, 'New light on Sterne: an old man's recollections of the young vicar', *PMLA*, vol. 80 (1965), pp. 549–53.

The standard edition of Sterne's letters, including his *Memoirs* and the *Journal to Eliza*, is Lewis Perry Curtis (ed.), *Letters of Laurence Sterne* (Oxford: Clarendon Press, 1935). This can be supplemented by the following works:

Cash, Arthur H., 'Some new Sterne letters' *The Times Literary Supplement*, 8 April 1965, p. 284.
Curtis, Lewis Perry, 'New light on Sterne', *Modern Language Notes*, vol. 76 (1961), pp. 498–501.
Monkman, Kenneth, and Diggle, James, 'Yorick and his flock: a new Sterne letter', *The Times Literary Supplement*, 14 March 1968, p. 276.
Shepperson, Archibald B., 'Yorick as ministering angel', *Virginia Quarterly Review*, vol. 30 (1954), pp. 54–66.
Wasserman, Earl R., 'Unedited letters by Sterne, Hume, and Rousseau', *Modern Language Notes*, vol. 66 (1951), pp. 73–9.

(4) BIBLIOGRAPHY AND REFERENCE

The publishing history is treated in appendixes to the Florida edition and in the following articles:

Curtis, Lewis Perry, 'The first printer of *Tristram Shandy*', *PMLA*, vol. 47 (1932), pp. 777–89.
Monkman, Kenneth, 'The bibliography of the early editions of *Tristram Shandy*', *The Library*, 5th ser., vol. 25 (1970), pp. 11–39.

For the history of Sterne's reputation, see the following:

Howes, Alan B. (ed.), *Sterne: The Critical Heritage* (London/Boston, Mass.: Routledge & Kegan Paul, 1974).
Howes, Alan B. (ed.), *Yorick and the Critics: Sterne's Reputation in England, 1760–1868* (New Haven, Conn.: Yale University Press, 1958).

Oates, J. C. T., *Shandyism and Sentiment, 1760–1800* (Cambridge: Cambridge Bibliographical Society, 1968).

The standard listings of modern studies are:

Hartley, Lodwick, *Laurence Sterne in the Twentieth Century: An Essay and a Bibliography of Sternean Studies, 1900–1965* (Chapel Hill, NC: University of North Carolina Press, 1966).

Hartley, Lodwick, *Laurence Sterne: An Annotated Bibliography, 1965–1977* (Boston, Mass.: G. K. Hall, 1978).

A concise listing will be found in 'Laurence Sterne', in *The New Cambridge Bibliography of English Literature*, ed. George Watson (Cambridge: Cambridge University Press, 1971), pp. 948–62.

For Sterne's library,, see *A Facsimile Reproduction of a Unique Catalogue of Laurence Sterne's Library, with a Preface by Charles Whibley* (London: J. Tregaskis & Son, 1930).

(5)　CRITICAL STUDIES: BOOKS

Cash, Arthur H., and Stedmond, John M. (eds), *The Winged Skull: Papers from the Laurence Sterne Bicentenary Conference at the University of York* (London: Methuen, 1971).

Conrad, Peter, *Shandyism: The Character of Romantic Irony* (Oxford: Basil Blackwell, 1978).

Dilworth, Ernest Nevin, *The Unsentimental Journey of Laurence Sterne* (New York: King's Crown Press, 1948).

Fluchère, Henri, *Laurence Sterne: From Tristram to Yorick. An Interpretation of 'Tristram Shandy'*, trans. and abridged by Barbara Bray (London: Oxford University Press, 1965). See section (iii) above.

Fredman, Alice, *Diderot and Sterne* (New York: Columbia University Press, 1955).

Freedman, William, *Laurence Sterne and the Origins of the Musical Novel* (Athens, Ga: University of Georgia Press, 1978).

Holtz, William V., *Image and Immortality: A Study of 'Tristram Shandy'* (Providence, RI: Brown University Press, 1970).

James, Overton Philip, *The Relation of 'Tristram Shandy' to the Life of Sterne* (The Hague: Mouton, 1966).

Jefferson, D. W., *Laurence Sterne* (London: Longman, 1954).

Lanham, Richard A., *'Tristram Shandy': The Games of Pleasure* (Berkeley/Los Angeles, Calif.: University of California Press, 1973).

Loveridge, Mark, *Laurence Sterne and the Argument about Design* (London: Macmillan, 1982).

Moglen, Helen, *The Philosophical Irony of Laurence Sterne* (Gainesville, Fla: University Presses of Florida, 1975).

New, Melvyn, *Laurence Sterne as Satirist: A Reading of 'Tristram Shandy'* (Gainesville, Fla: University of Florida Press, 1970).

Piper, William B., *Laurence Sterne* (New York: Twayne, 1965).

Stedmond, John M., *The Comic Art of Laurence Sterne: Convention and Innovation in 'Tristram Shandy' and 'A Sentimental Journey'* (Toronto: University of Toronto Press, 1967).

Swearingen, James E., *Reflexivity in 'Tristram Shandy': An Essay in Phenomenological Criticism* (New Haven, Conn.: Yale University Press, 1977).

Traugott, John, (ed.), *Laurence Sterne: A Collection of Critical Essays* (Englewood Cliffs, NJ: Prentice-Hall, 1968).

Traugott, John, *Tristram Shandy's World: Sterne's Philosophical Rhetoric* (Berkeley/Los Angeles, Calif.: University of California Press, 1954).

(6) BOOKS WITH SUBSTANTIAL CHAPTERS ON STERNE AND
TRISTRAM SHANDY

Alter, Robert, *Partial Magic: The Novel as a Self-Conscious Genre* (Berkeley/Los Angeles, Calif.: University of California Press, 1975), pp. 30–56.

Bagehot, Walter, *Literary Studies* (London: Dent, 1910), vol. 2, pp. 94–130.

Baker, Ernest A., *The History of the English Novel* (London: Witherby, 1924–39), vol. 4, pp. 240–77.

Battestin, Martin C., *The Providence of Wit: Aspects of Form in Augustan Literature and the Arts* (London: Oxford University Press, 1974), pp. 241–69.

Booth, Wayne C., *The Rhetoric of Fiction* (Chicago, Ill.: University of Chicago Press, 1961), pp. 221–40.

Brissenden, R. F., *Virtue in Distress: Studies in the Novel of Sentiment from Richardson to Sade* (London: Macmillan, 1974), pp. 187–217.

Carnochan, W. B., *Confinement and Flight: An Essay on English Literature of the Eighteenth Century* (Berkeley/Los Angeles, Calif.: University of California Press, 1977), pp. 119–27.

Connolly, Cyril, *The Condemned Playground: Essays: 1927–1944* (New York: Macmillan, 1946), pp. 21–6.

DePorte, Michael V., *Nightmares and Hobbyhorses: Swift, Sterne, and Augustan Ideas of Madness* (San Marino, Calif.: Huntington Library, 1974), pp. 107–54.

Fliegelman, Jay, *Prodigals and Pilgrims: The American Revolution against Patriarchal Authority, 1750–1800* (Cambridge: Cambridge University Press, 1982), pp. 60–6.

Forster, E. M., *Aspects of the Novel* (New York: Harcourt, 1927), pp. 157–80.

Frye, Northrop, *Anatomy of Criticism: Four Essays* (Princeton, NJ: Princeton University Press, 1957), pp. 308–25.

Kettle, Arnold, *An Introduction to the English Novel* (London: Hutchinson, 1951), vol. 1, pp. 81–7.

McGilchrist, Iain, *Against Criticism* (London: Faber, 1982), pp. 131–75.

McKillop, Alan D., *The Early Masters of English Fiction* (Lawrence, Kans.: University of Kansas Press, 1956), pp. 182–219.

MacLean, Kenneth, *John Locke and English Literature of the Eighteenth Century* (New Haven, Conn.: Yale University Press, 1936), passim.

Mendilow, A. A., *Time and the Novel* (London: Peter Nevill, 1952; New York: Humanities Press, 1965), pp. 158–99; reprinted in Traugott, pp. 90–107.

Muir, Edwin, *Essays on Literature and Society* (London: Hogarth Press, 1949;

revised and enlarged edn, Cambridge, Mass.: Harvard University Press, 1967), pp. 50–7.

Nuttall, A. D., *A Common Sky: Philosophy and the Literary Imagination* (Berkeley/Los Angeles, Calif.: University of California Press, 1974), pp. 45–91.

Paulson, Ronald, *Satire and the Novel in Eighteenth-Century England* (New Haven, Conn.: Yale University Press, 1967), pp. 248–65.

Preston, John, *The Created Self: The Reader's Role in Eighteenth-Century Fiction* (London: Heinemann, 1970), pp. 133–95.

Price, Martin, *To the Palace of Wisdom: Studies in Order and Energy from Dryden to Blake* (Garden City, NY: Doubleday, 1964), pp. 320–42.

Priestley, J. B., *The English Comic Characters* (London: Bodley Head, 1925), pp. 128–57.

Quennell, Peter, *Four Portraits: Studies of the Eighteenth Century* (London: Collins, 1945), pp. 139–94.

Read, Herbert, *The Sense of Glory: Essays in Criticism* (Cambridge: Cambridge University Press, 1929), pp. 123–51.

Reed, Walter L., *An Exemplary History of the Novel: The Quixotic versus the Picaresque* (Chicago, Ill.: University of Chicago Press, 1981), pp. 137–61.

Rothstein, Eric, *Systems of Order and Inquiry in Later Eighteenth-Century Fiction* (Berkeley/Los Angeles, Calif.: University of California Press, 1975), pp. 62–108.

Seidel, Michael, *Satiric Inheritance: Rabelais to Sterne* (Princeton, NJ: Princeton University Press, 1979), pp. 250–62.

Spacks, Patricia Meyer, *Imagining a Self: Autobiography and Novel in Eighteenth-Century England* (Cambridge, Mass.: Harvard University Press, 1976), pp. 127–57.

Tave, Stuart M., *The Amiable Humorist: A Study in the Comic Theory and Criticism of the Eighteenth and Early Nineteenth Centuries* (Chicago, Ill.: University of Chicago Press, 1960), pp. 140–63.

Van Ghent, Dorothy, *The English Novel* (New York: Rinehart, 1953), pp. 83–98.

Watkins, W. B. C., *Perilous Balance: The Tragic Genius of Swift, Johnson, and Sterne* (Princeton, NJ: Princeton University Press, 1939), pp. 99–156.

Woolf, Virginia, *The Common Reader: Second Series* (London: Hogarth Press, 1932), pp. 78–85.

(7) ARTICLES

Alter, Robert, 'Tristram Shandy and the game of love', *American Scholar*, vol. 37 (1968), pp. 316–23.

Anderson, Howard, 'Associationism and wit in Tristram Shandy', *Philological Quarterly*, vol. 48 (1969), pp. 27–41.

Anderson, Howard, 'Tristram Shandy and the reader's imagination', *PMLA*, vol. 86 (1971), pp. 966–73.

Baird, Theodore, 'The time-scheme in Tristram Shandy and a source', *PMLA*, vol. 51 (1936), pp. 803–20.

Booth, Wayne C., 'Did Sterne complete Tristram Shandy?', *MP*, vol. 47 (1951), pp. 172–83.

Booth, Wayne C., 'The self-conscious narrator in comic fiction before *Tristram Shandy*', *PMLA*, vol. 67 (1952), pp. 163–85.

Brady, Frank, '*Tristram Shandy*: sexuality, morality, and sensibility', *Eighteenth-Century Studies*, vol. 4 (1970), pp. 41–56.

Burckhardt, Sigurd, '*Tristram Shandy*'s law of gravity', *ELH*, vol. 28 (1961), pp. 70–88.

Cash, Arthur H., 'The birth of Tristram Shandy: Sterne and Dr Burton', in R. F. Brissenden (ed.), *Studies in the Eighteenth Century: Papers Presented at the David Nichol Smith Memorial Seminar, Canberra 1966* (Canberra: Australian National University Press, 1968), pp. 133–54.

Cash, Arthur H., 'The Lockean psychology of *Tristram Shandy*', *ELH*, vol. 22 (1955), pp. 123–35.

Cash, Arthur H., 'The sermon in *Tristram Shandy*', *ELH*, vol. 31 (1964), pp. 395–417.

Coleman, Anthony, 'Sterne's use of the Motteux–Ozell "Rabelais"', *Notes and Queries*, NS, vol. 25 (1978), pp. 55–8.

Davies, R. A., 'Annotating Sterne with the "Cyclopaedia"', *Notes and Queries*, NS, vol. 216 (1971), pp. 56–8.

Dyson, A. E., *The Crazy Fabric: Essays in Irony* (London: Macmillan, 1965), pp. 33–48.

Farrell, William J., 'Nature versus art as a comic pattern in *Tristram Shandy*', *ELH*, vol. 30 (1963), pp. 16–35.

Faurot, Ruth M., 'Mrs Shandy observed', *Studies in English Literature*, vol. 10 (1970), pp. 579–90.

Graves, Lila V., 'Locke's changeling and the Shandy bull', *Philological Quarterly*, vol. 60 (1981), pp. 257–64.

Harries, Elizabeth W., 'Sterne's novels: gathering up the fragments', *ELH*, vol. 49 (1982), pp. 35–49.

Hnatko, Eugene, '*Tristram Shandy*'s wit', *Journal of English and Germanic Philology*, vol. 64 (1965), pp. 47–64.

Holland, Norman N., 'The laughter of Laurence Sterne', *Hudson Review*, vol. 9 (1956), pp. 422–30.

Hunter, J. Paul, 'Response as reformation: *Tristram Shandy* and the art of interruption', *Novel*, vol. 4 (1971), pp. 132–46.

Jackson, H. J., 'Sterne, Burton, and Ferriar: allusions to the *Anatomy of Melancholy* in volumes five to nine of *Tristram Shandy*', *Philological Quarterly*, vol. 54 (1975), pp. 457–70.

Jefferson, D. W., '*Tristram Shandy* and the tradition of learned wit', *Essays in Criticism*, vol. 1 (1951), pp. 225–48; in Traugott, pp. 148–67.

Johnson, Maurice, 'A comic homunculus before Tristram Shandy', *Library Chronicle*, vol. 31 (1965), pp. 83–90.

Lamb, Jonathan, 'The comic sublime and Sterne's fiction', *ELH*, vol. 48 (1981), pp. 110–43.

Lamb, Jonathan, 'Sterne's system of imitation', *Modern Language Review*, vol. 76 (1981), pp. 794–810.

Lamb, Jonathan, 'Sterne's use of Montaigne', *Comparative Literature*, vol. 32 (1980), pp. 13–15.

Landa, Louis A., 'The Shandean homunculus: the background of Sterne's

"Little Gentleman"', in Carroll Camden (ed.), *Restoration and Eighteenth-Century Literature: Essays in Honor of Alan Dugald McKillop* (Chicago, Ill.: University of Chicago Press, 1963), pp. 49–68; reprinted in Landa, *Essays in Eighteenth-Century Literature* (Princeton, NJ: Princeton University Press, 1980), pp. 140–59.

Lehman, Benjamin H., 'Of time, personality and the author', *Studies in the Comic, University of California Publications in English*, vol. 8 (1941), pp. 233–50; in Traugott, pp. 21–33.

Lockridge, Ernest H., 'A view of the sentimental absurd: Sterne and Camus', *Sewanee Review*, vol. 72 (1964), pp. 652–67.

Maskell, Duke, 'Locke and Sterne, or, can philosophy influence literature?', *Essays in Criticism*, vol. 23 (1973), pp. 22–39.

Mayoux, Jean-Jacques, 'Laurence Sterne parmi nous', *Critique*, vol. 18 (1962), pp. 99–120; in Traugott, pp. 108–25.

Moss, Roger B., 'Sterne's punctuation', *Eighteenth-Century Studies*, vol. 15 (1981), pp. 179–200.

New, Melvyn, 'Laurence Sterne and Henry Baker's *The Microscope Made Easy*', *Studies in English Literature*, vol. 10 (1970), pp. 591–604.

New, Melvyn, 'Sterne, Warburton, and the burden of exuberant wit', *Eighteenth-Century Studies*, vol. 15 (1982), pp. 245–74.

Petrie, Graham, 'Rhetoric as fictional technique in *Tristram Shandy*', *Philological Quarterly*, vol. 48 (1969), pp. 479–94.

Posner, Roland, 'Semiotic paradoxes in language use with particular reference to *Tristram Shandy*', *The Eighteenth Century: Theory and Interpretation*, vol. 20 (1979), pp. 148–63.

Putney, Rufus, 'Laurence Sterne, apostle of laughter', in Frederick W. Hilles (ed.), *The Age of Johnson: Essays Presented to Chauncey Brewster Tinker* (New Haven, Conn.: Yale University Press, 1949), pp. 159–70.

Rawson, C. J., 'Two notes on Sterne', *Notes and Queries*, NS, vol. 4 (1957), pp. 255–6.

Reid, Ben, 'The sad hilarity of Sterne', *Virginia Quarterly Review*, vol. 32 (1956), pp. 107–30.

Rogers, Pat, 'Tristram Shandy's polite conversation', *Essays in Criticism*, vol. 32 (1982), pp. 305–20.

Rosenblum, Michael, 'Shandean geometry and contingency', *Novel*, vol. 10 (1977), pp. 237–47.

Rosenblum, Michael, 'The sermon, the king of Bohemia, and the art of interpolation in *Tristram Shandy*', *Studies in Philology*, vol. 75 (1978), pp. 472–91.

Shklovsky, Viktor, 'A parodying novel: Sterne's *Tristram Shandy*', in Traugott, pp. 66–89.

Sinfield, Mark, 'Uncle Toby's potency: some critical and authorial confusions in *Tristram Shandy*', *Notes and Queries*, NS, vol. 25 (1978), pp. 54–5.

Stout, Gardner D., Jnr, 'Some borrowings in Sterne from Rabelais and Cervantes', *English Language Notes*, vol. 3 (1965), pp. 111–17.

Towers, A. R., 'Sterne's cock and bull story', *ELH*, vol. 24 (1957), pp. 12–29.

Tuveson, Ernest, 'Locke and Sterne', in J. A. Mazzeo (ed.), *Reason and Imagination: Studies in the History of Ideas, 1600–1800* (New York: Columbia University Press, 1962), pp. 255–77.

Warren, Leland, 'The constant speaker: aspects of conversation in *Tristram Shandy*', *University of Toronto Quarterly*, vol. 46 (1976), pp. 51–67.

Watt, Ian, 'The comic syntax of *Tristram Shandy*', in Howard Anderson and John S. Shea (eds), *Studies in Criticism and Aesthetics, 1660–1800: Essays in Honor of Samuel Holt Monk* (Minneapolis, Minn.: University of Minnesota Press, 1967), pp. 315–31.

Wright, Andrew, 'The artifice of failure in *Tristram Shandy*', *Novel*, vol. 2 (1969), pp. 212–20.

INDEX

Single references, unless of special interest, are omitted from the index, as are all references in the notes at the end of each chapter.

DA？